A HUNDRED FEET
OVER HELL

FLYING WITH THE MEN OF THE
220TH RECON AIRPLANE COMPANY OVER
I CORPS AND THE DMZ, VIETNAM 1968–1969

JIM HOOPER

ZENITH PRESS

To all the Catkillers, but especially Jim Hudson and Doc Clement, who, when visibility dropped below minimums and I saw no alternative to turning back, kept me firmly on course.

Whenever I talk to someone who was in Vietnam, and especially someone I knew over there and haven't seen for thirty years or more, it's amazing how time and distance evaporate and we get slammed right back into the feelings and thoughts we had then. Sometimes a smell or sound will rekindle it. One fine spring day several years ago, we had the office windows open at Fort Monroe and a Huey flew over with that distinctive *wop-wop* sound that we heard so much in Vietnam. No one else seemed to notice, but when I looked up from my desk, absorbing the memories that invaded the otherwise placid morning, I saw a colleague and fellow vet staring at the window. We exchanged a knowing smile, acknowledging an awareness that escaped everyone else in the room. It wasn't necessary to say anything, but we both knew what the sound of that helicopter had awakened in the other. And we knew that it could not be explained to anyone who was not there.

—Glenn Strange, Catkiller 2

First published in 2009 by Zenith Press, an imprint of MBI Publishing Company, 400 First Avenue North, Suite 300, Minneapolis, MN 55401 USA

Zenith Press titles are also available at discounts in bulk quantity for industrial or sales-promotional use. For details write to Special Sales Manager at MBI Publishing Company, 400 First Avenue North, Suite 300, Minneapolis, MN 55401 USA.

To find out more about our books, join us online at www.zenithpress.com.

Library of Congress Cataloging-in-Publication Data

Hooper, Jim, 1944-

A hundred feet over hell : flying with the men of the 220th Recon Airplane Company over I Corps and the DMZ, 1968-1969 / Jim Hooper.
    p. cm.
ISBN-13: 978-0-7603-3633-5 (hb w/ jkt)
ISBN-10: 0-7603-3633-4 (hb w/ jkt)
1. Vietnam War, 1961-1975--Aerial operations, American. 2. Vietnam War, 1961-1975--Reconnaissance operations, American. 3. Vietnam War, 1961-1975--Personal narratives, American. 4. Air pilots, Military--United States. I. Title.

DS558.8.H65 2009
959.704'348--dc22
                        2008044749

Maps by: Phil Schwartzberg, Meridian Mapping
Cover montage: Napalm strike photographed from a Catkiller Bird Dog, *Don Long*; Catkiller Bird Dog in flight, *Charles Finch*.
On the back cover: L-R: Glenn Strange, Russ Blanchard, Bud Bruton, Charlie Finch, John Herring, Dale Moore, Terry Scruggs, Bill Hooper, Doc Clement, Fred Willis, Roger Bounds. *Charles Finch*

Printed in the United States of America

Contents

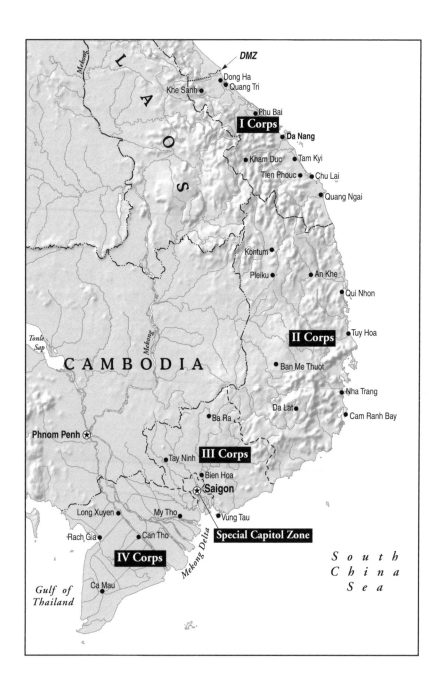

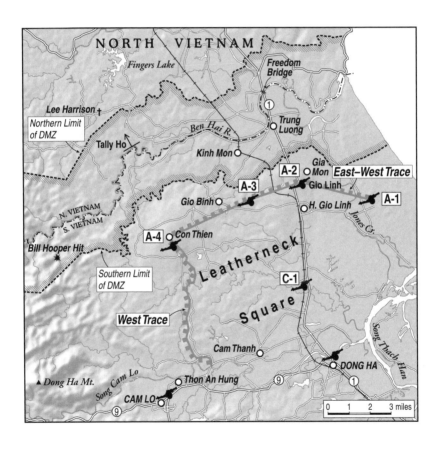

NORTH VIETNAM

Fingers Lake

Freedom Bridge

Lee Harrison +

Northern Limit of DMZ

Ben Hai R.

Trung Luong

Tally Ho

Kinh Mon

Gia Mon

A-2

East–West Trace

A-3

Gio Linh

A-1

N. VIETNAM
S. VIETNAM

Gio Binh

H. Gio Linh

Jones Cr.

Bill Hooper Hit

A-4 Con Thien

Leatherneck

Southern Limit of DMZ

C-1

West Trace

Square

Song Thach Han

Cam Thanh

▲ Dong Ha Mt.

Song Cam Lo

Thon An Hung

9

DONG HA

CAM LO

9

1

0   1   2   3 miles

Preface

SURROUNDED BY JETS, EXPLODING ARTILLERY, and enemy ground fire—a setting he already knew well—Bill Hooper's luck finally ran out. His struggle to remain conscious, aided by the steady voice of another Catkiller flying alongside, lasted long enough to reach a dusty airstrip, where he was eased from the cockpit into a waiting helicopter and rushed to a marine surgical team. Two days later, the twenty-three-year-old army pilot began a journey halfway around the world to Fort Gordon, Georgia. Now, a little less than eleven months after he left for Vietnam, and with the second in a series of operations to rebuild his arm behind him, my brother was home on leave from the hospital.

But his mood baffled us. Rather than sharing our joy at his return, Bill was angry. Not because of the crippling wound received in an unpopular war—he accepted that as part of what he had signed on for. The anger came from being *here*. In a demonstration of uncompromising loyalty over logic, it was, he believed, a betrayal of the warrior family he'd left behind. Held rigidly upright by the neck-to-waist cast, Bill's physical injury was obvious. What could not be seen were other effects of almost daily combat. The happy-go-lucky teenager I'd last seen four years earlier had metamorphosed into a mature and deadly serious man, unforgiving of error and curiously detached from everything around him.

Our mother, tearful and grateful for her youngest son's homecoming, had long since gone to bed; Bill and I remained at the kitchen table, a bottle of Jack Daniels close to hand. Outside, jasmine and orange blossoms sweetened the air, palms rustled, and the Anclote River flowed past our backyard to the Gulf of Mexico. But Florida was a foreign land, and the serenity of the night did nothing to soften his bitterness or the need to make me understand. He was still in Vietnam, the war too recent and raw to relate dispassionately. Pleas for help through his earphones.

Sonic booms of heavy-caliber bullets slamming past him. Blare of piston engine straining through violent maneuvers. All this and more, far more, remained vivid. *That* was where he belonged.

Places and phrases that meant nothing to me ricocheted around the room: Dong Ha, Ben Hai, Tally Ho, "dask," "from my mark," "cleared hot." Listening to the flood of words, I gradually realized that each represented part of a stage or a line from an ever-flexible script he knew by heart. Names of men I had never met tumbled out: Doc Clement, Sarge Means, Lee Harrison, Mike LaFromboise, and, the most repeated of all, Charlie Finch, all of them actors in a morality play based on duty, honor, and courage. Some had died, others finished their tours unscathed, the rest were still on that stage, where death was real and grief never feigned. These were the men against whom Bill measured himself; men who spoke the same language of the time and place; men who had shared the fear and exhilaration of combat with him. And here, tonight, his ties to them were stronger than to us.

They were the Catkillers of the U.S. Army's 220th Reconnaissance Airplane Company, based in Phu Bai, Quang Tri Province, Republic of Vietnam. Flying 100-mile-per-hour Cessnas, vulnerable to every weapon in the enemy's arsenal, they patrolled the most violently contested real estate on earth. Bullet and shrapnel holes in their tiny airplanes warranted little more than shrugs; maintenance crews riveted neat aluminum patches, and the next morning aircraft and boy pilots were again over the guns. As one commanding officer would write many years later: "Those who flew these missions were unique: self-reliant, aggressive, determined, and tenacious. And because they were virtually on their own from takeoff to landing, it also required a personality bordering on controlled recklessness." It is little surprise that their combat record was viewed with wonder. Insiders called them the Myth Makers.

The stories and names I heard that night remained with me for twenty years, but it was only after learning for myself the meaning of fear under fire that I began to record them. Assignments as a freelance journalist to various post-Vietnam conflicts made the writing a slow process, with many pauses, detours, dead ends, and reversals. Among the early difficulties was finding those my brother had lost contact with after leaving the army. The miracle of the Internet led me to a surprised

Sarge Means, who, understandably cautious about a writer claiming to be the brother of a cherished comrade, plugged me into the Catkiller network. The response was immediate, and over the next weeks Bill's telephone burned hot as they relived moments forever branded into their memories. My suggestion that those moments might make a book was met with guarded consent. Eventually, backed up by military commendations, orders, logbooks, faded photographs, diaries, and letters to wives and parents, all found stored away in attics and garages, the first thumbnail sketches began to develop density, motion, and personality. And the more I saw and heard, the stronger my conviction that what they had done was extraordinary; to forget would be an injustice—not just to them, but the history of the Vietnam conflict.

A more difficult task—and, given the passage of time, one in which I had little hope of success—was tracking down veterans of the ground war who had been supported by the Catkillers. Queries to a range of Vietnam websites were met by silence. Another dead end. But then fortune intervened in the person of Command Sgt. Maj. Gary Huber, a never-met cousin-in-law, Vietnam veteran, and webmaster for the Society of the 5th Infantry Division. Gary printed my request in the society's *Red Diamond* newsletter, and some weeks later an email arrived from former Platoon Sgt. Jim Roffers, whose recollection of a certain Bird Dog remained as clear in 2002 as it had been at the Battle of Kinh Mon. Through the efforts of Huber and Roffers, more men who had been there stepped forward to share memories that had been locked away for more than three decades; they would add an entirely new dimension to those of three Catkillers flying overhead that day.

The National Archives in College Park, Maryland, provided another treasure house of information on the Battle of Kinh Mon. When the envelope arrived, it contained not only the official after-action report on Operation Rich but the more revealing duty officer's log, which established a precise timeline for interweaving the accounts of infantry and airmen. Included were copies of penciled notes—"spot reports"—made in the Tactical Operations Center during the fighting; on them, scrawled in haste by a forgotten hand on 25 October 1968, was my brother's call sign, Catkiller 12.

No matter how graphic the telling, however, *A Hundred Feet Over Hell* must serve as a mere outline of what these men experienced. All lived through far more than is recorded here, and only they will ever know how much and how often they risked everything for their fellow Americans. Thus, it is by no means the complete story of the Catkillers, nor of the forward air controller's role in the Vietnam War. Not only did pilots in other platoons and other Bird Dog companies—army, marines and air force—exhibit astonishing bravery when called on: so did those who served before and after the men you will meet in these pages. The legacy they inherited from previous generations that answered the call to war survives among those who guard America today. All deserve to be remembered and honored.

—Jim Hooper
Dorset, England
January 2009

Chapter 1
The Mission

GRAYSON DAVIS: I WAS FAST ASLEEP IN MY COT AT Dong Ha when a brigadier general shined a flashlight in my face and told me I had twenty minutes to get to a briefing on Operation Thor, which was the start of our missions into North Vietnam. The army had moved massive amounts of artillery—entire batteries of 105mm, 155mm, 8-inch, and 175mm—around Dong Ha that day to hit areas in the DMZ and north of the Ben Hai River. Our usual arty missions with the marines saw us adjust with one gun and use two guns in fire for effect. When the operation kicked off the next morning, after the guns were adjusted and the data transferred to the other batteries, there must have been five batteries in fire for effect. Our marine backseats were in awe of the firepower, and we probably fired more arty that morning than we had in the past year. I was initially against the operation, believing that twin-engine airplanes—meaning air force O-2s—were better suited for the mission. But after seeing numerous secondary explosions coming from the bunkers north of the DMZ and none of us getting shot down that morning, I decided it was pretty cool, like I was finally doing some good in the war effort.

"Tank" Meehan: As the liaison officer between the 12th Marines and the army's XXIV Corps, it was my job to keep the Catkillers away from the political infighting of those who wanted to tell them how to fly and when to fly. I also ran interference for them when some senior officer, who knew neither air operations nor the taste of antiaircraft fire, wanted them at his beck and call. It gave me the opportunity to fly with and schedule Catkiller missions, day and night, in support of all ground combat operations. We covered the entire northern I Corps area, as well as North Vietnam, Laos, and the A Shau Valley. Today, the idea of sending unarmed O-1 observation aircraft over North Vietnam and Laos sounds unbelievable, but the Catkillers did it, time after time after time. These days the job is done by remotely controlled model airplanes.

FOR FRESH-FACED ARMY PILOTS ASSIGNED to the 220th Reconnaissance Airplane Company, the first surprise was finding themselves under operational control of the 3rd Marine Division, which oversaw all combat operations in the northernmost tactical zone of I Corps. Even more eye-opening was the mission. Officially, army Bird Dog units were limited to what they had trained for: visual reconnaissance and directing artillery fire. If air strikes were needed, only USAF forward air controllers—FACs—were allowed to call them in.* But the marines' one Bird Dog unit in I Corps, the VMO-6 "Fingerprints," was badly overstretched and welcomed the Catkillers, though not without a period of on-the-job training. Once they had mastered the techniques of close air support, Catkiller pilots, uniquely, received the marine designation of Tactical Air Coordinator (Airborne). As TACAs, they were authorized to control both artillery and air strikes in support of hard-pressed ground units. To ease the workload and increase their effectiveness, aerial observers drawn from the 12th Marines' G2 (intelligence) section and Artillery Regiment, or the army's 108th Field Artillery Group, rode with them. It was not unusual for a "back-seater" to be directing the big guns while, between salvos, the Catkiller pilot marked the target with white phosphorus smoke rockets and told the fighter-bombers where to place their ordnance. It was a steep learning curve.

Those assigned to the Catkillers' 1st Platoon faced a special challenge. Although based in Phu Bai with the rest of the 220th RAC, they staged out of Dong Ha, a small airstrip barely ten miles from the Ben Hai River, the border between South Vietnam and its hostile neighbor. This close-knit group's primary area of operations was the Demilitarized Zone, the theoretical buffer on either side of the Ben Hai. In a war notorious for peculiar euphemisms, none quite compared with "DMZ." Of the estimated seventy-eight thousand enemy soldiers in I Corps, that was precisely where thousands were to be found—and where the Myth Makers could expect ground fire from AK-47 assault rifles to 12.7mm antiaircraft guns. Demilitarized indeed.

Among the many things committed to memory was which pre-set button—"push" in the jargon—on their UHF radios connected them to

---

*When the tactical situation warranted it, Bird Dog pilots regularly ignored this restriction.

the Direct Air Support Control Center (DASC) at Dong Ha. Protected from enemy fire in an underground bunker, "dask" maintained landline or radio communications with every headquarters, air base, ground unit in the field, and aircraft operating over northern I Corps. Co-located with a navigation beacon known as Channel 109, DASC's most vital role was scrambling air support when the Catkillers announced they had "troops in contact"—a phrase guaranteed to receive immediate attention. By giving their bearing and distance from Channel 109, the Catkillers told Dong Ha DASC where the bomb- and napalm-laden jets were needed.

The 1st Platoon was not limited to the southern side of the DMZ. Even more perilous was Tally Ho, the codename for North Vietnam, where daily missions took them across the Ben Hai River in search of enemy artillery, troop concentrations, and supply lines. Here, the authority to scramble jets belonged to Hillsboro, a radar-equipped C-130 orbiting at twenty-five thousand feet south of the border. Sending single-engine Cessnas over the Communist motherland may have been an expedient first line of defense, but it placed the slow-flying Catkillers in the sights of mobile antiaircraft guns of up to 57mm. Tally Ho was not for the faint-hearted.

Their tactical area of responsibility (TAOR) was relatively small, some sixty miles from the South China Sea to Laos and less than twenty miles wide, only part of which demanded day-to-day coverage. Rarely did it take more than half an hour—often only half of that—to reach an assigned patrol area. Despite its limited size, however, a lack of natural terrain features made navigation difficult, particularly during the heavy rains of the monsoon season when ceilings often dropped to a few hundred feet and visibility to well under a mile. Among crucial landmarks was Highway 1, the colonial-era two-lane blacktop that passed Dong Ha on its way to the blown "Freedom Bridge" over the Ben Hai River. Equally important was the East-West Trace, a defoliated, kilometer-wide strip linking a string of U.S. artillery bases that began near the coast, crossed Highway 1 north of Dong Ha, and continued to the fire-support base at Con Thien, where it turned south to become the West Trace. In bad weather these landmarks provided crucial references for locating American units needing air support, and could be equally important in the Catkillers' finding their way home again. The area of operations may have been compact, but in I Corps the enemy was never far away.

FIRST LIEUTENANT EDGAR "DOC" CLEMENT was straight out of flight school when he set off for Vietnam in early May 1968.

Doc Clement: I left McChord Air Force Base in Washington on a Boeing 707 packed with GIs. We stopped in Japan for four hours to refuel and change crew, but no one was allowed off the aircraft in case he decided not to come back. When we landed in Cam Ranh Bay, they herded us on to what looked like prison buses. I asked why there was heavy wire over the windows. "To keep the gooks from throwing grenades in the bus," they said. "Welcome to Vietnam!" I was there for two days and they said, "You're going to Da Nang." "Where's that?" I asked. When they said, "As far north as you can go," I thought, "I'm in it now," and boarded a C-130 to watch GIs puking their guts up all the way there. In that heat the smell was terrible. At Da Nang I was assigned to the 212th Combat Support Aviation Battalion.

That night I was at Marble Mountain having a cold beer with pilots of the Black Cats helicopter company, listening to some loud rock and roll, when someone stuck his head in the club and yelled, "INCOMING!" The place suddenly emptied around me. I'd never heard of "incoming" before, so I walked outside and saw them diving into a bunker. I looked around at all the excitement and thought, "Wow, this is just like being on a movie set." About then—*kaBAM!*—a 122mm rocket hit, and I could not get into that bunker fast enough. I was there another day, and they said, "You're going to Phu Bai." Well, I was as far north as I could go and on the coast, so I asked, "How far west is that?" and they said, "It's as far north as you can go." So back on a C-130 to Phu Bai, still on the coast. When I got to the Catkillers, they told me I was assigned to the 1st Platoon at Dong Ha. "How far west is that?" And they said, "As far north as you can go. Hell, you can *see* North Vietnam from there." That's when I knew I was in a world of shit.

A MAN WHO LIKED HIS CREATURE COMFORTS, Doc was dismayed by the living conditions.

Doc Clement: Besides being so hot and muggy that you could hardly breathe, there was the stink of dried sweat, latrines, dust, all mixed with the smell of cordite from the incoming enemy rockets and artillery. I picked up my bedding from the supply room and the sheets were stale and as stiff as if they'd been starched. The hooches were concrete-floored Quonset huts divided into ten-by-ten-foot cubicles, each with a single cot and a metal locker. Three-foot cinder block walls topped with screened wooden slats kept mosquitoes and other insects out, but let the hot, muggy air in, while the corrugated metal roof turned the sparse interior into an oven soon after the sun rose. I sadly contemplated the prospect of spending the next year in this hellhole.

That first night, I was lying on those stiff, stale sheets, sweat running off me, and wondering how I was ever going to get any relief from the heat. I had finally drifted off when there was a hell of an explosion and I woke up to see guys running for the door. *Shit!* I grabbed my steel pot and flak jacket and was right behind them. When I got to the bunker, everyone else was dressed and there I was, stark naked except for my helmet and flak jacket. When I asked them how they'd gotten dressed so fast, they said, "Dumbass, you gotta sleep in your clothes, because you never know when we'll get incoming." I figured that if I had to wear my flight suit in bed, I'd definitely never get any sleep.

FOR ALL HIS TRIBULATIONS, Doc buckled down to the job. He was given his new call sign of Catkiller 18, along with maps, lists of frequencies, and different terminologies the marines and air force used for the same bombs. A gifted pilot, Doc's confidence took a blow when he realized that the training at forts Stewart and Rucker had not fully prepared him for the job. This was made abundantly clear on his first combat mission with marine 1st Lt. Bob Happe in his back seat.

As was common with many aerial observers who wore the eagle, globe, and anchor, Happe had already served a combat infantry tour as a senior NCO before receiving a direct commission. A few years older, this crew-cut, no-nonsense veteran struck Doc as the prototypical storybook marine. Sitting at the picnic table in the Dong Ha line shack, Happe opened his map case. This morning's destination was Leatherneck Square, a block of heavily bombed terrain between Dong Ha and the

DMZ, where they'd spend the next three hours looking for the enemy. He finished the briefing by stating that he would handle all radio calls. Doc breathed a little easier; the fewer tasks he had this first time out, the better. Happe snapped the map case closed, slung his M16 over a shoulder and strode toward the flight line, his nervous pilot alongside. Doc waited until Happe settled into the back seat of the Bird Dog and then hoisted himself into the cockpit.

Doc Clement: I hooked up my harness, started the engine, and sat there. After a couple of minutes, Happe said in his deep marine voice, "What the hell are you waiting for?" I told him I was waiting for him to call the tower for clearance. "You FNG," he said, "*you* call the tower!" Damn, did I feel stupid. Anyway, we took off and headed out to Leatherneck Square. Happe spotted some rocket emplacements aimed at Dong Ha, but I couldn't see a thing. He called up Dong Ha DASC and asked for snake and nape and then told me that when the air got on station he'd talk to them, fly the aircraft, line up on the targets, and tell me when to fire a rocket. Sure enough, as soon as the F-4s arrived, he worked the radios, aimed the aircraft, and I fired the rockets. I didn't know what the hell was going on. By the time the mission was over, I was wondering how I was ever going to learn to fly, spot the targets, call the air in, give the coordinates, and run air strikes and artillery all at the same time.

By the time I'd been flying the DMZ for a month, I'd shot some artillery and run a few flights of air, but the heat and humidity were still killing me. You couldn't get away from it, not even when flying. With the sun coming through the overhead Plexiglas panel, the cockpit became a sauna. It wouldn't have been so bad if the pilot opened his windows like the observers could in the back. But if he did, the wind would blow their maps all over the place. There was a pull-out air vent in each wing root and I'd fly with one hand on the stick and the other on the cross bar so the air could blow down my sleeve into the flight suit.

It was worse on the ground. The picnic table in the line shack at Dong Ha had an FM radio on one side and some wooden storage boxes on the other. I'd strip off that hot Nomex flight suit and stretch out on them in my shorts and boots to get some shuteye between missions. That's where I was one morning when my marine observer Ken Anal showed up with the op orders. To my dismay, it was convoy cover out to the Rockpile and Vandergrift fire-support bases. I'd already done a few of these and hated them. Everyone hated them. It was three hours of flying circles over a bunch of deuce-and-a-halfs driving at forty miles per hour down Route 9. We were supposed to be there to call in air and artillery in case they were attacked, but nothing ever happened.

About twenty trucks and some jeeps were just pulling out of the Dong Ha gate when we took off. Ken established comms with the convoy commander, and I called Dong Ha DASC to check in and give them our area of cover for that mission. Then I tuned my ADF to Armed Forces Network Vietnam to listen to the latest rock and roll. I set up a racetrack pattern at a thousand feet over the convoy, just boring holes in the sky. We'd search areas that looked like ambush sites, but the vegetation was pretty thick, and it was hard to see anything through it. With the drone of the engine and the sun beating into the cockpit, after about two hours it was all I could do to stay awake.

Then I was wide awake, the FM radios filled with voices shouting that the convoy was under attack. Trucks were hit at the front and rear of the column by mortar shells, effectively pinning the rest of them in place. Ken was trying to calm the commander down long enough to tell us where it was coming from when he saw a puff of smoke to the north. He cranked up the artillery while I called Dong Ha DASC. The mortar position was right at the top of a tree-covered ridge line, making a direct hit very difficult for artillery. By now the convoy had some wounded, and they were calling for a medevac. Then they started taking small-arms fire from about half-way up the ridge. Ken immediately adjusted the artillery with firecracker rounds, air bursts that exploded just above the treetops. That seemed to stop most of the small-arms fire, but the mortar was still dropping shells around the convoy. Right after that we saw smoke from a second mortar about two hundred meters farther west. The convoy was getting picked to pieces by them.

That's when I got a call on my UHF radio from a flight of four Gunfighters, air force Phantoms out of Da Nang. I gave them a target brief and rolled in to shoot a Willie Pete smoke rocket that hit just short of the first mortar tube. Dash 1 came in and set the ridge top ablaze with napalm, followed by Dash 2, who hit the same general area. I waved off

Dash 3 and 4, telling them to stay in the same pattern, and went in again, this time taking some small-arms fire. I punched off another rocket at the second mortar position, aiming low to keep it from overshooting the top of the ridge. Dash 1 came in with another nape and hit short. Dash 2's hit was a little closer, and Dash 3 put one right on top of it. The convoy commander said the mortars had stopped, but I had the F-4s empty the rest of their ordnance on the two sites just to make sure. The convoy pushed the disabled trucks off the road and started moving again. We stayed with them until another Catkiller arrived to take it the rest of the way. When I turned toward Dong Ha, my flight suit was wringing wet. I'd gone to college on a football scholarship and was used to tough, summer training sessions, but football practice never left me feeling as physically exhausted as one of these missions did.

After running air strikes and arty all day, I grabbed a can of C-rations at the line shack and then strolled down to the transit overnight tent, where we had our cots. A couple tents farther along was one occupied by Capt. Tom Jones, who was in charge of Dong Ha DASC. Located in an underground bunker with controllers talking on radios, DASC had maps of our TAOR painted on Plexiglas panels, which were continually updated with grease pencil, showing where our troops were, and where Catkillers and other aircraft were flying—basically anyone doing business in DASC's area of responsibility.

Tom was a great guy, a marine F-4 pilot temporarily assigned to ground duty. I had taken him up several times to get a feel for the area he was responsible for. The first time, he arrived with more survival gear than you could imagine, even a sawed-off M1 carbine, and said he wanted to go up to Tally Ho. As we crossed into North Vietnam, just for fun, I fired off two Willie Pete rockets each side of his head. I hadn't warned him, and he about came out of the back seat. I got a kick out of that. He finally settled down, and we flew around so he could see what the place looked like.

When I got to Tom's tent, he was sitting outside smoking a cigar. I pulled up an old log, sat down, and we discussed the day's operations. Finally I said, "Let's go get a cold one," so off we went to the marine officers club. We started with boilermakers. I kept hearing a strange noise and eventually realized it was coming from a marine at the end of the bar. He had this really wild-eyed look and was grinding his teeth. Tom told me the guy had spent the last month in the bush and lost half his company in an ambush.

After more boilermakers, Tom dragged four tables end-to-end for a game the marine and navy pilots called "Aircraft Carrier." The object was to take a running dive, land on your belly, and see how far you could slide down the tables without spilling your drink. I thought it was great, and after each attempt I'd be on downwind again, ready to follow him. Our enthusiasm wasn't appreciated by everyone, and before long things got rowdy between us and the other drinkers. There was some pushing and shoving, and for a moment it looked like we were about to take on the whole club. They finally told us that they'd had enough of our carrier landings and to get the hell out. We headed back to the tents, but pretty soon were on our hands and knees praying to the barf goddess. We eventually made it to our dusty cots and passed out. It was tough getting up to fly at first light.

THE EFFECTS OF CARRIER LANDINGS NOTWITHSTANDING, twenty-one-year-old Doc continued to hone his skills in the air. By now the holder of a Distinguished Flying Cross, his ability to run close air support impressed even Bob Happe. The two of them were teamed up again when Doc took off for a visual reconnaissance along the DMZ. As he headed up Highway 1, a voice from the DASC bunker crackled in his earphones. The mission had changed: a marine Force Recon team was in trouble in the foothills southwest of Con Thien and needed immediate help. In the back seat, Happe, call sign Southern Hotel, was already dialing in the team's radio frequency. Minutes after the Bird Dog turned toward the reported position, he keyed his microphone.

"Mustang, Mustang, this is Southern Hotel. Over." Nothing interrupted the static in his earphones. He waited. Silence. "Mustang, Mustang, this is Southern Hotel. Do you copy? Over."

There was another long pause, then a whispered reply: "Southern Hotel, this is Mustang 6. Copy you Lima Charlie. How me? Over."

"Mustang 6, Southern Hotel copies Lima Charlie. Over."

"Southern Hotel," the team's radioman said quietly, "we got gooks all around us. No contact yet, but we need some air right quick."

In the front seat, Doc alerted the DASC controller to put air support on standby, adding that he would give them an update as soon as he was over the recon team. At the same time, Happe was telling the nearest artillery battery at Con Thien to prepare for a fire mission. He switched back to the recon team's push. "Mustang 6, this is Southern Hotel, we're an O-1 Bird Dog approximately one thousand feet above the terrain. Advise when you have us in sight. Over."

A few more minutes passed. "Southern Hotel, we're at your two o'clock." Doc swung the Bird Dog to the right. Thick undergrowth and bomb craters passed slowly below. "Southern Hotel, we're at your eleven o'clock." A little rudder brought the nose back to the left. "Mark, mark," said the recon marine even more softly. Doc dipped the left wing to see a figure lying in an old bomb crater, an orange panel spread over him. Still in a left turn, he brought the throttle back. Engine noise faded, and they were dropping through five hundred feet when the whispering stopped.

"Contact! We're taking fire!" Behind the voice were sharp bursts from automatic weapons. The six-cylinder Continental bellowed as Doc added power. Rudder pedal in, stick over and back to hold a tight orbit, he counted at least twenty-five enemy soldiers in the open and muzzle flashes from more concealed in the undergrowth. Some had closed to within twenty meters of the crater. The North Vietnamese called it "grabbing the enemy by the belt," a tactic designed to prevent American air strikes for fear of killing friendlies. He hit his mike button.

"Dong Ha DASC, this is Catkiller 1-8. Over."

"Roger, Catkiller 1-8, this is Dong Ha DASC. Go ahead."

"DASC, this is Catkiller 1-8. We have troops in contact on the 292 out of channel 109 at fourteen nautical miles. I need that air now!" When DASC asked how many flights he wanted, Doc told the controller, "Just keep 'em coming."

"Mustang," Happe called, "this is Southern Hotel. How's your cover? Over."

"Southern Hotel, we got good cover, but we can't hold on long!"

"Roger, Mustang, we'll have arty on the way ASAP!" Happe switched his radio back to the marine artillery battery at Con Thien. "Cherry Buster 6, this is Southern Hotel. Fire mission. Over." He was giving the battery commander the coordinates when DASC confirmed that the first flight would be wheels up out of Chu Lai in less than two minutes. Doc shook his head. Chu Lai was 150 miles to the south, at least twenty minutes flying time for the jets. Something needed to be done now: anything to buy time. He lifted his M16 from where it was slung on the map light and chambered a round. A quick glance over his shoulder showed his backseater doing the same. "Ready to go, Hap?"

"Let's do it, Doc!"

The Bird Dog came around in a steep, descending turn and leveled off at 150 feet. One hand on the stick and the other holding the M16 across his chest, Doc pushed the barrel out the window. Passing over the position, he rolled to the left, and army pilot and marine observer emptied their magazines into the attackers. Taken by surprise, the enemy faltered. Snapping back to level flight, Doc edged the stick forward to gain speed and then hauled back in a steep, climbing turn to clear the area as Happe was calling for one gun in adjustment. The battery commander, target coordinates already cranked into the M114 howitzer, answered immediately.

"Southern Hotel, Cherry Buster 6. Fire. Over."

"Roger, Cherry Buster. Fire. Wait."

Forty seconds later, they heard the moan of the approaching 155mm shell, followed by the muffled *whump!* of its explosion three hundred meters from the crater. Out of the cloud of smoke and earth, splintered trees spun through the air. Happe hit the mike button. "Cherry Buster 6, this is Southern Hotel. Drop two hundred, right one hundred. Repeat." The next round detonated seventy-five meters northwest of the marines. Happe walked the shells around the backs of the NVA while Doc flew a horseshoe pattern to avoid the incoming artillery and keep the target in view. Then came the call he was waiting for.

"Catkiller 1-8, this is Lovebug 202. Flight of two Fox-4s with four Delta 9s, eighteen Delta 2-Alphas, and thirty minutes' play time. Over." Somewhere above him two white Phantoms, "MARINES" painted large on their sides, were carrying a total of eight napalm canisters, thirty-six 500-pound high-drag bombs—"snakes"—and enough fuel to remain over the target for half an hour. Hermetically sealed in their sophisticated cockpits and pushed by two powerful jet engines, they waited for the sweaty army pilot to answer. When he did, they could hear the sounds of piston engine and wind through his open windows.

"Roger, Lovebug 202," Doc acknowledged. He scrawled the call sign on his windscreen with a grease pencil. "Is this the 'Indian' I'm talking to?" Two weeks earlier, he had been the guest of honor at the marine officers club in Chu Lai. The hangover had lasted two days, but he was sure he recognized the voice.

"You got him, Catkiller."

"Roger that, Lovebug. Say your position. Over."

Strapped tightly into his ejection seat, Indian rolled the 50,000-pound F-4 into a steep bank and keyed the microphone switch. "Catkiller, this is Lovebug. I have a Bird Dog in a left-hand turn at my ten o'clock. If that's you, we're ready for a target brief. Over."

Doc leaned forward and scanned the sky. Two Phantoms, trailing their signature dark exhausts, were curving over him at four thousand feet. He sat back against the parachute propped in his seat.

"Roger, Indian, we got a major shit sandwich on hand. We got gooks within twenty meters of friendlies, so I'm gonna need some real precision bombing here. My heading will be 270. Your run-in heading is 090, with a right break. Understand that you're not dropping this close to friendlies unless you have me in sight. I will be over the friendlies. I say again, the only way to drop this close to friendlies is on top of me."

By protecting the recon team with his own aircraft, Doc ensured that Indian and his wingman knew the exact location of their people below. Giving them a west-to-east bomb run placed the South China Sea straight ahead; if either Lovebug was hit—and a single bullet could result in one of the delicately balanced jet engines tearing itself apart—"feet wet" was a far safer place to eject than over terrain teeming with the enemy. Instructions on which way to turn after the bomb runs also kept them out of range of mobile antiaircraft guns in North Vietnam, less than a minute's flying time away. The safety of the men on the ground and that of the marine pilots was paramount. So there would be no confusion over which Lovebug he was talking to, from now until they dropped their last bomb, Indian would be Dash 1, his wingman Dash 2. Doc turned toward the target.

"Lovebug Dash 1, are you ready for my mark?

"Roger, Catkiller, Dash 1 ready to observe your mark. You copy, Dash 2?"

"Dash 2 copies."

Happe cut the artillery as Doc armed one tube and pushed the nose over. "Hap, tell 'em to keep their heads down, this is gonna be close!" He lined up and, at a slant range of about a thousand feet, pulled the trigger. The solid-fuel motor ignited in a shower of sparks, and the 2.75-inch folding-fin aircraft rocket streaked away. Seconds later, it hit thirty meters from the crater, exploding in a spray of burning phosphorus that instantly became an expanding cloud of brilliant white smoke. "Dash 1, do you have my smoke?"

"Roger, Catkiller, I have the mark."

"Dash 1, from my smoke, twelve o'clock, twenty meters with one nape."

"Twelve o'clock, twenty meters, one Delta 9," Indian confirmed. "Dash 1 turning final."

Both men were pressed into their seats as Doc made a tight 360-degree turn and leveled out at five hundred feet on an east-to-west heading that would take him directly over the marines. Tracers passed to one side. Ignoring them, he looked up to see Indian a mile and a half away at 1,500 feet and descending toward him at 350 knots. "Dash 1, this is Catkiller 1-8. Do you have me in sight? Over."

"Affirmative, Catkiller."

"Dash 1, the only way you will drop this close to friendlies is on top of me. You're cleared hot with one nape on my position." He watched the Phantom getting bigger and pass below his horizon. Four hundred feet from the target and less than three seconds from hitting the ground, Indian triggered the release and immediately started climbing. The 500-pound canister separated from the wing station, and Doc hauled the Bird Dog around to be in position for Dash 2. He was halfway through the turn when it hit about fifty meters north of the marines. A dark-orange fireball boiled upward and across the landscape, one of the magnesium igniters emerging in a long white arc. The twisted remains of the ruptured canister, dragging a short tail of burning napalm, came spinning out of the still-swelling maelstrom, scythed through the top of a tree, touched the ground, bounced in another long leap, and slammed to a stop 150 meters beyond its impact point.

"Doc!" said Happe. "Mustang said that was a good hit, good hit!" He centered his controls. Jet-black smoke capped the two-thousand-degree inferno to his right. The Bird Dog bucked when it passed the edge of a rising column of super-heated air, and Doc caught a whiff of the jellied gasoline. As the crater and its marines disappeared under the Cessna's cowling, Indian's wingman was head-on toward him in a fifteen-degree dive. "Dash 2, this is Catkiller. Do you have me in sight? Over."

"That's affirm, Catkiller, I have you in sight."

"Roger, Dash 2. The only way you're dropping this close to friendlies is on top of me. Let's go with one nape at twelve o'clock, twenty-five meters from Dash 1's hit. Your approach is good, you're cleared hot."

"Roger, Catkiller. One Delta-9 at twelve o'clock, twenty-five meters, and dropping on your position. Dash 2 is in hot." The F-4 pilot released below three hundred feet and brought the control stick back in a climbing turn to the south. Doc broke to the right. More tracers rose from AK-47s. He had completed his turn and was watching Dash 1 heading toward him when the second flight of air reported inbound.

"Catkiller 1-8, this is Hellborne 412. Over."

"Stand by, 412. Dash 1, do you have Dash 2's hit?"

"Affirmative, Catkiller."

"Then let's go three o'clock, twenty-five meters, with one nape. Do you have me in sight?"

"That's affirm."

"Then you're cleared hot." Doc added the Hellborne call sign to his windscreen as the napalm's oily flame rolled over the enemy position. He looked over his shoulder at it. "Good hit, Dash 1!" he barked. Then, to make clear that the next transmission was not for Lovebug: "Break, break. Hellborne 412, say your position." The marine A-4 Skyhawks were on the 120-degree radial, twenty-five miles from Dong Ha at eighteen thousand feet. Doc made a quick trigonometry calculation in his head. He needed to position them safely outside Lovebug's pattern but close enough to take over as soon as the F-4s were finished. "Roger, 412, proceed to the 350 at eight miles, Channel 109, descend and maintain ten thousand. I will call you shortly. Break, break. Lovebug Dash 2, do you have me in sight?"

"Affirmative, Catkiller."

"Then let's go from Dash 1's hit, three o'clock, seventy-five meters with one nape."

Sunlight glinted off the Phantom's canopy. Three hundred feet above the ground, the incendiary bomb left its multiple-ejection rack. Dash 1 added power and climbed away. Tumbling end over end, the teardrop canister followed the same course, losing speed and altitude until a gush of flame ripped through the undergrowth and trees north of the marines. Doc saw a North Vietnamese soldier, burning napalm clinging to his back, running frantically away from the firestorm. Without the Bird Dog overhead, the enemy would have already overwhelmed and killed the six Americans. Their plans thrown into confusion by the air strikes, the survivors were trying to regroup. More runs finished Lovebug's napes, and Doc brought in the two F-4s one after the other with their snakes. Trees and undergrowth were burning, and green and red tracers from attackers and defenders blazed through the smoke. At five hundred feet the small, slow Cessna seemed an easy target, and dozens of tracers rose toward it. Doc held his course and watched Dash 2 make his last run.

"Catkiller 1-8, Lovebug 202 is Winchester," Indian said to confirm that the racks on both Phantoms were empty. Doc acknowledged and advised that he would relay the BDA—bomb damage assessment— later. Indian clicked his mike switch. "Understood, Catkiller. You have your hands full. Lovebug 202, out." The marine aviators advanced their throttles. Light on fuel and no longer burdened by the weight and drag of almost six tons of ordnance under their wings, the two McDonnell-Douglas Phantoms were soon receding dots. Thousands of feet behind and below them the next act of the drama was unfolding.

"Doc," Happe said, "Mustang says the gooks have moved up and to put the next ones closer!"

Doc glanced at his windscreen to remind him who was waiting to the east at ten thousand feet. With Lovebug clear of the area, he vectored the smaller Skyhawks into his position. They had been monitoring the fight and were fully aware of the situation on the ground; there was no need for a detailed target brief. "Hellborne 412, this is Catkiller 1-8. Are you ready for my mark? Over."

For the next forty-five minutes, with chatter going in and out of three radios and between Doc and Happe on the intercom, Doc ran two more flights of Skyhawks, followed by a pair of Gunfighter F-4s. But the sun was dropping toward the mountains, and shadows were lengthening. They had to get the team out before dark. Happe had already identified an open area large enough to accommodate a rescue chopper, but it was a good four hundred meters to the northeast and blocked much of the way by almost impenetrable scrub. Doc used Gunfighter's last bombs to clear the worst of it, opening a ragged escape route visible only from the air. Happe and his pilot agreed on the next step of the rescue. Minutes later, two more call signs joined the chaotic mix of radio traffic.

"Catkiller 1-8, this is Chatterbox 3-2, flight of two orbiting five miles east of your position, with two Seaworthy guns. Over." This was the recon team's ride home, marine CH-46 Sea Knight helicopters escorted by Huey gunships.

"Roger, Chatterbox, this is Catkiller. Stand by. Hap, get those guys moving!"

"Mustang, this is Southern Hotel. Choppers inbound! Get going to your east!" The marines broke out of the bomb crater, heading across freshly churned earth, before Happe turned them north through a maze of splintered trees and burning undergrowth. He switched to the artillery push.

"Cherry Buster 6, this is Southern Hotel. From the last gun target line, add three hundred, right fifty, four rounds of whiskey papa. Repeat. Over." Five miles away the battery commander shouted instructions as sweating crews rammed the 97-pound shells and powder charges home and slammed and locked the breech blocks. The gunners took a twist of the heavy lanyards around wrists and held them taut, waiting. "Fire!" There were four staggered roars, the guns rocked under the massive recoil, and shells went moaning down-range. White phosphorus rounds impacted in quick succession, the clouds swelling to screen the approaching helicopters behind a wall of dense smoke. Happe saw a small group of enemy soldiers set off in pursuit and immediately adjusted the artillery, calling for high explosives and dropping the shells behind the marines.

One Chatterbox Sea Knight orbited away from the action, ready to take over if the other was hit. The lead chopper came in low to flare hard over the edge of the clearing. Before the wheel struts had bottomed, six young Americans were diving into the open tailgate, and Chatterbox was off again. A quick pedal turn swung them away from the artillery and pursuing enemy, the nose dropped, and they were thudding toward safety before the smoke screen had dissipated.

"Hap, let's teach those fuckers a lesson," Doc said, turning toward the enemy. The next flight of air was waiting and had him in sight. Doc acknowledged with, "Lovebug 305, this is Catkiller 1-8. Are you ready to observe my mark?"

WHEN THE LAST FLIGHT OF SKYHAWKS headed back to Chu Lai, Doc made a final low pass for a BDA and set course for Dong Ha. He lit his first cigarette since taking off that morning and replayed the encounter in his mind. It had been the most intense mission he had yet flown. But god*damn!*—he and Happe had pulled it off. Fifteen minutes later, he was chopping the throttle and easing the stick back, back, back until the wings lost lift and wheels touched down in a soft, three-point landing, the runway matting clicking and rattling on the rollout. Toes at the top of the rudder pedals, Doc braked to an easy stop. Soaked with sweat and feeling utterly drained, he shut down next to the fuel bladder to top off the wing tanks before taxiing to a revetment. When he and Happe walked into the line shack, six marines were slumped at the picnic table. They wearily got to their feet. It was the recon team.

Doc Clement: They looked like hell warmed over, all of them covered in mud and dust, a couple of them with singed hair from the napalm, their fatigues in shreds. They crowded around us, shaking our hands and thanking us. Then one of them said, "When we saw you that low with tracers all around your plane, we were sure you were going to get shot down, and that would be the end of our air cover. We couldn't believe that you kept doing it! If that's what your job is like, lieutenant, you'll never get *me* in one of those Bird Dogs. No *way!*"

As tired as I was, I had to grin. I guess everyone has his own natural element that he's comfortable in, and mine was definitely in the air. There wasn't enough money in the world to get me to do what those guys did.

DOC CAME THROUGH THE DOOR of the Catkiller officers club wearing his favorite Bermuda shorts, flip-flops, and a blue T-shirt that said "I'm Playing All Night." At the poker table were Lee Harrison, Glenn Strange, and Jim Hudson. Doc took a long pull from an ice-cold Budweiser and shook a Winston out of a fresh pack. "Yeah, we hosed the shit out of 'em. Six flights of air, and Happe laying the arty on 'em in between."

"Take much ground fire?"

"Fair bit." He expelled a cloud of smoke. "So what are we playing here, Stranger?"

"Kansas City."

"Sounds good to me. Let's go."

Chapter 2

The Apprentice

HAD BILL HOOPER WORKED A LITTLE HARDER IN college, he might have missed the war altogether. As it was, his first year's grades failed to impress the draft board, and the letter inviting him to attend army basic training duly arrived. For many young men during the Vietnam War it was a dreaded event; for Hooper, it would be the catalyst for a dramatic transformation from the lackadaisical to ferocious self-discipline. Two years later, having completed Officer Candidate School at Fort Sill, Oklahoma, and a year's purgatory at Fort Bliss, Texas, he was a first lieutenant halfway through pilot training. Those who had made it this far stood in a half circle next to the small airplane at Fort Rucker, Alabama. The instructor settled his baseball cap and put his hands on his hips.

"Gentlemen, this is the Cessna O-1 Bird Dog. It has no armor. It carries no offensive weapons. It is slower than the front-line fighter aircraft of the First World War. But those of you who end up flying this aircraft in combat will log more hours in your first three months than the jet jockeys will during an entire tour in Vietnam. Here, more than anywhere else in your training, you will learn the lessons that will keep you alive."

Finishing in the top third of his class, Hooper could not have been more proud when the silver wings were pinned on his uniform. Orders for Vietnam came with them. Given thirty days' leave, he returned to Florida. A high school friend just back from the war stopped by to shake his hand and whisper, "Don't be a hero." On the morning of his departure, Bill was awake long before the alarm rang. His mother, heartbroken at seeing her youngest son going to war, gave him a hard, desperate hug, saying little lest she dissolved in tears. Too awkward for much conversation, they headed for the airport and National Airlines Flight 27 to San Francisco, where he boarded Pan Am for Vietnam. On arrival, he was sent to the 21st Reconnaissance Airplane Company—the Black Aces—at the southern edge of I Corps. The next three months would serve as little more than an apprenticeship before reassignment to a far more demanding unit—the 220th RAC.

10 JUNE 1968

Some 170 miles south of the Catkillers, Hooper swept his eyes across rice paddies and forested mountains passing slowly below. Control stick and rudder pedals vibrated behind the six-cylinder engine, its throaty roar penetrating the hiss of earphones. With both windows open, the wind through the cockpit brought only slight relief from the heat and humidity on the ground. Just ahead and to his right, a second olive drab Bird Dog cruised at eighty-five knots, both aircraft floating slowly up and down like skiffs on an invisible sea. The white skull and crossbones overlaid on the black ace on the tail fins suggested more deadly intent than warranted by the aging Cessnas, yet Hooper couldn't help glancing with satisfaction at the underwing rocket tubes loaded with HEs—high explosive warheads. Twenty-two years old and untried by enemy fire, knowing he was armed and in search of the enemy added to the nervous excitement of his first combat patrol.

"Black Ace 3-7, this is Black Ace 3-4. Over."

Hooper thumbed the mike button. "Roger, Black Ace 3-4, this is 3-7. Over."

"Three-seven, there it is at twelve o'clock, about two miles."

Staring over the faded paint on the engine cowling, Hooper spotted the grass landing strip at the apex of an L-shaped valley. A low pass brought CIA-paid Montagnard mercenaries out of their huts to move the grazing buffalo. He touched down, feeling the rumble of the spring-steel wheel struts flexing rapidly over the uneven ground, then swung around with rudder and a burst of power, taxied back, and shut down. Hot exhaust manifolds ticked in the silence, the humidity closed around him again, and sweat darkened his jungle fatigues. A special forces sergeant appeared for the bag of mail they'd brought and led them to the old French hunting lodge under the trees. Hooper was politely ignored, as befitted his newcomer's status, while the other pilot spent the next half-hour gossiping with them.

The second part of the mission was to scout the east-west leg of the valley. Because the area was an important source of food for the

Viet Cong and a route for moving weapons and supplies down to the coastal plain, it had been declared a free-fire zone. Anyone found there was assumed to be enemy and therefore a legitimate target. The two Bird Dogs had made a slow sweep and turned for the coast when the special forces camp reported that a Main Force Viet Cong unit had been seen moving a herd of water buffalo. They banked toward the map coordinates and within minutes spotted a dozen dark Asian cattle and five herdsmen in black peasant clothing and conical hats. Three bolted for the nearest tree line. Hooper saw arms rising and falling as the last two whipped the animals toward the trees. Reporting their discovery, the pilots were told to engage the target. Black Ace 3-4 acknowledged the order, rolled in quickly, and snapped off a rocket that missed by more than a hundred meters. Now it was Hooper's turn.

Bill Hooper: I had fired one rocket in flight school, a final exercise over a peaceful range in Alabama barely six weeks earlier. Mouth so dry I could barely swallow, I reviewed the classroom lecture. A little stick and rudder swung the nose until I could just see the two Viet Cong down the right side of the fuselage. Pulling up, I waited for the first shudder of a stall, then released back pressure on the stick. The nose dropped below the horizon, and my first live targets came into view through the windscreen. Time slowed and my senses seemed to expand, eyes recording their every movement, hand intimately aware of the control stick and trigger, ears drumming to engine, wind, and my own pulse.

He glanced at the air speed indicator: ninety knots and increasing. Optimum speed for firing a rocket was one hundred. He remembered the instructor emphasizing that when firing two rockets at the same time, they had to be from opposite sides of the airplane to prevent them colliding with each other. Beyond the sun-crackled windscreen, faces turned toward him. *Run!* he thought. He lifted his hand to the overhead panel and armed the outboard tubes. Another glance at the air speed: ninety-five knots. *Forget those stupid animals and run!* But they were still there. The needle reached one hundred knots. Time had run out. He squeezed the trigger. Two rockets ignited with a fluid *bang!* and shot forward in a sparkling shower of propellant. His eyes followed their flight. One exploded between, and the other just ahead of the two figures. He recovered at three hundred feet and looked back to see the buffalo loping awkwardly out of the cloud of earth and smoke. As he climbed away, Black Ace 3-4 was shouting excitedly that he'd gotten both of them.

Bill Hooper: "Gotten both of them?" I thought. Celebration was the farthest thing from my mind. I had just killed two people, and suddenly I wanted it to be a movie. Come on, isn't it time for everyone to get up and brush themselves off? "Black Ace 3-4, this is 3-7. Cover me, I'm going back down!" I had to see what I had done. To make sure.

"COVER YOU?" HE LAUGHED into his mike. "What am I supposed to cover you with?"

"Just watch me, I'm going back down!" Hooper chopped the throttle and crossed the controls. These were the enemy, he kept telling himself, and this was what he was here for. Recovering from the slip, he broke toward the bodies and crossed over them at seventy-five feet. The transition from the war films of his youth to reality came with the sight of the first crumpled figure. Only feet away a smaller body lay face down in the grass. He had just slaughtered a child.

Muzzle flashes sparkled in the tree line, and Black Ace 3-4 shouted to break off. Hooper looked toward the source of the tracers just as two men on bicycles appeared under his left wing, assault rifles slung over their backs and pedaling furiously down a well-worn path toward a hillock.

Why hadn't they taken the boy? Why did they leave him to die?

He stood the Bird Dog on its wing and held the stick in his gut, head craning over his shoulder. The horizon spun past the nose, and he snapped the wings level behind them. It wasn't his fault, but theirs, and he focused his fury on them, slamming the throttle forward and descending through fifty feet. Green tracers spilled from the trees and 3-4's voice shouted in his earphones, but Hooper was too bent on revenge to consider how dangerously exposed he was. He armed both inboard tubes, closing the range until he couldn't miss. Just before they reached cover, he squeezed the trigger. One rocket overflew into the trees, but the other exploded on the edge of the hillock, knocking both men off their bicycles. Passing over them at twenty-five feet, he saw one crawling frantically on his hands and knees into thick foliage. He hauled the Bird Dog around in tight 180-degree turn and flew over the position once more. They were both gone, and the engagement was over.

Bill Hooper: I formed up in a loose echelon with 3-4, who was reporting the engagement and body count to the special forces camp, and followed him back to Quang Ngai in silence. After we had parked the planes in the revetments, he started to congratulate me, saw my face, and stopped. I can't remember more of that day, save weeping in the privacy of my room. Perhaps the saddest thing of all was that I would learn to be unemotional about killing, eventually joining others who were very good at it.

THE 3RD PLATOON OF THE 21ST Reconnaissance Airplane Company was billeted in a former French citadel in Quang Ngai, its whitewashed walls, gun ports, and enormous wooden gates a legacy of the departed colonial army. They shared it with a few U.S. Air Force FACs, who flew Cessna O-2 Super Skymasters, and a team of Australian army advisers. Under operational control of Military Assistance Command, Vietnam (MACV) Advisory Team 2 and tasked with supporting the 2nd ARVN Division, they flew out of a small airfield some five kilometers west of the Beau Geste fort. The senior officer at the citadel was air force Lieutenant Colonel Sterling.

Probing attacks by Main Force Viet Cong and North Vietnamese Army units on Quang Ngai were almost nightly affairs, and soon after Hooper's arrival it was decided to strengthen the citadel's defenses. Army engineers arrived to construct heavy frames for bunkers and observation towers clad with thick planks. When not flying, the Black Aces were tasked with filling and stacking sandbags around the eight-foot-high huts. A passing marine's comment that their size made them easier to hit was frostily ignored by their designer, Lieutenant Colonel Sterling. No goddamn marine was going to tell him how to build a bunker. Hooper's team was assigned to one that faced a wide gap bulldozed out of the wall by the French when they withdrew twelve years earlier. Given the enemy threat, the Americans needed little encouragement to complete their last-stand position, though Hooper couldn't understand the colonel's order that the side facing the hole be the last to receive its sandbags. The rolls of concertina wire that filled the breach might slow an infantry assault but not bullets.

"Sir," he asked, "could I make a suggestion?"

"I don't know, I don't know. Okay, what? What's your suggestion?"

"Colonel, since that's where we're most exposed"—Hooper pointed toward the gap in the wall—"shouldn't we stack the sandbags in front first?"

"You'll place those sandbags where I tell you, lieutenant."

Between flying and sleeping, it took three days to sandbag the back and each end of the bunker. The most vulnerable side hadn't been started when Friday afternoon arrived and the work parties were stood down for the weekend. Hooper was tempted to point out that the NVA and VC worked seven days a week, but his blistered hands overrode the temptation.

At one o'clock on Saturday morning he lay awake in his bunk, listening to the sounds of incoming when the wail of the emergency siren jerked him upright. They'd broken through! Hauling on boots and flak jacket, he grabbed his M16 and a bandolier of magazines and ran for the bunker in his underwear. As Sterling's assistant gunner, he dropped alongside to help set up and load the M60 machine gun, and then prepared to start feeding the ammunition belt. Marine Corporal Rackhart, who flew with the Black Aces as an observer, scampered up the tower. The sounds of the enemy assault were intensifying from every quadrant of the city. Automatic weapons fire grew closer and sharper, while mortar shells and 122mm rockets exploded across Quang Ngai. After a long, tense moment, Hooper glanced to his right to see Sterling glaring at his boxers.

"Lieutenant Hooper, after we secure from this drill, you and I are going to have a serious discussion about being out of uniform."

Over the sounds of battle, a taut voice somewhere in the bunker muttered, "Somehow, colonel, I don't think this is a drill."

Beyond the barbed wire fence a streetlight illuminated a paved intersection. Sweating bodies attracted mosquitoes, which they tried to brush away without taking their gaze from the lighted area beyond the concertina wire. Everyone was psyching himself for face-to-face ground action, something they were neither trained nor prepared for. Acutely aware that the two-inch planks between the approaching enemy and themselves would do little to slow down an AK-47 bullet, Hooper had already decided that at the first shots he was abandoning Sterling and his machine gun to fight from behind the bunker.

"They're coming down the street!" Corporal Rackhart shouted from above.

Safeties snapped down and saucer-sized eyes stared over gunsights. There! Something moved! Whispers: "Where, for fuck's sake?" "There. Just to the left." "Yeah, I think I saw it." "Oh, shit." Fingers took up slack in triggers. Any second now. And at that moment a little brown and white dog trotted into the light. He stared directly at the bunker for a moment, sat down for a good scratch, then turned and disappeared into the night. An hour later, the explosions stopped. Covered in sweat, dirt, and mosquito bites, they stumbled back to their rooms. The next morning, Lieutenant Colonel Sterling had them busy stacking sandbags against the front of his bunker.

A NORMAL WORKING DAY STARTED SOON AFTER sunup when the duty jeep joined carts, foot traffic, and motor scooters for the slow drive to the airstrip. The congestion often reduced its speed to a crawl, making the pilots easy targets for someone with a grenade, and it was always a relief when they crossed the Quang Ngai River and entered the gates of the airfield. They would fly a morning mission, return to refuel and fill out their flight reports, then fly an afternoon mission before heading back to the citadel. There was also a rotation for night missions to locate the muzzle flashes of enemy mortars. On one of these missions, Hooper came under fire by a .50-caliber machine gun manned by their allies, the Army of the Republic of South Vietnam. Imbued as he was with the culture of John Wayne and Duty, Honor, and Country, it was the first of many lessons that led to an increasingly tainted view of the ARVN. Stories of incompetence, corruption, and cowardice were legion. Away from the battlefield, their arrogance infuriated those risking their lives to support them. ARVN soldiers swaggered through Quang Ngai, webbing festooned with grenades, hollow chests crisscrossed with ammunition belts, and weapons slung from hips and shoulders. Given their diminutive stature, Hooper sometimes wondered how they could stand under the weight of it all.

Listening to the morning briefing, he noticed the ring pin from a smoke grenade on the floor. Identical to those used in hand grenades, it went into his pocket. On the way to the airfield he spotted two ARVNs on a Honda motor scooter and asked the jeep driver to ease alongside. The Vietnamese soldier on the back looked across the two-foot gap and Hooper gave him comradely smile. The ARVN answered with an indifferent stare and looked away. Hooper leaned over and tugged his shirt next to one of his grenades. The head snapped around, and Bill lifted his hand to show him the pin.

A sudden convulsion caused the driver to look over his shoulder and do a double take. Panic ensued. In a blur of motion, the passenger began unloading every grenade he could reach before the one in question blew him to smithereens, while the driver, trying to retain control of the Honda with one hand, was desperately trying to shove him off with the other. Hooper was still wiping the tears from his eyes as they drove through the gate of the airfield.

When he returned to the citadel late that afternoon, there was a message to report to the senior American advisor. He grabbed a jeep and made it to the MACV office an hour after sundown. Sitting behind the desk was a large U.S. Marine major, sleeves rolled up to reveal massive forearms. He picked up a memo. "I received a complaint about you harassing a couple of ARVN troops. Want to tell me what happened?" When Hooper finished, the major tried hard to keep a straight face. "Yep, that's exactly what they said, and I promised to take swift and decisive action." He looked up from beneath thick eyebrows. Hooper waited. The major cleared his throat. "As soon as I think of something, I'll let you know."

"Hey, Lieutenant Hooper, you ready for another beer?"

Mouth full of steak, Bill mumbled "Yessir" and accepted the ice-cold Bud from his CO, who was celebrating the completion of his second tour in Vietnam. Most the 21st RAC's officers and NCOs had gathered at the Chu Lai headquarters to bid him farewell and welcome his replacement. Six pilots and two crew chiefs had flown up from Quang Ngai at noon. A third crew chief had drawn the short straw and stayed behind to mind the store. T-bones sizzled on smoking barbecues, and a mountain of beer was steadily dwindling as the Black Aces and assorted guests ate and drank to their hearts' content. Sitting on an ammo box next to Hooper, Matt Barlow peeled the pop-top off a fresh beer and took a long, satisfying pull. "I think this is gonna be my last one," he said. "We still gotta fly back."

Hooper nodded. The never-to-be-broken rule enshrined somewhere was No Drinking Within Twenty-Four Hours of Flying. "This is only my third," Bill shrugged, feeling very grown up. "Besides, you know what they say: No Drinking Within Twenty-Four Feet of the Airplane."

"That's it," Barlow giggled. The conversation lapsed. The Beach Boys were singing "California Girls." "Whadja think of Ten Fucks?" Barlow asked, referring to their flight that morning to the remote fire-support base at Tien Phuoc with a load of mail and paperwork. It had been Hooper's first visit, and the jeep ride from airstrip to camp revealed impressive defenses. Sited on a low hill, the base faced a wide, shallow river to the west, while the balance of the perimeter looked over rice paddies with fields of fire out to three hundred meters. Inside a minefield and concertinas of razor wire, interconnecting trenches led from machine gun bunkers to mortar positions and four 155mm guns. The route to the command bunker of reinforced concrete was via a twisting, sandbagged passageway overlooked by gunports and ending at a steel door. But, however muscular in appearance, Tien Phuoc's Achilles' heel was the single overland road to it. If the NVA attacked at night or during the monsoon season, when American air support would be limited at best, the camp was on its own until ground forces could fight their way through. The flaw was so obvious that good manners precluded asking, "What if?" Coffee mug in hand, Hooper followed one of the gun commanders around the base. They stopped next to his 155. "How often do you get hit?" Hooper asked.

"Pretty regular. Mortars, rockets sometimes, snipers. Nothin' we can't handle," he said. "They haven't gotten real serious yet."

"What's real serious?"

"Human-wave shit at night. I'd like to see the little bastards try, though. We got enough flares and ammo to keep going 'til daylight, and then we'll have the air force up there calling in tacair, right? Hey, no problem." His confidence seemed a little forced, and Hooper breathed a small sigh of relief when he and Barlow lifted off for Quang Ngai.

"Man," Barlow said, cracking another beer, "can you imagine being stuck out there? Wouldn't be my idea of a hot time. No sirree, not this boy."

It was late afternoon and the sun had begun its descent. Quang Ngai airstrip had no runway lights, and halfhearted suggestions that they should head back were met with, "Okay, just one more for the road." Suddenly, the sun was perilously close to the horizon, and they still had a thirty-minute flight ahead of them. Six pilots and two crew chiefs stumbled for the flight line. With four aircraft, the first decision was that the most sober pilots had to fly. Inasmuch as two of their number had passed out, this was a simple matter of elimination. Those two were poured into the back seats, and the olive drab Cessnas fishtailed toward the runway, pilots denying responsibility for the broken taxiway lights in their wake.

"When the sun disappeared behind the mountains, it was like someone had switched off the lights," Hooper said. They followed the coastline south to the mouth of the Quang Ngai River and followed it inland, looking for the second bridge that led toward the airfield. Totally befuddled, they turned at the first bridge, which took them over the center of the blacked-out city, and played follow-the-platoon-leader as he flicked on his landing lights and descended to a hundred feet in search of the runway. That all four aircraft missed all three of Quang Ngai's two-hundred-foot radio masts and their cables was a miracle.

The short-strawed crew chief stepped out of the line shack to see landing lights wandering round the sky and raced a jeep to the end of the runway. Spotting the headlights, the platoon leader came under sniper fire on short final, but bounced to a landing and taxied back to the approach end. With his aircraft's landing light and the jeep's headlights illuminating the threshold, the rest of the Bird Dogs wobbled in. Shutting down, they helped their drunken comrades from the back seats.

"Some people just can't handle it," someone said beerily. "Hell, I probably fly better when I'm drunk." "Yeah, me too." "Anyone see me grease that landing?" "Which one? The way your lights were bouncing you must have made three or four." "Fuck you." "Who the hell almost ran into me?" "Not me." "It wasn't me." "Me either."

The sober crew chief made a quick check of the aircraft, stomped back to the jeep, and delivered them in brooding silence to their quarters. He climbed out and walked around the jeep to see a pilot fall from his seat to the ground. A fresh roar of laughter shook everyone. When the pilot swayed to his feet, the crew chief could contain himself no longer. "What I want to know, sir," he demanded grumpily, "is who's going to clean up the puke in the back of that airplane?"

Chapter 3

Catkiller on Crutches

After an earlier tour with the 219th RAC Headhunters at Pleiku I was assigned as executive officer to the 220th in early '68, and took over as CO from Millard Pedersen in August. By this time our focus was on A Shau Valley interdiction and the destruction of artillery and antiaircraft positions in North Vietnam. Those who flew these missions were unique: self-reliant, aggressive, determined, and tenacious. And because they were virtually on their own from takeoff to landing, it also required a personality bordering on controlled recklessness. Several men didn't make the grade and were reassigned to other units that had less demanding missions.

—Jim Wisby, Catkiller 6
August 1968–January 1969

CHARLES FINCH: WHEN MAC BYRD AND I ARRIVED at Phu Bai in late July '68, I was assigned to the 2nd Platoon. I had already learned that flying out of Dong Ha guaranteed action and lobbied Major Wisby to move me to the Myth Makers. He was easy to convince, as he was getting ready to rotate some of the 1st Platoon guys who'd been getting their asses shot off for the last six months.

A few days after my check ride, I sprained an ankle playing volleyball and was taken off flying status. This coincided with increasing numbers of engagements between the NVA and American forces across I Corps. The 1st Platoon was already stretched between supporting the marines and army. Flying six to eight hours a day was exhausting enough; dashing into bunkers while on the ground to shelter from the night-and-day rocket attacks left everyone fatigued and on edge. Seeing new guy Finch hobbling around on crutches or sitting in the officers club writing letters did not make a good impression.

On August 10, I was in the hospital for more x-rays when I heard choppers coming in. Doctors and medics ran to meet the dust-off Hueys filled with wounded. "I had never seen so much gore, guts, and people in severe pain in all my life," I wrote to my wife Nancy.

No one seemed to have enough morphine. I saw two die from massive head wounds while others were inside having limbs amputated. Body bags were being tagged and sent to the morgue.

Here I was, never having seen combat, in a nice clean flight suit and all I could do was hand out cigarettes to these poor shot-up paratroopers from the 101st Airborne. I felt so damn uncomfortable and useless. They told me they'd been in a firefight near the Ta Bat outpost in the A Shau Valley when the air support arrived. Whether the air force F-100s had a bad mark from a FAC or just blew the target no one could say, but these kids had been hit with 20mm and rockets. Eight were killed and something like fifty wounded. I heard over and over about one GI that had only two weeks left in country. His buddies were bitterly asking why he was allowed to go back in the bush.

They were sweeping blood out of the helicopters. The boys are all so young. They haven't been clean in weeks and their uniforms were rotting off their bodies, they'd had them on so long. . . . It is really a pitiful sight. I have been here two weeks now and I am doubtful whether the war is really worth it. I have seen very few Vietnamese whom I could have any compassion for. . . . Talking to some of them up here I get the impression there is no real desire to end the war. . . . I just don't know the answer.

I never forgot what I saw that day, and it probably accounted for my being so careful whenever I ran air strikes near friendlies. Some weeks later, when Bill Hooper arrived at the 220th, we had troops in contact, and I broke in on the radio and aborted a flight that he had cleared hot. The NVA got away. When we landed, Bill was so angry I thought he was going to hit me. I didn't bother explaining.

I was more excited than nervous the first time I flew up to Dong Ha. I didn't know that much about calling in artillery or running air strikes, but Doc Clement and Roger Bounds told me to just watch and listen. Doc gave me a card with the marine and air force designations for all the different types of ordnance they carried, the locations of all our artillery batteries, the frequencies, everything.

Over the next few weeks, instead of flying back to Phu Bai at the end of a mission day, I took to hanging around the flight shack to pick up tips, toured Dong Ha DASC to listen to their radios, reviewed photos of the area, and was briefed on the NVA artillery and their gun target lines. I colored my map more than anyone and eventually knew more about where the marines were in our area of operations than my marine back seats did.

Although I got my share of ragging from the old-timers and had to pay my dues, I became very comfortable real quick and decided that I preferred flying low ship on Tally Ho missions. High ship flew at five thousand feet while low ship was supposed to fly around three thousand feet, but I started going a lot lower, which pissed off the high ships because they couldn't keep track of me. I became increasingly aggressive, and those who flew with me gave me a lot of grief about what they considered to be dangerous tactics. I wasn't a daredevil or a cowboy, but I hated seeing marines in body bags loaded onto those helicopters. If I was going to fly two three-hour missions almost seven days out of ten, then I wanted to kill as many NVA as I could. We enjoyed incredible independence as Catkillers, and I stretched it to the max.

Marine backseaters like Russ Cedoz, Mike LaFromboise, and others had confidence in us. We knew the TAOR and they trusted us to take the fight to the enemy. When our 108th observers needed to find the NVA guns north of the Ben Hai River, they relied a lot on our knowledge of the terrain. It was a dangerous job, and we were all afraid at times, but no amount of ground fire would keep us from supporting the marines or army grunts and bringing hell down on the enemy. We were all proud of what we did and proud of each another.

Chapter 4

Black Ace to Catkiller

The marines had been fighting hard and taken casualties. I saw some bodies and asked them if they'd recovered all their wounded. They said they had, but I decided to make a low pass to check if there were any still between the lines. I was about five feet off the deck and maybe thirty feet from the bodies when a dozen NVA suddenly stood up, firing at me from the hip. I could see the whites of their eyes. I thought, "What a dumbass move *that* was!"

—Doc Clement, Catkiller 18

BILL HOOPER: THOUGH WE DIDN'T TAKE FIRE ALL that often flying out of Quang Ngai, our observers pointed out that if the pilot was hit, they were helpless. We took their point and decided to give them enough basic instruction to get the airplane down in one piece. It was on one of these training sessions that I almost killed Corporal Rackhart and myself.

Finishing our mission early one day, I decided to introduce him to stall-spin recovery. Rackhart, who had a black belt in tae kwon do, had been giving me karate lessons, and his teaching techniques regularly left me bruised and sore. A little payback was in order. Climbing to 2,500 feet, I explained over the intercom how a right spin was counteracted somewhat by the torque of the engine, while a left spin was accelerated by it. Leveling off, I brought the throttle back to idle and pulled the nose up until the Bird Dog started to shudder. I kicked right rudder and, true to the immutable laws of aerodynamics, the right wing dropped and she fell off into a spin.

A phenomenon of a spin is that with each rotation there will be a distinct *whoosh* from the wings as the spin becomes tighter and faster and finally reaches its maximum rate. To get out of it, the pilot releases back pressure on the stick to allow the wings to start generating lift again, kicks opposite rudder, and then gently pulls the stick back to return to level flight. We recovered at a thousand feet and started climbing again. "See how easy that was?" I said over the intercom. There was a queasy response from the back seat and I smiled.

"Now we'll try one to the left." Throttle and stick all the way back, she starts to shudder, full left rudder, the wing drops abruptly, and we fall off in the spin. *Whoosh.* "See how much tighter this one is than the last one, and how much faster we're losing altitude?" I inquired calmly. *Whoosh . . . whoosh.* Skipping mention of the obvious first step to recovery, I said with extreme cool, "Now, to get out of it we kick opposite rudder." I hoofed in rudder, but nothing happened. *Whoosh-whoosh.*

My enjoyment of Rackhart's discomfort had seen me allow the spin to accelerate, and I was suddenly anxious to get out of it. I shoved the rudder pedal to the firewall again. No response. *Whooshwhooshwhoosh.* A third time and nothing. What the hell was going on? Then I looked at the ground coming up. I closed my eyes, took a deep breath, and thought, "What are the steps?" First step: release back pressure on the stick. I looked down and saw the stick in my gut. Idiot! I shoved it forward. Second step: opposite rudder.

We came out of the spin and I hauled back on the stick. The nose lifted abruptly, and we were once more out of control, buffeting in a high-speed stall. We were going in! I eased the stick forward, and then back again, forward, then back, the ground rising to fill my peripheral vision. I braced for the impact.

Suddenly we were straight and level, the windscreen filled by a thatched roof in front of thirty-foot-tall trees. I hauled back on the stick, clawing for altitude as the hut flashed by inches below the landing gear. I was staring at the trees, teeth clinched, when we hit. There was a crash as my wheels tore through the top branches, and I blinked in amazement. We were still flying. I turned for Quang Ngai and climbed gratefully to a thousand feet. After landing and finishing our debriefing, I led Rackhart outside. "Did you understand what was going on out there?"

"Oh, yes, sir," he said cheerfully. "I'll have to practice a little bit—if you'll let me—on getting into one of those stalls and getting out again. But that last spin you did? You were just fucking with me, weren't you?"

I stared at him for a second, then managed a rueful shrug. Convinced he had seen through my transparent attempt to scare him, a grinning Rackhart threw a comradely salute and turned for his billet. I headed shakily toward the officers club and a stiff drink.

26 AUGUST 1968
Awakened by an unusually heavy mortar and rocket barrage, we had gathered in the ops room to monitor the radios. By 0300 we heard that enemy forces had penetrated the city limits and were engaged in street-to-street fighting with units of the 2nd ARVN Division. This didn't sound good, and we all ran to grab M16s, flak jackets, and steel helmets. The next tense radio message was that both bridges over the Quang Ngai river were under heavy attack. Just after dawn we heard that the main bridge had been blown and the other heavily damaged. The order came to launch a single aircraft to provide reconnaissance and fire support.

I waited for someone to do a Robert Mitchum routine like, "Them cross-eyed little bastards couldn't hit me if they tried," and head toward the airfield, but the silence was broken only by the sounds of battle and requests for air support crackling from the radio. When it seemed everyone had taken an odd interest in the ceiling, I stepped forward. There was a collective sigh and someone ran to get the jeep. Surrounded by well-wishers, I zipped up my flak jacket, snapped the chinstrap on my helmet, and settled behind the wheel, the first twinges of doubt beginning to weigh. Maybe I'd been a little hasty. Dropping two bandoliers of magazines on the passenger seat, I laid the M16 across my lap and turned the key. More men gathered to ask what was going on.

"The new guy, he's going by himself."

"Good on ya, mate," an Aussie grinned. "Don't think ya want to give me that nice watch for safe keeping, do ya?"

Mouth too dry to spit, I was on the verge of switching off the engine when someone asked if I was ready. Trapped by the youthful folly of my own *beau geste*, I nodded mutely. The gates swung open and my supporters scattered. Alone in the center of the compound, I stared down an empty boulevard and thought of the scene through the periscope in the film *On the Beach*. I closed my eyes for a second, took a deep breath, and floored the accelerator. Shoulders hunched and neck pulled down, my eyes flicked back and forth, trying to pinpoint the sources of the gunfire as I raced through the center of the town, hearing the ebb and flow of battle at each intersection.

Approaching the river, I saw the bodies of three Main Force Viet Cong lying alongside the road, hands and feet tied around bamboo poles. Just beyond them, ARVN troops were shoring up the remaining bridge with temporary bracing. I crossed and entered the gate. The 1st Americal Division had secured the airfield during the night, and none of our aircraft had been damaged.

Taxiing out of the revetment, I listened to reports of increased enemy activity in the southwest quadrant of Quang Ngai. Minutes later I was overhead and talking to Australian and U.S. advisers, who explained that the enemy had already lost the initiative and were attempting to escape across the river. Marine A-4s orbited overhead, unable to attack because of the proximity of enemy and friendly forces to each other, and the fact that, as an army pilot, I wasn't allowed to run them. Only air force FACs could do that, and they were committed elsewhere. By 1000 hours there were at least a dozen contact points, and I was flying from one to another to provide updates on enemy locations, access routes, and potential ambush sites. I continued on my own until late morning, when another pilot joined me, followed by two more in the early afternoon.

I had been flying all day over a hamlet that lay about five hundred meters west of the airfield. What no one knew was that a group of VC was trapped there and waiting for nightfall to make their escape. Coming in for my second refueling, I looked down on an ARVN platoon in a skirmish line. They were moving across a dry rice paddy toward the hamlet. I saw one man fall and the others turn to run. Then I spotted muzzle flashes winking in the hamlet. Reporting that I had troops in contact, I hauled the Bird Dog around in a tight bank, leveled the wings, lined up, and fired two rockets into the grass huts. They exploded with hard, bright flashes, sending confetti clouds of dry thatch into the air. One hooch was already burning as I rolled in a second time and triggered my remaining two rockets. As soon as I radioed the situation, ARVN M113 armored personnel carriers roared in on three sides of the hamlet and opened fire with their .50-caliber machine guns. Hearing that no helicopter gunships were available, I explained to the U.S. advisor with them that our rockets packed roughly the same punch as a 105mm howitzer shell, and he enthusiastically pressed us into service as his tactical air support.

Back on the ground, I directed the line crew to set up an arming post on the taxiway. This allowed us to turn off the runway, stop for fresh rockets and be airborne within three minutes of touching down. Taking off, we'd turn cross wind, turn again on the downwind leg, roll in on the target, and fire closely spaced pairs of rockets at a slant range of 150 to 200 meters, before reestablishing the downwind leg. A tight turn to base leg and final and we'd be back at the arming post again. It was almost dusk when all return fire from the village finally ceased. The after-action report listed one ARVN wounded and nineteen NVA killed or wounded. I was earning my spurs.

Badly bruised, the NVA pulled back from Quang Ngai, and things returned to the normality of boring night patrols. I was ruefully contemplating serving out my time here when the army realized that because many aviation companies had deployed to Vietnam as a unit, they would lose their experienced pilots at the end of their twelve-month tour. To balance this, it was decided to spread new arrivals throughout the companies of the 212th Combat Support Aviation Battalion. One of us would be reassigned to the 220th Reconnaissance Airplane Company in Phu Bai. This was my chance. I marched into my CO's office. He reluctantly closed a Superman comic book, laid it on a pile of others in his in-tray—the only items on an otherwise clean desk—and listened to my request with a look of genuine astonishment. He nodded and was already engrossed in his Superman by the time I marched out the door. If he'd asked why I was volunteering, I could have said that, as a bachelor, I had less to lose than those with wives and children. More honestly, I was becoming addicted to combat and wanted more. The action I had been craving was fast approaching.

19 SEPTEMBER 1968

I'd arrived in Phu Bai the day before, met my new CO, Maj. Jim "Gee" Wisby, and gone through all the administrative horseshit, before drawing my equipment and lugging it to my assigned hooch. Now it was just after sunup and I waited on the ramp for the company instructor pilot. Regardless of experience, having one's flying skills graded was standard procedure for any new arrival in an aviation unit. I started to yawn and almost choked at the unexpected voice. "You Hooper, the new guy?" I twisted around to see a short, barrel-chested first lieutenant planted like a tree stump in front of me. "Doc Clement," he said in a gravelly North Carolina accent, taking my outstretched hand in a crushing grip. "Ready for your check ride?"

"You bet."

When he brought his cigarette up for a drag, the sleeve of his flight suit stretched tight around his biceps. That, and a sturdy, shoulder-swinging swagger, suggested he was not someone to mess with. On the way to the flight line, I listened to a story about carrier landings and being thrown out of a marine officers club. Impossible. No one got thrown out of marine officers clubs. We stopped at his airplane.

"Let's get a few basics out of the way first, okay? A Bird Dog's a good airplane, but with all the radios, rockets, the armored seat and full fuel tanks, she's so heavy, she'll ground loop on ya in heartbeat if you're not on the ball. Ever ground looped?" I shook my head. "Well, I'll tell ya a little secret, Ace. There are those who've ground looped a taildragger, and those who will, so don't think your shit don't stink, okay?" I nodded, thought better of it, and shook my head to confirm I wouldn't dream of thinking my shit didn't stink. Doc worked his way into the back seat. "Okay, let's get this over with."

Three hours later we were back on the ground. Doc had put me through the wringer with high-angle approaches, engine-outs, and spin recovery; picked targets for the rockets; and shown me techniques with the Bird Dog I'd never even heard about. "I don't want someone going up north who has to think about flying," he'd barked over the intercom. "You got to wear an O-1, or you're gonna get hurt. Okay?"

We climbed out and headed for the operations room. "That wasn't too bad," he said grudgingly. Two pilots were leaning over an aerial chart spread on the table when we entered. Doc made the introductions. "Captain Anderson, the company ops officer, and Lieutenant Harrison." We shook hands. "He's okay, Andy," Doc said, heading out the door, "so put him to work."

Anderson motioned me to a chair. "Let me give you a few basics first," he said in an east Texas twang. "The 12th Marines give us most of our DMZ missions and the 108th Field Artillery gives us counterbattery missions north of the Ben Hai." He turned the map toward me. "Headquarters is here at Phu Bai, but the 1st Platoon stages out of Dong Ha, which is straight up Highway 1 about sixty miles. We're tasked with three missions a day: early morning, noon, and afternoon, each one three hours long. Late afternoon missions fly from Phu Bai, stop at Dong Ha to pick up observers and operational orders, then head north. We land back at Dong Ha at last light, remain overnight, then fly an early morning and a noon mission. We drop off our observers there and refuel, then come back to Phu Bai. The next shift takes over and does the same thing. I hope you like to fly, because you're going to be doing a lot of it until the monsoon season starts. By the way, the Old Man has just moved Jim Hudson out of the 1st Platoon to supply officer, so you'll be taking his call sign of 1-2."

"What sort of missions were you flying out of Quang Ngai?" asked Lee Harrison, another Texan.

"Pretty much general reconnaissance."

"Take much ground fire down there?"

"Not a lot," I said cautiously.

"What Lee's leading up to—mind if I butt in, Lee?—is that the 1st Platoon works the hottest area for O-1s in-theater." Anderson traced the wandering blue line of the Ben Hai River and the clearly marked demilitarized zone. "You can forget about the DMZ being demilitarized. You're likely to get shot at anywhere, anytime. As soon as you cross the river, though, the threat gets real serious.

"How often do you take fire?"

"What do you reckon, Lee? Maybe 70 to 80 percent of missions north of the river?"

"Something like that." Harrison uncoiled his heavy, six-foot frame and rummaged through a C-ration pack. "They're so damn good at camouflage," he said, cutting into a can of peaches with practiced twists of a P38 opener. "You never know where they are, because they move the guns around. And they like to wait until you're flying away from them. That way you miss the muzzle flashes and don't see the tracers 'til they're all around you." He speared a peach and lifted it out of the thick syrup.

"I know you had some defensive flying at Rucker," Anderson interrupted. I nodded. It was something Doc had also lectured me on.

Cross-controlling by pushing the rudder one way and holding opposite aileron with the stick put the Bird Dog in a skid and held its nose a few degrees off its actual flight path. If the enemy gunners tried to lead the aircraft by aiming directly ahead of the nose, their first burst would, hopefully, pass to one side. "I can't emphasize it enough here," Anderson continued. "You've got to cross-control and constantly change heading and altitude when you're up there. Fly straight and level over Tally Ho and you're going to get your ass shot off."

"How often do you actually take hits?"

"Regularly," Harrison shrugged, as if to say that bullet holes were just part of the job, then added, "We've lost three pilots and two observers this year to ground fire." I stared. "When the gooks overran Hue Airfield during Tet, they blew up seven of our Bird Dogs"—I must have stared even harder—"but we haven't lost anyone for a while." He drank the last of the syrup and wiped his chin. "Ready to go to work?"

An hour later the interlocking aluminum matting of the Dong Ha runway rattled like castanets as I touched down behind Harrison and taxied to a partially buried fuel bladder surrounded by sandbags. We topped off our wing tanks and strolled toward the line shack. A deuce-and-a-half raised a trail of dust on the other side of the runway as a Huey settled on the ramp behind us and a C-123 cargo aircraft squatted on the taxiway doing a run-up and mag check. The smells of turbine and piston-engine exhausts made the muggy air seem even thicker.

When we entered the line shack, our two aerial observers were sitting at the picnic table. "Bill Hooper, meet Bill Norton from the 108th Field Artillery Group. We shoot their big guns a lot." I had no reason to suspect that on the day I'd fly my last mission in Vietnam, this lean officer would save both of our lives. "And this is Steve Bezold," Harrison said, lifting his chin toward the other aerial observer of the 108th. "So what do you have for us today?"

Bezold handed over the op orders, and Harrison opened his map case to show me where we were going. My first mission as a Catkiller would be up to Tally Ho, with Bezold in my back seat. As high ship, we'd cross the Ben Hai River at five thousand feet, two thousand feet higher than Harrison and Norton. "Never lose track of the low ship," Harrison cautioned. "If he goes down, you have to provide command and control for the rescue. You can believe that if I'm down and you can't tell a Jolly Green where I am, I'm going to be pretty pissed off." Within a few weeks I would spend hours looking for him and Bezold.

We were walking toward the flight line when three Bird Dogs entered the pattern on the tightest downwind, base-to-final approaches I'd ever seen. Their wheels chirped, the matting rattled and the three were rolling down the runway together. They taxied up to the fuel bladder and shut down. Whoops of laughter reached us as pilots and observers climbed out and began examining their airplanes. "Finch, you crazy bastard, I thought he had you!" someone shouted.

"That's the noon flight," Harrison said. "Come on, let me introduce you." We stopped at the nearest Bird Dog. A slight Huckleberry Finn–type was standing with one boot on the footplate below the cowling and reaching over the leading edge of the wing to untwist the fuel cap. His movements were fast, almost jerky, and I could see he was pumped on adrenaline. "How'd it go, Charlie?" Lee asked.

"Last time those gooks shoot at anyone," he grinned. "Man, I put those bombs right down their fucking throats." He looked down at my name tape, then at me. "You must be the new guy. Hi, I'm Charlie Finch. Welcome to the big time. You play poker?"

I bridled slightly, not sure what to make of him. Everything this guy said was like a direct challenge. "Yeah, a little." But he was already reaching for the nozzle and fuel hose held up by his observer. I'd seen the backseater lean an M16 against the wheel strut, and through the open door of the Bird Dog I saw another hanging by its sling from the map light. At Quang Ngai we strapped on .38 revolvers, but no one ever flew with his M16.

"Great," Finch said. He slid the nozzle into the wing tank. "See you in the club. Hope you've got some money to lose."

The sun was approaching the top of the mountains as I shut down next to the fuel bladder. I couldn't shake the picture of swarms of big, orange tracers. Concentrating on keeping my eye on the low ship, I'd listened in astonishment to Harrison's almost clinical voice as he briefed the marine pilots above us, marked the target, and evaded the streams of tracers, all, it seemed, at the same time. It was a long way from flying the nightly mortar watch over Quang Ngai.

"Today wasn't that bad," Harrison said. He looked at the sun touching the distant mountains. "What say we get these old girls topped off, then go and write up our debriefs. After that, I think I know where we might find a couple of cold beers."

I had found my home.

Not long after my arrival, I was patrolling the DMZ one quiet Sunday. Not a cloud marred the sky, and visibility was unlimited. A few kilometers away in North Vietnam lay Fingers Lake. Flying straight and level toward the Ben Hai, I saw a series of flashes near one of the splayed fingers of the lake. I continued my course for a few moments, before making a slow 180 back to the south. Seconds later, half a dozen flak rounds exploded where I would have been.

Each morning at Dong Ha was much the same. Reveille was 0500, and after a breakfast of C rations we waited for our marine or army observer to bring the op orders specifying which areas of the DMZ or North Vietnam we'd be covering. An hour later the temperature was already in the low eighties and everything was dusty. The hooch we lived in was dusty, the air was full of dust, clothes were full of dust, and everything smelled of stale sweat. The typical light-hearted conversations, bullshit conversations, which always filled the evening hours, were noticeably absent in the morning. In the morning, with pilots and observers focused on the mission ahead, things got very serious.

I would preflight my aircraft before 0600, and then buckle on my gear. An emergency first-aid kit was slung from the hip and tied down on the leg. This rested on my left thigh and contained morphine, bandages, and other paraphernalia I might need if I was downed. An emergency radio and beacon went into the breast pocket of my fatigue jacket. Next came the flak vest, and over that a shoulder holster with a Colt .45 semi-automatic pistol.

While most pilots carried only the pistol, a few of us added our M16s loaded with alternating ball and tracer ammunition. Officially, this was for self-defense in the event we went down, as engaging the enemy "out the window" was absolutely forbidden due to the possibility of empty shell casings jamming the control cables. (Doc had once suffered this inconvenience, and it was only his skill and knowledge of the Bird Dog that got him back on the ground safely.) The M16 would be slung from the map light in front of my right knee. A canvas bag with twenty magazines, three fragmentation grenades, two smoke grenades, and one white phosphorus grenade went under my seat. More smoke grenades were stored on a shelf in the door.

Going into combat almost daily, I had little time to reflect on whether or not I could do the job, and I settled quickly into the routine, drawing on lessons from the likes of Doc, Harrison, Finch, Andy Anderson, and Roger Bounds and learning from my own experiences with a capable and dangerous enemy. The route from Phu Bai to Dong Ha became as well known to me as Riverside Drive in front of my home in Tarpon Springs, Florida, and the Ben Hai as familiar as the Anclote River that flowed behind it. Leatherneck Square, Fingers Lake, The Horseshoe, and the Tennis Racket entered my vocabulary as places of particular peril in a cratered landscape where the enemy waited patiently to kill us. We took hits, but luck saw them pass through our aircraft without striking flesh or engine, and we returned to Phu Bai to count the holes, play a few hands of poker, and prepare for the next day's mission. War was our life. It was what we did.

I had parked my aircraft after a morning mission and was walking toward the line shack when I flinched at the low, muffled impact of two artillery rounds exploding some six hundred meters north of the runway. I came out of my reflexive crouch and stared in disbelief at the clouds of smoke and debris rising out of Dong Ha village. I looked up to follow the sound of a second pair of shells shrieking overhead and thought, "Oh shit, we've been bracketed!" just before they detonated in dry rice paddies three hundred meters south of me.

A law of physics states that no two objects can occupy the same space at the same time. This, I realized, was patently untrue when five bodies burst simultaneously from the door of the line shack and dove for the nearby bunker. I ran after them, stuck my head inside and screamed for an observer, then sprinted for my aircraft with Bill Norton right behind me. He threw himself into the back seat and I followed, hitting the starter switch. Keeping the airplane rolling in more or less a straight line with the rudder pedals, I pulled on my helmet and firewalled the throttle. We lifted off without the formality of clearances from the tower, wondering if the next shells were going to land close enough to knock us out of the air. We were still buckling into our harnesses as we cleared through Dong Ha DASC and headed for Tally Ho. Fifty feet off the ground, we spotted three large muzzle flashes on the horizon. Bill was already telling a 175mm battery to prepare for a fire mission while I called the next tasking agency to request air support.

"Hillsboro Control, this is Catkiller 1-2. Over."

"Roger, Catkiller. This is Hillsboro. Go ahead."

"Roger, Hillsboro. Catkiller 1-2 is off channel 109 at this time. We have active arty, I say again, active artillery. I have Sundowner Whiskey in my back seat in aircraft 2646. Scramble two flights of air. I want high delivery Delta-3s with Daisy Cutters. Will rendezvous with air on radial 345, Channel 109, at fifteen nautical miles. ETR to be advised. Over."

I trimmed the aircraft and began the slow climb to altitude. For the next fifteen minutes we observed the muzzle flashes of our intended target situated about five miles north of the Ben Hai. As soon as we crossed the river we started picking up 37mm flak. Though not too close, I began making radical course changes while climbing and descending. These maneuvers were impossible to predict and prevented the enemy gunners sending the shells to intercept us. But it was hell on an observer. In the back seat, Bill was being thrown from side to side by the violent maneuvers and fighting the nausea brought on by constant changes in G-loading. One second we'd be pressed into our seats, the next lifted against our harnesses, and then back into our seats again while the horizon tilted, rose, and fell without stop. During the zero-G moments, sand floated up from the floor like a thin haze and we squinted to keep it out of our eyes. Another five minutes went by before we were close enough to get a fix on the target, which belched more staggered flashes as the gunners yanked the lanyards on three Soviet 152mm howitzers.

Bill initiated the fire mission and we watched the rounds edge closer, until he ordered the battery to fire for effect using airbursts. The 175mm was not known for its accuracy, but today it was perfect. The shells exploded a hundred feet directly above the target, shotgunning the crews with cones of lethal shrapnel. Whether the guns had been damaged or the crews were dead and wounded, they stopped firing. Minutes later the first flight of Gunfighter F-4s arrived a few thousand feet above us. I warned the flight leader about the heavy ground fire, then lined up and fired a smoke rocket. I located the guns relative to the mark and Dash 1 confirmed he had it. Because there were no American troops involved, the green and brown air force Phantoms chose their headings and rolled in to release their Mk 83s. The 1,000-pound bombs plummeted almost a mile to explode just outside the berms. Racks empty, the Phantoms were replaced by a second pair of Gunfighters. Their bombs landed inside, turning the long-range Soviet-supplied guns into scrap metal. The flight leader rogered my bomb damage assessment as he and his wingman accelerated out of sight toward Da Nang. Far below and behind them, a satisfied Bird Dog crew chugged contentedly back to Dong Ha.

Charles Finch: When Hooper arrived, it was like he had been there for months. Sarcasm in the 220th just dripped, and normally the new guy would take it and not come back at you. Not Bill. He wasn't cocky, just very confident and sure of himself. Within days, everyone knew him. Pilots were talking about Hooper, Wild Bill, Hoops; Hudson was calling him "Billy" like he had known him for years. He gained instant respect. Maybe it was because he was younger and better-looking than most of us, but I remember Doc telling me he was a good pilot, and Andy Anderson said he liked his spirit. And it turned out that he was just as capable at the poker table as he was at the controls of a Bird Dog.

The poker table is one of the places you can judge character. Bill would not take my bullshit, which everyone else seemed to buy. He wasn't as good a player as Hudson or Stranger, but you could not run him if there were more than four players in the hand. But, God, could he be irritating. When he won a pot he had this annoying way of sticking his elbows out and just moving his forearms to pick up the chips and stack them very methodically. He looked like some kind of goddamn insect. I think the only reason he did it was because he knew it pissed me off. When I'd tell him, "Count your money on your time, deal on mine," he wouldn't even look up as he kept stacking his chips very slowly, which pissed me off even more.

And he was such a straight arrow. He would never allow a lie to go unchallenged, never back off from the truth, nor ever fail to take the blame if he screwed up. He had a quick temper and would get right in your face if you pissed him off, but he was equally quick to forgive. He was never full of praise for anyone. Major Wisby wrote in my OER that I was the finest combat aviator he knew. If I had ever heard that from Bill it would have made my day. Hell, I could have won the Medal of Honor and he would have just thought it was a normal part of the mission.

Every time Bill was annoyed, he'd get this "I-am-not-happy-look" that, whatever was the cause of it, made me feel it was somehow my fault. If I was late getting to the jeep that took us out to the flight line, or was trying to figure out whether to declare "high or low" in a game of Kansas City, Hooper would give me that look, which was always unsettling.

He was moody at times, but that was usually because of bad weather or an unserviceable airplane. And though you didn't see him smile every day, when he did, it made the room light up. If you made Bill Hooper laugh, it was a good day. Some people saw the two of us as competitors. Certainly we were both very focused, very determined, though we approached the job very differently. When I got to the flight line, I cranked and was gone: I knew where the enemy was, could always find a fight, and didn't worry about where the 108th or the marines wanted me to go. If I was supposed to fly high ship in North Vietnam, I could usually talk the low ship into swapping. I hated just watching the low ship, particularly if he wasn't looking for a fight.

Bill, on the other hand, was meticulous about planning, preflight, briefing his backseater, and following the mission orders to the letter. Everything he did had a sense of purpose. Bill is alive today because of his attention to detail and his knowledge of his aircraft and his abilities. He was always prepared for an emergency, and some months later when he got hit, all of his self-discipline paid off. He wasn't lucky—he was prepared.

Chapter 5

The Lighter Side

The thing is that the 220th was not *like M*A*S*H*, it *was M*A*S*H*! The back of the officers club looked out on the morgue, and almost any night a lot of sobering sights in the form of shadows on the covered windows could be seen. Once, an enlisted guy went off the deep end in there and shot up the place. We did crazy things: bartered lobsters, steaks, and freeze-dried shrimp from the general's mess; stole jeeps from the 101st Airborne; traded airplane rides for AK-47s. Mike Sharkey once traded a ride to a Seabee for enough aluminum runway matting for us to have a volleyball court. When that was discovered, we had to give it back, so I traded a ride into North Vietnam to another Seabee in return for a concrete replacement.

—Jim Hudson, Catkiller 12

MIKE SHARKEY: MY FIRST Z MISSION WAS a classic. After doing the mandatory milk runs and convoy cover and finding out the coastline really didn't run north and south, I was sent to the Z with marine Major Mulkey in my back seat. Arriving on station I was awestruck by the sight of the tracers and all the other activity associated with a major contact. After Mulkey briefed the fighter-bombers, I made two rocket runs with a mouth so dry I could hardly swallow (fear took on a new meaning that day), but each run resulted in a misfire.

It was then that Mulkey uttered his immortal words: "Well, Captain Sharkey, we now know the fucking intercom works. If you would squeeze the right switch up there, we can get on with this fucking war." With the hissing noise of the intercom side tone ringing in my ears, I made another run and squeezed the correct switch this time—only problem was, both overhead switches on the same side were still armed, and the rockets collided coming out of the tubes and headed off in opposite directions. Needless to say, the fighter pilots and Mulkey were not impressed with the location of my marks.

Then there was the time I came in from a late-night mission when I'd used one rocket, and parked the aircraft next to the fuel pit. After refueling the next morning, I cranked up, turned the airplane toward the portable tower, and called for takeoff clearance. Problem was—I had left the overhead switch armed and had not replaced the trigger safety pin. As I keyed the mike button, I squeezed the trigger and fired a rocket right past the tower. All I could see were assholes and elbows as the two guys in the tower made a hasty evac, thinking they were under a rocket attack—which, in a way, I guess they were. When they finally figured out it was me, they radioed and asked what the fuck I thought I was doing. I told them that I was going to take off now and if that rocket hit any friendlies, my family could reach me through a North Vietnamese postal address.

Some months later, I was on a solo recon when I got a radio message to proceed to a place in the foothills and destroy all the water buffalo there. Apparently some tactical genius (probably a West Point grad) had determined that they were potential pack animals and had to be killed. When I arrived, sure enough there were about two hundred buffalo grazing around an enormous water hole. With much pleasure I called in an artillery mission on a spot about five miles away and single-handedly blew the shit out of about one square mile of jungle.

The mission I was most proud of occurred one day when I was just nosing around the foothills about five miles north of Camp Carroll. After being shot at by a new AA site, I scrambled a Da Nang flight to dispatch the bad guys. Knowing that fighters were very vulnerable to the AA, I decided to try something I hadn't done before. Waiting for the F-4s to arrive, I flew down to Camp Carroll and took a magnetic heading to the target, then flew back and took up a position ninety degrees and a mile from the target. When the fighters arrived, I directed them to the tin roofs of Camp Carroll and gave them the heading to the target. I marked the target at the very last instant and had the fighters drop all their nape, then make as tight a 180 as possible and drop all of their snakes. The whole thing went off like a dream. The gooks were concentrating on me and didn't even know the fighters were in the area until it was too late. I don't think they ever got a shot off.

Living with John Kovach was a hoot, though he wasn't called Bear because his first name was Teddy. Being a devout Catholic, he was very concerned that my over-developed libido was going to ruin my chances of getting past the pearly gates. Consequently, he was always trying to sabotage my rendezvous with missy whatever. Once he even stooped to harassing me from outside the hooch window during one of my romantic interludes—I guess you could call that sexual harassment.

One day John and I flew the beloved Beaver down to Marble Mountain to do some scrounging. After a few beers we decided we deserved some time off, and he stormed into the company orderly room and demanded R&R orders to Australia. The clerk informed us that the only passes available were to the Jungle Survival School in Subic Bay, and the aircraft was taking off in less than an hour. Soon thereafter we found ourselves on a C-130 on the way to the Philippines with no luggage, not even a toothbrush—just the wilted fatigues we had on. When we landed at Subic naval station, I used the phone in the arrival hall to call for transportation, identifying myself as Captain Sharkey. We were impressed by the swift arrival of a staff car in search of a navy captain—equivalent to an army colonel. The driver was nice enough to give us a lift to the O-club even though we were just a couple of junior army officers.

The club was beautiful and full of men and women in their dress whites. As we walked into the main dining area, the music stopped and everyone turned to stare. A real navy captain called out, "Where are you guys from?" When we informed him that we were from Nam, we became instant celebrities and couldn't buy a drink. During the course of the evening we discovered that we knew the call signs of some of the carrier pilots there. They were the ones who used to come down from the north on bad-weather diversions, and we'd run them on targets of opportunity. The next day we were invited to their carrier and given a first-class tour of the ship. It was quite an impressive thing to see.

During the party the first night, John and I decided to dance together—we did that a lot in Phu Bai. In the confusion as to who should lead, we fell across a chair, and I injured my ribs. This prevented me from attending the five-day, living-in-the-jungle school from hell. Of course John had to stay with me and nurse me back to health. So for the next five days we were forced to eat hot dogs, drink beer, and go to that awful red-light district across the Olongapo River.

I used to fly mail and cold beer out to the small base camps. I'd make a low pass, hold the stick between my knees, and throw the goodies out the window. Shortly after we installed the smoke grenade holders on the outside of our planes to help the fighters find us as they came on station, I made a run out to a base camp near Khe Sanh. When I tossed the mail bag out it got caught on the grenade holder, opened, and spewed letters and parcels all over the camp's mine field. Needless to say, I was not the most popular guy after that and didn't return for a while, for fear of being shot down by the inhabitants.

When Kovach and I got to be the senior captains in the company, we were entitled to share a big room. Another captain, who was the scheduling officer when I was with the platoon in Hue, joined us for a while. One night I was awakened by a bright light in my face and this guy (who shall remain nameless) pointing a flashlight at me and yelling. Gradually I realized that I was standing at the end of his bed pissing all over his feet. I remember him as the kind of guy who would take all the safe missions for himself and leave the dangerous ones to the rest of the pilots. I guess my subconscious took over. Kovach, of course, loved every minute of it.

John and I took the Beaver down to mid-country on another scrounging mission. It was a large base camp in the middle of nowhere, but he had some friends there who could get us the things we needed. During the course of the evening (and after the mandatory few beers) we began launching flares from our survival kits. Well, the place went crazy, everyone thinking they were under attack, and went to full alert. When they found out it was coming from inside the compound, they began a systematic search to catch and probably lynch the culprits. To save our skins we had to sneak back to the airstrip and take off in the dead of night without much fuel. We ended up landing at another camp to refuel and file a proper flight plan. I remember that night very vividly.

John was the originator of the dreaded Catkiller Puff initiation, a tradition reserved for the new guys. It is pretty much the same as the Cardinal Puff thing we did in college: a repetitive drinking sequence where if you messed up, you have to chug your drink and start over. Kovach was the chief judge and demonstrator, and no matter how well the guy did the first few times around, John would always find some fault. Eventually they'd be knee-walking drunk. It was his way of making the new guy feel accepted.

Charles Finch: Kovach and Sharkey always seemed to be around when the sacrifice ritual began. The first person I saw sacrificed was Mac Byrd when a bunch of guys hoisted him onto the bar and began pouring drinks on top of him. The funniest one was when Lee "Gaper" Harrison, still a lieutenant, was being loud, sarcastic, and irreverent to the captains. Captain Bud Bruton suggested it was time to sacrifice the Gaper, and Lee said something like, "Yeah, Bud? You and what army?" In about three seconds we had slammed him on the bar and were pouring everything in sight on him, with Lee cussing and saying how he was gonna kill all of us one at a time. A few minutes later, Lee was ensuring that half of those in the club that night were sacrificed. Major Wisby just stood to one side and laughed.

One night we were right in the middle of a poker deal when we started taking incoming. Wisby was yelling at us to get to the bunker, but we just sat there because of all the cash on the table. There had to be $500 in that pot! Rockets were impacting everywhere. Then the lights went out. Everyone had a Zippo, and we got a candle lit and finished the hand. I thought we were going to die for sure.

Grayson Davis: Right after we started flying north, the word spread about the mission and what a good job we were doing. Several senior officers from down south came up to see us. One was a chicken colonel from Saigon. After a few drinks, we explained the Catkiller tradition of being sacrificed. He thought it was a capital idea and hopped on the bar. Gee Wisby came in as the first drinks were finding their mark and must have thought his career was going down the drain. He rushed over to stop the melee, but the colonel would not let us stop.

I don't know what was worse, being sacrificed or having to become a Catkiller Puff, because Kovach made it his personal business that everyone should be indoctrinated the first night in the 220th. One of our new 1st Platoon pilots eventually made Catkiller Puff and then struggled to the latrine, threw up so hard that he dislocated his jaw, and passed out with his head in the commode. When found, he was unable to talk. Finally, the flight surgeon figured out what had happened and fixed the jaw.

Sarge Means: I'd already been sacrificed, so when it came to cards, I had a choice to make: lovemaking at the 85th Evacuation Hospital or heavy losses at the 220th poker table. One way or the other I was going to get screwed, so why not go next door and enjoy it so much more! I remember the many trips to the hospital with Paul Brennan and John Hillman as we courted three gorgeous nurses. And being shaken awake by them at o-dark-thirty to sneak back to our hooches before the sun came up. War really became hell when the hospital finally encircled the compound with concertina wire and broken glass, and we had to navigate through all that just to go home to get some rest.

HAIR STILL WET FROM THE COLD shower and wearing fresh fatigues, Hooper stepped out of the sandbagged Quonset hut into a muggy night and made his way to the officers club. A dart board hung on the inside of the door. He knocked, listened for the okay, and opened the door to see Major Wisby waiting to throw his next dart. A cloud of cigarette smoke, mingled with the smell of sweat and beer, rolled over him as he headed to the bar to grab his first Budweiser. A tape deck thumped rock and roll, and the nightly poker game had already started. Card shark Charlie Finch, still in his marine flight suit, flashed him a predatory grin.

"Hey, Hoop! You ready to lose some money?"

Hooper raised his beer. "Next hand."

A mixed group of the company's noisier pilots were working themselves up to a sacrifice. The newcomer among them smiled wanly, knowing something was coming but not what. Charlie skipped the last card across the table. Doc, Stranger, Hudson, and Lee Harrison scooped up the hands and brought them to their chests. There was a loud knock on the door. Major Wisby held fire, and Sarge Means, with the two bars of a captain on his collar, entered, passed under the bent Bird Dog propeller, and took a stool next to Hooper. "I'd been a little bewildered the first time we'd been introduced," Hooper later recalled, "until learning he'd been given the name Sargent at birth, a moniker that had caused no end of confusion since he'd joined the army. Meeting a Captain Sarge Means still saw people scratching their heads. He was one of my favorite people in the 220th."

"How's it going, Sarge?"

"We were working the A Shau today," he said in his distinctive Maine accent, shaking his head. "Brutal. Hell, since the 101st pulled out, the gooks have moved right back in." Six weeks earlier a major battle had taken place in the A Shau Valley between the NVA and the 101st Airborne Division, with the Catkiller's 2nd Platoon providing round-the-clock cover. When the ten-day battle finished, the Communists had lost hundreds of men, but taken many American paratroopers with them. From the safety of Saigon, General Westmoreland had declared a victory and withdrawn his battered forces, allowing the enemy to reoccupy the valley from their sanctuary in Laos. Many more battles would yet be fought for control of the A Shau.

The adjacent table was growing rowdier by the minute. They all stood, grabbed the FNG, and carried him to the bar. He was slammed down, arms and legs pinned. The platoon members began their ritual chant, and a torrent of beer soaked him to howls of laughter. Wisby gave them an avuncular glance and threw another dart.

"You're bluffing, Doc," Harrison laughed at the poker table. "I'll raise you."

"Suit yourself, Gaper."

"Heard you had a brutal time today," Sarge said. *Brutal* was one of his favorite words.

"Fuckers hosed us pretty good."

"I still think you're bluffing!" Harrison shouted gleefully. "I'm calling!" I looked over to see a deadpan Doc laying down his cards one by one. Harrison watched expectantly as each appeared face up, until the last one was revealed. His jaw dropped. "Shit!" he yelled. "I was sure you were bluffing. *Shit.*"

Sarge laughed. "That boy will never learn," he drawled. "He'll hang in there and call every hand, no matter how much is in the pot. Then when he sees the other guy's cards, he says the same thing every time. 'I thought you were bluffing!' Someone once told him, 'You're always sitting there with your mouth open when I turn over a full house and you're holding a pair of threes. Quit gaping so much!' That sort of stuck, and he's been the Gaper ever since."

Tall, round-faced, and a little chubby, Lee Harrison was the quintessential big kid: loud, exuberant, and possessed of a face so comically expressive that he could reduce everyone to helpless laughter whenever he wanted. He also had a penchant for elaborate schemes to circumvent pointless regulations, and regularly drew his friends into them. Once he got in the air, however, the kid they knew on the ground underwent a classic Jekyll and Hyde transformation, calling in air strikes and artillery with cold, clinical precision.

"Come on, Hooper," Finch shouted over the noise, "it's time you took some of the Gaper's money."

Hooper tilted his head toward the poker table. "You playing?" he asked Sarge.

"Not me. I got a date at the 85th Evac."

Hooper dragged a chair to the table and sat across from Charlie as he shuffled the cards and set them on the table. Hooper tapped for the cut. "Let's make this one seven card draw," Finch said, sending the cards around the table with quick snaps of his wrist.

The party boys surrounded the table. "These guys are the 'Myth Makers,'" the ringleader explained to the beer-soaked FNG. "All those missions up north and shit." None of the players said anything. "I was already aware that the 1st Platoon had a reputation for aloofness," Hooper said. "What they didn't understand was that the stress of those missions bound us so tightly to one another that, with rare exceptions, we preferred our own company."

"Two," Hooper said, slapping his discards down. Finch lifted his eyes briefly, trying to read this new competitor, and then dealt the cards. Lifting the corners, Hooper frowned disappointedly and sat back in the hope that when he began to raise, it wouldn't be only Harrison who thought he was bluffing.

"Look at 'em, they're still dry," the drunk giggled. He began waving a hand, and his fellow pilots took up the monosyllabic chant, "Ya-da-de . . . "

Doc cast them a withering look. "I'm only going to say this once, okay?" he warned. "Pour beer on me and I'm going to knock you on your ass." The guy stood there for a moment, a silly grin on his face, before withdrawing into a huddle with his buddies. From it rose their ritualistic chant, and they broke to stand behind Doc. Stony expressions only served to raise the volume of their chant. With a final, rising, "Daaaaa!" beer rained down to soak Doc. There was a growled "sunovabitch" as he came out of his chair and landed a single punch that dropped his taller tormentor like he'd been pole-axed. Doc turned to the next one, but the fun had suddenly paled, and they backed away, mumbling darkly about "fucking Myth Makers." From across the room, Major Wisby gave the dazed pilot a distant examination and threw another dart.

"Two," Doc said, sliding his wet discards toward Charlie.

Charles Finch: An Australian floorshow came to Dong Ha with six girl dancers and singers. Roger Bounds and I found a viewing port where we could watch them change costumes while Briscoe and a bunch of the 108th back seats were trying to push past us to get a look. The girls had incredible figures and started dancing naked with one another in the changing room. Roger was going crazy. The rest of the show had started, and I tried to get him to come back to our seats, but he wasn't moving. He had the target, stayed in his orbit, and extended his viewing until they finally got dressed.

We met them the next day, and I ended up getting drunk with one, putting her in the Bird Dog and flying up to North Vietnam that night, and then back to Da Nang to see her boyfriend. We landed at around midnight, with her in the front seat on my lap and the drummer's twelve-year-old kid in the back. This was another time that I thought my career had ended, as the crew chiefs at Dong Ha knew I had taken off with three in the airplane—two of them civilians—and definitely under the influence. I did a lot of dumb things, but that must have been the dumbest.

Glenn Strange: One night in the club, we were raising our usual hell when Bob LaFerriere, a former Catkiller who had transferred to flying

U-21s, came in with his co-pilot. The new guy was staring in disbelief at the rowdiness when I heard Bob tell him, "If you knew what these guys do in the daytime, you'd understand why they carry on like this at night."

Yet, for all the frivolity, jocularity, and good humor in the 220th, there was always an undercurrent of anxiety, despair, fear, and just plain hopelessness. After my first mission out around Khe Sanh, where I took my first hit from ground fire, I remember thinking that I would never get out of there and so just resigned myself to my fate. We were just kids in our early twenties, and coming face to face with mortality was difficult, very difficult, to handle. A few turned inward and imploded. There's no reason to mention names, but I can think of five that were taken out of the situation and sent home or reassigned.

Most of the rest of us brooded out loud. Late one night after being awakened by incoming, we were crawling into the bunker when Bob Domine said, "If Lyndon Johnson had to do this just once, this shit would stop!" We resented the unfairness, the political crap, and the fact that we were pawns in a stupid game of power struggles and greed. (We saw all the money that was going to Dynalectron, Pacific Architects and Engineers, and other contractors.)

I think it was Jim Hudson who coined the phrase "hate session." It didn't take much to set off a round of bitching, moaning, and griping, and then all those underlying negative thoughts and feelings would surface, and it was impossible to cut them off. There were certain individuals who stirred up the hate and got the sessions going. Hudson (somehow always a cooler head) was able to observe those sessions more dispassionately and intelligently than the rest of us. I remember him talking about them and some of the instigators, concluding that they served to blow off steam and avoid an uncontrollable detonation of tempers.

Jim Hudson: We were a mixed group. I was a physicist, Arrington was a barefoot skier from Cypress Gardens, Doc was determined to be an airline pilot, Glenn claimed to have won his car in a poker game, and Mike Sharkey was running a bass- and racing-boat company when I saw him after the war. We were good for each other. I am now a molecular biologist, and we would call it "hybrid vigor."

I was older than most of the pilots and I was married, expecting a second child. My view of the "right" way to be a FAC was in conflict with Finch. As I saw it, Charlie was a great pilot, a good poker player, and a bad influence on new guys. We often got into heated discussions about it.

Glenn Strange: One night a middle-aged newspaper correspondent came to the club. He had a coupla' beers and played poker until one of those hate sessions started at the bar, and he went over to listen. Later, when things calmed down and we were having a nightcap, he told me that it reminded him of sessions he and his buddies had in 1942–1944. He said that his World War II experiences were being repeated, with only cosmetic differences, in Vietnam.

Doc Clement: I was finally getting a little more acclimatized to the heat, but still could not manage a restful night. When my flight school class-mates Jim Hudson and Glenn Strange got permission to move into a larger hooch adjacent to the officers club, I talked them into letting me room with them by saying that I'd convert it into the best damn quarters in I Corps.

Once I'd drawn up some plans, the first priority was to get it wired for air-conditioning. The guys from the Navy Construction Battalion, the Seabees, were the ones who could do that—if they had the right motivation. Fortunately for me, they were not allowed to buy alcohol. As an army officer, I could. And being the company instructor pilot, I had unlimited access to an O-1, so on my first day off operations, I flew down to Da Nang for a case of Jack Daniels. This was enough for the Seabees to wire the place for 220 volts, tile the floor, and slip us thirty-two sheets of marine plywood. Our construction project got cranking. When not flying, I'd work on the Super Hooch, as would Hudson when he could break away from supply. Strange, kept busy by the CO in operations, had a harder time getting away.

As soon as it was wired and tiled by our crew of grateful sailors, the next step was installing a couple of air conditioners to start cool-ing things down. This presented a problem. Spare air conditioners were nowhere to be found in I Corps. There is always a solution to a problem, however, and it dropped in my lap when I was sent to jungle survival school in the Philippines. As soon as I got there, I went shopping for air conditioners. The rest of the time I spent drinking and chasing women. The jungle survival school never saw me.

At Subic Bay naval air station, I talked the air force crew of a C-130 into loading my unauthorized cargo. When I got back to Phu Bai, we partitioned off the Great Room, installed a 220-volt air conditioner, and packed insulation into every nook and cranny. Along the back wall we put up shelves that could be covered with a fold-down table to hide crucial supplies from the prying eyes of visitors. We stained the walls, and I hung up some *Playboy* centerfolds. That's what I called serious art. Each of our private bedrooms got a 110-volt air conditioner, and we built the beds about four feet off the floor so we could fit a refrigerator and more storage shelves underneath. Finally, we hung a double-reinforced front door and put our names on the outside so everyone would know who lived in the Super Condo Hooch.

It was so well insulated that we were never bothered by the sounds of airplanes taking off and landing. A few times we'd be having breakfast in the mess hall, and everyone would be talking about the mortar or rocket attack the night before. We'd look at each other and then at them and say, "What mortar attack?"

When important food stocks ran low, I'd fly down to Da Nang and fill the back seat with wine, champagne, and crackers. I even found a Smithfield ham that I hung up to save for my DEROS party. My father, who was a captain with Piedmont Airlines, had the flight attendants save anything the passengers didn't open on their trays, and then sent me shoeboxes full of little individually wrapped cheeses. Hudson was not only the supply officer, but the mess officer, too, and he could get cans of dehydrated shrimp. So with Hudson's tape deck playing, we would have our wine, cheese, and crackers with shrimp in air-conditioned comfort in the middle of Vietnam.

Glenn Strange: Pizza was just one of the things we missed, and, though it sounds trivial when piled on top of all the other things and people we missed, it made a significant gap in our lives there. (When Mac Byrd got back from R&R in Hawaii with his wife, he told us that on about the fourth day she said, "Mac, I know it's been a long time since you've had any and it will be a long time before you get any more, but can't we eat something besides pizza today?")

When the Super Hooch was finished, we started talking about how we could treat ourselves to this much-missed college tradition. It was Hudson who came up with an ingenious solution. First, he traded something for pizza mixes. Then he built an oven from a potato chip can, a hot plate, a popcorn popper, and a wire coat hanger. He cut a hole in the top and the bottom of the potato chip can and inserted two lengths of the coat hanger through the middle to make a rack. With the can sitting on the hot plate and the pizza on an aluminum plate on the rack, he put the popcorn popper upside down on the top and *voilà!*—we were cooking pizza. If not the best pizza we'd ever had, it was certainly the most memorable.

Whenever anybody got a food package from home, Doc would take it and announce, "I'll be in charge of this." Depending on what was in the package, sometimes the rightful owner could get it, or some of it, for himself. But if it was chocolate-chip cookies, forget it. Chocolate-chip cookies were Doc's favorite, and he told everybody that since he didn't have a wife to send him cookies, he should get cookies from everyone else's wife. He did share them, but it was one cookie at a time, and he handed it out personally. No one else could get in the box. One time we wound up with a can of smoked oysters. Doc was the only one who liked them, so he got to eat them all himself. Then he said that didn't mean he wasn't going to get any more chocolate-chip cookies that came in.

Doc Clement: We let it be known that entry to the Super Hooch was by invitation only. Occasionally we'd invite some of the guys in for wine and cheese, but not often. If someone showed up about the time we were ready to open a bottle, we'd crank up the air conditioner all the way. They'd eventually get so cold they'd be shivering and have to leave. We'd turn it down, flip the table up, and enjoy our wine and cheese.

I liked it cold in the hooch, so we had our folks send us electric blankets. I'd sometimes play poker in the officers club until late at night and when I'd get back, Stranger and Hudson would be sound asleep. Just for fun I'd turn the air conditioner up and unplug their electric blankets. While the rest of the company were tossing and turning and sweating in their hooches, Glenn and Jim would be in a tight ball in the morning trying to stay warm.

We should have collected admission to the Super Hooch, because everyone visiting the Catkillers wanted to see it. I was having my wine and cheese one night when there was a knock on the door. Several guys from the 1st Cav were standing there. They had dropped in at our club for a few drinks, heard about the Super Hooch, and wanted a look. I invited them in and started talking to one that looked familiar. After a few beers, it turned out to be Sam Robinson, who had dated my sister in high school back in Winston-Salem, North Carolina. He was a captain with the 1st Cav and stationed on a firebase just north of Phu Bai. From then on when I headed up to Dong Ha, I'd freeze a case of beer and wrap and tie it up good. Then I'd call Sam on the radio, fly over his firebase, and drop it to him.

So that's how we survived in Phu Bai the last half of our tour. It was tough but we managed.

Glenn Strange: While Doc and Hudson were working on the Super Hooch, I was in operations. One day, a young sergeant came in and asked how far west we flew. I showed him the wall map and explained that we went just a few kilometers into Laos. Looking disappointed, he pulled a map out of his pocket and showed me where he and other members of a LRRP (long-range reconnaissance patrol) team were going to be inserted the next morning. He was hoping that we had some flights out that way so he could hitch a ride and get a look at the area.

I thought, "Geez, if this guy is going to be inserted way out there in the jungle, the least I can do is give him a ride so he can see where he's going." We took off, passed over the A Shau Valley, and, as we crossed the border, he asked me to get as low as I could. Dropping down, I continued into Laos for fifty or sixty miles, navigating by dead reckoning. When we crossed a large stream, my passenger asked me to climb so he could orient himself with the aerial photo he had. Once he got a good view of the area, we went back down to the treetops, and he directed me over the specific area where his LRRP team was to be inserted. After a second pass, he said, "OK, let's go home." We landed, he thanked me for the ride, and went off to get ready for his patrol.

Maybe a week later, a major from XXIV Corps HQ came in and asked me the same question: How far west did we fly? When I told him, I saw the same look of disappointment I'd seen on the LRRP sergeant's face. He said they were worried about a patrol that was deep in Laos, and thought maybe if we went out there we could confirm that they were still functioning. He didn't want to officially request a mission out there, but had heard the Catkillers were a rowdy group not overly concerned about protocol. Was there any chance of a strictly informal ride?

"What the hell, I guess I'm going back to Laos," I grinned just as Andy Anderson, the operations officer, came in. I started to tell Andy what was going on, but the major interrupted with a bland reason for his presence. On the way to the aircraft he told me that this flight was definitely off the record, and then gave me details of the cover story he'd given Andy so that I would be able to answer any awkward questions.

When we reached the area where I had taken the sergeant, the major gave me an FM frequency to tune in for him and began calling, "Spring Lake 47, acknowledge." Before long I heard what sounded like someone keying a microphone twice very quickly, and then the major said, "Spring Lake 47, confirm." I heard a microphone keyed once, and then the major said, "Let's go home." On the way back to Phu Bai, I asked why he and the sergeant picked the 220th, since Air America and certain other special operations outfits could easily have handled such a mission. He pretty much clammed up, so I just took him back to Phu Bai.

A couple of weeks after that second flight into Laos, we had occasion to go over to XXIV HQ for an intelligence briefing. That same major was there but pretended not to recognize me when we were introduced. As we were leaving the briefing room, the major caught my eye, and put his index finger over his lips for the "shhh" sign. I'll always wonder what was going on over there in Laos.

Chapter 6

Yellow Brick Road

I was out on the flight line one day and saw a lieutenant colonel looking in the cockpit of one of our Bird Dogs. When I walked up, he commented that it was outfitted with one of the new "black boxes" and asked how it worked. Noting that he had identified the battery as the new black box, I told him that it was highly classified and I had not received the briefing on it yet. But, I added, the pilots qualified to fly with it were really sold on its effectiveness.

—Grayson Davis, Catkiller 45/3

BILL HOOPER: THE DESERTED COMBAT BASE LAY DIRECTLY ahead of us, and I listened to its dramatic history from my backseater, Mike LaFromboise. I always liked having Mike with me. The athletic twenty-five-year-old from Seattle was typical of our observers from the 12th Marines—extremely professional, good company, and very knowledge-able about Vietnam. The moment Khe Sanh appeared on the horizon, he had begun a commentary on the seventy-seven-day siege of the marine base by the North Vietnamese Army. It had been another of General Westmoreland's "masterstrokes," costing more than 700 American dead and 3,200 wounded by the time it was abandoned about two months before I arrived in country. Crossing over the ghostly camp, I could see that the jungle was already creeping back. It disappeared behind us, and Mike was still talking over the intercom as I adjusted the trim wheel, beginning a slow climb to clear the steeply rising mountains ahead of us.

Our destination was Laos, and the mission we'd been given was a reconnaissance of the Yellow Brick Road. Better known as the Ho Chi

Minh Trail, this was the enemy's primary logistics route running from North Vietnam down the length of Laos and into Cambodia. Along the 1,600-mile route were regular transshipment points for men and materiel entering South Vietnam to reinforce and resupply NVA and Viet Cong units. Most of what reached I Corps came from where we were heading. Because of the Geneva Accord of 1962, which forbade any foreign troops from operating in Laos, our presence here, along with regular bombing missions, was top secret. Not that we were the only ones violating international law: the People's Army of Vietnam were in there, along with Chinese and Soviet advisors. They were the aggressors; we were just trying to stop them from killing American troops.

We crossed the unmarked border in line with the section we'd been assigned to recon, a dogleg that cut from the west side of the Annamese Mountains to the east before resuming its southerly route near the South Vietnamese border. It was a well-maintained gravel highway wide enough for two-way traffic and lay in the center of a fairly narrow valley. On the south side of the road a tumbling river ran below a 1,500-foot ridgeline. The north side, bordered by a wide expanse of elephant grass, rose abruptly to about eight hundred feet before flattening into a wide plateau. From the air it was a beautiful, pristine area unmarked by the overlapping bomb craters along the DMZ.

We had penetrated no more than four or five miles when Mike spotted faint truck tracks leading into the elephant grass. I immediately began cross-controlling and came around for another look. I saw one clear track and a less distinct set that disappeared about forty meters from the road. We were discussing whether or not the trucks were still there when a burst of 12.7 tracers ripped toward us. I evaded hard to the left as a second gun opened up. Turning away and dropping the nose, I scurried out of range, talking to Hillsboro.

Within minutes Blue Diamond 304, a flight of navy A-7s, was overhead at seven thousand feet and trying to spot my Bird Dog. I told Mike to pop one of the three smoke grenades attached to the outside of the fuselage. Diamond quickly spotted our smoke trail. I briefed him on the target and terrain, warning that we had already been engaged by two AA sites. I also advised that if he were hit, he should turn northeast and go feet wet, or head for Phu Bai, eighty-five nautical miles to the east-south-east, which had a five-thousand-foot runway and arrestor gear for their tail hooks. With the preliminaries out of the way, I rolled in and at 1,500 feet fired a rocket and broke hard left. Blue Diamond said he had the mark.

"Roger, Blue Diamond Dash 1. Your target is five-zero meters due north from the mark."

With no American troops to worry about, he was free to choose his own heading for the attack. I watched his approach, saw the bombs release and then condensation pouring from the tops of his wings as he pulled off the target. Seconds later, there were two bright flashes followed by clouds of gray smoke. The bombs blew away the camouflage to expose three vehicles. Dash 2's bombs ripped away the rest of the camouflage and revealed a fourth truck, all of them line abreast and separated by low berms, but their second runs failed to put bombs directly on the target. Mike focused his binoculars and gave them a closer look. Although all the trucks must have been hit with shrapnel, only the first one showed significant damage. To our surprise, neither of the 12.7 positions opened fire.

A second flight of A-7s arrived. Their attacks, again without interference from ground fire, resulted in direct hits on the two outside trucks, which sheered the bodies off the others. Pleased with the BDA I gave them, the pilots of the chunky Corsair IIs headed for their aircraft carrier in the South China Sea. I turned west again, continuing deeper into Laos, as Mike and I discussed the curious lack of ground fire. It didn't make sense, unless the first bursts had been the result of trigger-happy crews. Someone had ordered them to stop, which suggested they didn't want to draw more attention to the area. Instinct told us there had to be an NVA logistics base nearby. With two hours of fuel remaining, I reversed course and returned to the still-smoking trucks, making slow S-turns as our eyes swept the area.

Two miles beyond the trucks, the road and river turned sharply south around the ridge line. We reached the bend in the road without spotting anything. South Vietnam lay another three miles ahead. I checked the fuel and reluctantly brought the nose toward Khe Sanh— then ducked when a swarm of fat orange balls ripped past just over our heads from astern. I kicked left rudder, saw tracers going by, and kicked it right, but they were on that side, too. A quick glance down—more of them there! Between those I could see there were another four or five non-tracers, all of them followed by the distinctive and very frightening *thud!* of a 12.7mm or 14.5mm round breaking the sound barrier. Each had the energy to pass completely through the aircraft and our armored seats with ease, blowing both of us into fragments of flesh and bone. By sheer good fortune I had given the NVA gunners the smallest target possible, but found myself inside the natural dispersion pattern of what had to be a twin- or four-barreled weapon. By the time we were out of range and my heart was under control, I knew we had a fight on our hands.

LaFromboise clicked the intercom and I heard an explosion of breath into the boom microphone touching his lips. *"Fuck!"* I knew what he meant. Then he told me that he'd gotten a fix on the position.

I hit Hillsboro's push, described the target, and emphasized that because of fuel I had only a limited time to run an air strike. The controller told me that a flight of two marine A-6 Intruders, call sign Armourplate, was being diverted to me and should be on station in just over ten minutes. With my left fuel indicator nearing the red, I turned the selector to the right tank, which was showing three-quarters empty, and leaned the mixture as much as I dared. A simple calculation gave us a maximum of one hour in the air. Flying time back to Dong Ha was forty minutes, allowing me only twenty to twenty-five minutes to put bombs on that triple-A position.

Right on time, the gray and white A-6s, each carrying almost seven tons of 500-pound bombs, passed 1,500 feet above and picked me up immediately. I explained that the target was halfway up the ridgeline south of my orbit and warned that this crew was very good. Armourplate Dash 1 acknowledged my warning in a bored voice and said they were ready to observe my mark. Given my initial experience with that gun, I had no intention of getting too close. If I took a hit in a wing and lost what little fuel remained in either tank we'd never make it home. From a slant range of at least two thousand feet, I squeezed the trigger and watched the rocket streak away. A combination of distance and the four-foot-long rocket's notorious inaccuracy saw it hit wide of the target. When Armourplate said he had the mark, I admitted it was way off and told him where to deliver his ordnance relative to the smoke. He rogered, rolled in from the north, and the gun opened up on him. I hit my mike button.

"Armourplate Dash 1, you're taking fire on your nose!"

Replying with a laconic "Roger," he continued his run. Mike and I were astounded at how close he was to the target when he finally released the first two of his twenty-four Delta-2s and broke hard left to avoid the ridgeline. The bombs arced through the air to detonate about a hundred meters short of the gun emplacement. The enemy position had been chosen very carefully and was going to be difficult to hit. Any approach other than from the north would be attacking on a downslope, and the slightest delay in releasing the bombs would see them overshoot by a large margin, while an early release would place them well above the position. Making runs against a position on steeply rising terrain also made the A-6s a much easier target for the enemy gun crew.

"Dash 2, go south one hundred meters."

Watching the tracers passing above, under and to both sides of him, I couldn't believe he wasn't taking hits. Determined, he pressed in close before releasing his first two bombs. They impacted fifty meters short, no doubt shaking the gun crew with the concussion, but still ineffective because of the slope. The two-man Grumman A-6 was an exceptionally accurate attack bomber, something the NVA gunners were well aware of, and common sense suggested they abandon their weapon for a deep bunker. But they seemed just as determined as the marine pilots to play the ultimate game, one that was unlikely to end in a draw.

Although I was keeping a close eye on the fuel gauges, Mike made a light-hearted reference to the steadily dropping needles, noting that if we ended up eating fish heads and rice in a POW camp, he'd definitely cut me out of his will. It was a reminder that reinforced my own concern. This fight could go on for another fifteen minutes, by which time we might not have enough gas to get home. But we knew where the target was, and if one of the A-6s was hit and the crew ejected, we had to be there to direct an extraction team. Having brought them out here, it did not cross our minds to abort the mission. As Finch would tell me later, it was a day of choices for everyone, and no one was taking the easy one.

The two Intruders came in one after the other, their bombs stripping away the heavy forest below and to either side of the gun. After ten runs,

Dash 1 had taken a single hit in the tail, and my fuel situation was critical. I could still reach one of the two fire-support bases east of Khe Sanh if I left now. I advised Armourplate that they could make one more run each before we had to head for home. Dash 1 took a little extra time lining up and attacked straight down the center line of the ridge. Eight 500-pound bombs trailed behind him, and condensation poured off his wings as he hauled back on the stick to climb. The gun crew followed him upward, their tracers all around the Intruder. Just as he disappeared over the ridge, three of the bombs straddled the gun emplacement. When the debris settled, there was nothing left to suggest it or the men who'd been there ever existed.

The bombs revealed a series of trenches snaking up the ridge. Dash 2 placed the rest of his ordnance a hundred meters above where the gun emplacement had been, exposing more trenches and small bunkers. But the fight was over and Armourplate turned for Chu Lai. With both fuel indicators now deep in the red, I pointed the Bird Dog toward Khe Sanh. From the back seat, Mike gave me updates on bearings and distances to the various fire-support bases. We must have picked up a tail wind, for when we passed over Camp Carroll my right tank was still showing about an eighth. I soon picked out Dong Ha on the horizon. Playing it safe, I stayed over Route 9 in case I needed a place to put her down. With normal mission times seldom over three hours, my wheels touched the runway four hours and twenty-two minutes after we'd lifted off that morning. It would be the longest mission I ever flew. As Mike and I walked away from the aircraft, our mood was a little somber. I should have felt good about what we'd done, but I didn't. As courageous as the marine pilots, those NVA gunners could have retreated with honor soon after the attack began, but they chose to stand and fight. Some very brave men would never go home.

Coming back from Tally Ho, Lee Harrison and I crossed the mouth of the Ben Hai River and began descending. Three miles south of the river we leveled off about twenty feet above the beach. Up to seventy-five meters wide and with a fairly shallow gradient, the white sand beach was free of obstacles as far as we could see. At a thousand feet the Bird Dog was so slow it seemed to hang in the air, but here there was actually an impression of some speed. A few klicks farther south I started seeing the occasional fishing boat and bamboo racks for drying nets. I was just beginning to relax a little when Harrison's voice came through my earphones.

"Catkiller 1-2, this is Catkiller 4-9er, over."

I thumbed my mike button. "Roger, 4-9er, go ahead."

"Catkiller 1-2, this is 4-9er. How tight and low do you want to make this?" Harrison was issuing a challenge. How close could I fly formation on him at absolutely minimum altitude?

"As tight and low as *you* want to make it, 4-9er. Over." Challenge offered and accepted, we formed up in a right echelon, and I edged in until three feet of my left wing extended behind his right wing, with his tail directly opposite my cockpit. The turbulence coming off his wing had me holding lots of left aileron to maintain my position.

"One-two, this is 4-9er starting my descent, over."

"Roger, 4-9er." I kept my eyes on his Bird Dog, matching speed, course and the gradual descent with constant, tiny adjustments of throttle, stick, and rudder. Though this sort of flying required maximum concentration, five to eight hours a day in the cockpit made the Bird Dog almost a natural extension of our minds and bodies. We eased lower, settling out at about five feet above the sand. I saw Lee snap a quick look over his shoulder and grin.

"Nice work, 1-2."

"Roger that, 4-9er," I grinned back. My peripheral vision picked out something ahead. It grew larger and became a sampan pulled up on the beach. Now less than a klick away, I saw a figure standing in front it. My eyes flicked back to see something resting on his shoulder. Any moment now and he'll scamper away or hit the deck, I thought. But he stood facing us and now commanded as much of my attention as I could give him and still stay on Harrison. My thoughts went from "He'll get out of the way" to "Why isn't he moving?"

"We have traffic on the beach."

"He'll move," Harrison said.

"Four-niner, I'm getting ready to break off."

"Hold your position, 1-2. He'll move."

Even at only ninety knots, we were eating up 140 feet per second as we closed on this lone, motionless figure. At about one hundred meters

I saw it was a young boy. Resting on his shoulder was a bamboo pole at least twenty feet long.

"He'll move," Harrison repeated calmly. At which point the kid raised the pole and planted the butt in the sand.

"*Shiiit!*" We broke hard in opposite directions, the pole passing neatly between us. I caught my breath, the scene running through my mind. The little son of a bitch had suckered us in and then ambushed the hell out of us. Suddenly I found the whole thing hilarious. I came around in a tight 360, looking over my shoulder to see him watching me fearlessly. The pole now lay on the beach, and I leveled off at ten feet, passing within fifty feet of him. He stood there with his hands at his sides, and I waved merrily. My wave was returned with an expressionless stare. . . .

Finch, Doc, Lee and I were at the poker table when Mac Byrd walked into the club, popped a beer, and drained it in one long swallow. "Need that first one just to cut the dust," he said, opening another. "Hoop, you were with the Black Aces, weren't you?"

I glanced up from my hand, vaguely annoyed at the interruption. "Yeah," I mumbled. I drew another card and looked at it in disgust. Things weren't looking too hot for the home team. I shot a look at Charlie sitting across from me, wondering what he was holding. It was impossible to read him. Did I raise or fold?

"You hear about Tien Phuoc?"

I folded and picked up my beer. "What about it?"

"It was overrun last night." All four of us looked up at him. "Seems they got hit about two o'clock this morning and went off the air a couple of hours before dawn. One of the guys from the 21st was over it when the sun came up. Said it looked like the command bunker had been blown in with satchel charges and everyone was dead."

Many of our sorties over the DMZ were standard visual reconnaissance missions, flying over a designated area in search of the enemy. When nothing happened, these quickly became unbearably boring, and any sort of action went a long way to breaking the monotony. On one such mission two of us were patrolling a twenty-kilometer line just south of the Ben Hai while two high ship–low ship pairs were working north of the river.

An hour or so into the mission I was over the loop in the Ben Hai River that we called the Horseshoe, when I was contacted by one of the 8-inch artillery batteries dug in along the East Trace. Because factors such as wind, temperature, and humidity affect the accuracy of long-range artillery, the battery commander wanted to register one of his guns. Within a few minutes I spotted a small bunker dug into the river's south bank. Flanked by heavy foliage, its poorly camouflaged entrance showed evidence of recent use. Checking my map to determine its coordinates, I thumbed my mike button.

"Issuewood Kilo, this is Catkiller 1-2. Precision fire mission. Over."

"Roger, Catkiller 1-2, precision fire mission. Over." I gave them the description and grid reference and called for one gun in adjustment, one gun fire in effect. The coordinates were repeated back to me. I orbited about half a mile away to wait for them to crank them into the artillery piece.

"Catkiller 1-2, this is Issuewood Kilo 6. Fire. Over."

"Roger, 6. Fire. Wait."

The first round impacted well to the left and short. I began the adjustment. "Issuewood Kilo 6, Catkiller 1-2. From the gun target line, right 1-0-0, add 1-5-0. Repeat." The second round impacted. "Left 5-0, drop 7-5. Repeat." The third round buried itself less than twenty meters from the bunker, the soft earth heaving upward a few feet from the deep explosion. This was close to enough to begin giving them adjustments that were measured in less than one-mil increments.

"Short, left." Next round. "Over, right." The last round landed less than ten meters from target, well within the intrinsic dispersion of the weapon. Good enough for government work. Registration complete, I had just started to bank away from the target when I caught movement. Two men had run out of the bunker, seen me, and run in again. "New game," I thought grimly, thumbing the mike button.

"Issuewood Kilo, Catkiller 1-2, we have troops in the bunker. Over."

"Roger, Catkiller. Troops in the bunker. Fire. Over." Well off to one side, I heard the faint but distinctive shriek-moan of the incoming round and then saw it strike. "Short, right." The mission continued and with each finely tuned adjustment, the rounds edged closer and closer to the target. The two soldiers re-emerged, then again disappeared inside. The next two hundred pounds of high explosive and steel slammed into the ground. "Over, left." That one landed closer, and from my vantage point I saw the shock wave ripple through the bunker. The men inside finally made a very timely decision. As the next round left the tube a few miles away, three men suddenly appeared at the entrance. They hesitated for what appeared to be a short discussion, then scattered. One ran west and the other northeast along the river bank. Within moments both vanished in the heavy undergrowth. Inexplicably, the third headed due east toward a kilometer-wide area that offered virtually no cover. A few seconds later the last round went through a corner of the bunker, obliterating it. I terminated the fire mission while keeping my eyes on the one NVA soldier hoofing it across open terrain.

By this time the other five Bird Dogs, whose pilots had been bored witless over their assigned patrol areas, were orbiting around the Horseshoe. Watching the lone soldier sprinting eastward, I advised the other Catkillers that I had one troop in the open, then chopped my throttle and pulled the nose up hard to bleed off my airspeed. I saw him run out underneath me at my two o'clock just as the airplane starting to stall. As the nose dropped I armed one tube, eased the stick forward, and from four hundred meters centered him in the grease-penciled cross hairs. Given the inherent inaccuracy of our 2.75-inch rockets, there was little chance of hitting a stationary target, much less a moving one. I squeezed the trigger, sending an electrical impulse that ignited the motor's propellant. There was that familiar *bang!* and the rocket shot out of its tube and burned toward him. It hit about one hundred feet short and to the left, an orange flash followed by a brilliant-white cloud of expanding smoke. As I turned and climbed for a new firing position, I heard Charlie Finch advising that he was rolling in from my northeast. His rocket also missed, and the next Bird Dog announced his intentions. Another miss and another pilot rolling in from the east, then a fourth.

The impromptu free-for-all was getting out of hand. Charlie suggested a little more order, and within a minute or two our six Bird Dogs had formed a Lufberry circle around the fleeing soldier, whose path was marked by a ragged trail of dissipating smoke clouds. Having started at a good clip, especially after the first rocket, he was now beginning to flag.

But after about twenty minutes of this arcade game, each pilot had fired all four of his rockets, leaving this North Vietnamese soldier unscathed. None of us gave a second's thought to what our lone enemy was suffering at our young hands. Why should we? There was no question that he was trained to kill Americans and would have no hesitation doing so if given the opportunity. If any of us were shot down and he was there, would he allow us to run away? He'd kill us. The rules were as simple as they were old: some days you eat the bear, and some days the bear eats you.

Rocket tubes empty but unwilling to admit defeat, Finch and I were the first to roll in with our M16s out the window. One hand on the stick and the other around the pistol grip of the assault rifle, we walked the tracers toward him, the bullets kicking up dirt all around, but none hitting. By now the poor guy was pretty well spent. He would run about fifty meters and drop to his knees, gasping for breath. Then another tracer spewing Bird Dog grumbled past to send him another fifty meters or so. Following our example, the other four made two passes each, pilots and observers spraying bullets and, as far as we could tell, not so much as scratching him. No Carl Lewis, the soldier was now utterly exhausted. I was on the far side of the circle when I saw him collapse against a dry rice paddy dike, where, chest heaving, he waited for the inevitable.

I'm not sure at what point we began to recognize what a cruel game this was, but when Charlie Finch suggested that we disengage, everyone concurred. Charlie's next suggestion, however, received even more agreement from the Catkillers. We formed up in line astern and one last time headed toward our quarry. When he looked up, he had to know there was no escaping this time. His luck had run out.

But as each Bird Dog low leveled past him, instead of having an M16 at the ready, the pilot snapped a salute in recognition of the soldier's luck. Climbing away, I hoped the others felt as happy as I did that he was still alive. On our return to Phu Bai, we headed to the club and toasted this one foe until well into the night.

Doc Clement: A guy from the 108th said he wanted to fire on a target north of the river and asked if I would take him. I said sure. Well, about half an hour later he showed up with an M60 machine gun and said that's what he was going to shoot out the back window, and what's more, he wanted to be straight and level at four hundred feet over the target. "Are you nuts?" I asked him. He said he'd be able to shoot better from that height. Okay. I figured if he had the balls to do it, so did I. We took off and I called DASC to tell them where we were going and left the channel open.

So there we were, four hundred feet straight and level, when I heard him open up. It kept going on and on until I thought he was going to burn the barrel out. Suddenly he smacked me on the back of the helmet. I twisted around and he was freaking out, trying to talk to me on the intercom, but in his confusion he was transmitting on DASC's channel. He hadn't fired the first round—it was all ground fire I was hearing! I dove for the trees and we got out of there. When I came up on Dong Ha DASC, they said they'd heard the whole thing and wanted to know who'd been shot down. I told them everyone was okay and then asked the backseater if he wanted to make another run, but he said, "Hell no! Let's go back and land." Just some of the crazy things we did.

THE NORTHERNMOST EDGE OF the Catkillers' tactical area of responsibility lay two and a half kilometers north of where the Ben Hai River entered the South China Sea. This was the eighty-five gridline, beyond which no Catkiller was supposed to fly. Doc had already penetrated deeper than was prudent on occasion, but still wondered how far into North Vietnam he could go to give the NVA the finger. The challenge proved irresistible.

It was a quiet Sunday in the Dong Ha line shack. Strapping on his gear in preparation for the two-ship noon mission to Tally Ho, Doc decided he was going to "nudge that eighty-five a little more." As high ship he crossed the mouth of the Ben Hai into Tally Ho, keeping careful watch on Jerry Bonning below him. An hour passed. No targets, no ground fire, just the drone of the engine. Bored and frustrated, he abandoned Bonning and common sense and headed north along the coast. Half an hour and fifty miles later, he and his 108th observer Steve Bezold were approaching Dong Hoi, the first enemy town of any size. Far ahead and to the right they could see the battleship USS *New Jersey* steaming ten or twelve miles off the coast.

"I had no business going that far," Doc admitted. "Usually by the time you were a few miles north of the river, they were really hosing you down, but not today. I figured I was going to put some hurt on them."

With the Bird Dog orbiting just west of the town, Bezold scanned the ground with his stabilized fifty-power binoculars. "We got one," he said, passing the binos to Doc. "Three o'clock, just next to Highway 1." A supply depot was swarming with soldiers loading ammunition crates on at least twenty heavy trucks. Catkiller 1-8 had caught them flatfooted, never expecting an unarmed reconnaissance airplane this deep inside the country. Doc also saw some AAA sites.

Steve checked his map and noted the coordinates on his kneepad. The *New Jersey* was in an ideal position to engage the target with her 16-inch guns. "Onrush, Onrush, this is Sundowner Bravo. Fire mission. Over."

"Roger, Sundowner Bravo, this is Onrush. Over."

Five thousand feet below, warning sirens had gun crews racing to their weapons. Radar sets were engaged, sending electronic signals to multi-barreled flak machines. Small men in the light-green uniforms of the People's Army of North Vietnam stood poised to feed the guns with ammunition clips. Gyros whirred and muzzles lifted and swung toward the frail Bird Dog. Bezold was talking to *New Jersey*'s fire-control center when flame erupted from the muzzles of a dozen enemy antiaircraft guns. The opening salvo should have torn the trespasser apart. Miraculously untouched, Doc reacted instinctively, shoving the stick and rudder to one side in a diving turn as the next shells exploded around them in puffs of gray smoke and shrapnel.

Twisting, turning, climbing, and descending, but all the while edging toward the open sea, Doc was using every trick he knew to evade the streams of high-explosive rounds trying to bring him down. It was, as Doc said later, "like being suspended in the middle of a room with cherry bombs going off all around us."

But instead of cherry bombs, these were 57mm antiaircraft shells, each with a diameter of two and a quarter inches and four inches long, directed by radar-controlled guns capable of tracking jets flying 500 miles per hour. The 100-mile-per-hour Cessna would be easy pickings, only one shell needed to tear it apart and send the wreckage spinning earthward. Doc dove and the shells exploded where he had been. He shoved the throttle forward and hauled back on the stick in a climbing turn as the radar rapidly recalibrated and sent more shells to detonate below him.

Doc Clement: We could see the *New Jersey* steaming wide open, but she couldn't fire because we were on the gun target line, up to our ass in smoke from the triple-A and just trying to get the hell out of there. I had that O-1 pulling everything she had. I would spiral down in a 360 and slam the stick back in my lap with full throttle in a forty-five-degree bank, then slam it to the side, then slam it full forward in a turn and pull the power back, each maneuver lasting not more than two to five seconds. I was doing everything I could—not thinking, just reacting. Steve was hanging on to anything he could grab when his map was sucked out the window. It was like having a swarm of killer bees after you, and you're running with nowhere to hide, and they just keep coming and coming until they get you or someone just gives up. The cockpit was full of the smell of explosives. It was like the films of Kamikaze pilots trying to get through the flak to hit American ships during World War II. Steve was on the radio to the *New Jersey*, shouting, "We're going down! We're going down! Keep us in sight!" If I had been in the back seat, I'd probably have thought we'd been hit, the way I was flying that O-1, pulling all the Gs the airplane could take.

FIVE MINUTES HAD GONE BY since the flak machines locked on to them, and it seemed incredible that they were still alive and flying. The *New Jersey* confirmed they were tracking Catkiller 1-8 by the cloud of bursting flak and that the search and rescue team at Quang Tri had been alerted. After what seemed an eternity, Doc crossed the beach and dove for the water, still throwing the Bird Dog through uncoordinated maneuvers as he made desperately for the *New Jersey*. Soaked in sweat and legs trembling so badly he had trouble keeping his feet on the rudder pedals, he turned south before reaching the battleship and announced he was returning to Dong Ha. "It was really quiet in the aircraft on the way back," Doc said.

By the time the prop jerked to a stop, everyone on the flight line was there to meet him. When Doc, who feared no man, climbed out, the terror of the ordeal still gripped him. "I really thought we were going in. It just kept moving with us. Shit, I thought I was going to throw up." Doc's bubble of immortality had burst. He passed a hand over his sweating face. "I can't do it anymore," he said. "I just can't do it anymore." He would, of course, but later people said that was the day Doc got religion.

"When Bezold and I walked around the airplane," Doc said, "we couldn't believe there wasn't a single hole in it. Someone was looking after us."

Chapter 7

My People Need Help

There is no such thing as a small battle or tiny war at cockpit, squad, and platoon levels.
—Col. Jack L. Mullen, Road Runner 6

WHILE RESEARCHING THE EVENTS of 25 October 1968, the author sent a query and rough draft of Bill Hooper's view of the action that day to the website of the 5th Infantry Division. The reply from Jim Roffers saw the recollections of Catkillers Hooper, Finch, and Stewart develop into something else entirely:

> Yes, sir, I remember YOU VERY WELL!! I have waited all of these years to say THANK YOU. I have always thought that I would not be alive today if it hadn't been for your very timely "air strike" on that NVA 12.7 machine gun. I was a sergeant with Recon 1-61. A 12.7 was chewing us UP—I had crawled to within fifty meters from it and stood to fire my LAW at him. He spotted me and adjusted to me. I fired the LAW and it said "CLACK"—misfire—sir, that 12.7 had me cold—you swooped in and GOT him, just in time for me!! I also remember the M16 firing out the side window and the hand grenade "bombs". It has taken me a long time to finally get to say this, THANK YOU, Sir.
>
> Jim Roffers
> Recon Platoon
> 1-61

Twenty-year-old Jim Roffers from Marshfield, Missouri, had returned from Vietnam and reported to the 5th Infantry Division at Fort Carson, Colorado. Learning that the division's 1st Brigade was deploying to Vietnam, he volunteered for a second tour and was assigned to the Reconnaissance Platoon of Headquarters Company, 1st Battalion, 61st Infantry Regiment (Mechanized) under command of newly-commissioned 2nd Lt. David Merrell.

Jim Roffers: On 22 July 1968, we loaded up in C-141 Starlifters and flew from Colorado Springs to Anchorage, Alaska, and from there directly to Cam Ranh Bay. We were ferried to Quang Tri in C-130s, then by trucks out to Wunder Beach. We were there for several weeks, and recon started out as armored cavalry, keeping the road between Quang Tri and Dong Ha open at night for the marines. We had some skirmishes and the companies saw some good firefights, but it was mostly fairly small scale, nothing like what we would experience during Op Rich.

As the official after-action report (AAR) would later record: "Operation Rich was conceived as a Reconnaissance in Force to search out and destroy enemy forces and materials in a designated area between Con Thien and the Ben Hai river . . . Enemy strength and exact locations and dispositions within the area of operations were not known prior to starting the operation. Order of Battle data indicated that the area was believed to be the area of operations for the 27th and the 138th Independent Regiments (AKA 132nd Independent Regiment)."

While Bravo and Charlie Companies and the battalion HQ group waited at Con Thien, Spc. 4th Class Joe "Ski" Krawcykowski, twenty-two years old, from Dunellen, New Jersey, was with Alpha Company at A3 fire-support base near Gio Linh.

Joe Krawcykowski: One of the things that I remember in the few days prior to going into the Z was an Air America chopper that landed and shut down. Official-looking people climbed out and went into the command bunker. It seemed an awfully long time for someone to park a chopper where we got mortared every day. As the radio operator for Captain Haddigan, CO of Alpha Company, I was with the command group, and the skinny coming down was that something big was in the works. On 22 October, A Company was told to be ready at 2400 to move out on foot alone; we'd meet up with the rest of the battalion in the DMZ. After getting my gear ready, I played horseshoes with the mortar platoon. The stakes could not be seen from the pitching end, but being with the mortar platoon, we called in adjustments and actually had a decent game. But the tension in the air could be cut with a machete.

Then mail call came. I received a men's magazine. The inside lead story was "Marines Battle Near DMZ." It was about Operation Buffalo and the marines getting their asses kicked in 1967 right outside our base camp! Bad vibes, ugly omen. After chow, most people hit their racks to get some rest. The bunker for the command group was heavy with something in the air; when you thought that you were the only one awake, you would hear someone whispering. The air had something in it. Oppressive.

Jim Roffers: Recon was with HQ Company at Con Thien. As we were breaking up that last evening before moving up to the DMZ, Lieutenant Merrell was extremely worried about our lack of radio gear and on- and off-again commo. I think we had only three PRC-25s and two PRC-6 radios. Most of the time we were passing "the word" back and forth, up and down the line, verbally. Before we left Con Thien, we had scrounged all over the battalion, trying to beg or borrow radios . . . no go. I even had to steal a radio from our so-called allies, the ARVNs, down in Cam Lo.

Joe Krawcykowski: Alpha Company started out from A3 at about 2345 hours. Dark as hell. Walking through the water up to my neck behind the captain and the group, I became separated by a little bit and no longer had visual contact. I thought, "Great, dark, can't see, can't yell and I don't want to be out here alone. This shit is insane. How can I find them?" Then I realized that they had left a phosphorescent wake though the water, so I just followed that. What a hump through the water to make up time! Then I thought, "Wait, if I can see the trail, so can the gooks! This is insane!" Nothing to do but hump on. Caught up with the group and humped until daylight.

THE MEN OF THE 1st Battalion, 61st Infantry Regiment moved north under radio silence. The NVA could usually expect American forces to prep an objective with artillery before an attack. Operation Rich, however, began with a deception as army and marine batteries sent shells to the west and northwest of 1-61's intended area of operations. At the same time, elements of the 9th Marines and 2nd ARVN Regiment were launching a separate armored and mechanized infantry attack into the DMZ, eight miles to the east of 1-61.

When the sun rose, the advancing battalion began receiving inaccurate mortar fire. Bravo Company overran the mortar position, and an hour later, Recon Platoon stumbled on the first NVA bunker. Then more appeared, many containing weapons caches and food stores, one with a hot meal hastily abandoned by the enemy.

As the American troops continued under sporadic mortar fire, push-pull Cessna O-2s from the USAF 20th Tactical Air Support Squadron at Quang Tri, call sign Barkey, were orbiting above them, calling in artillery on enemy positions and marking targets for air strikes. They were also starting to draw ground fire. A NVA gunner behind a camouflaged 12.7mm antiaircraft gun centered one of the Barkeys in his ring sight and opened fire.

Corporal Alan Ogawa, eighteen years old, from Honolulu, Hawaii, was with 3rd Platoon, Charlie Company.

Alan Ogawa: I looked up and saw a plane flying low, marking the area with white smoke rockets. Then it seemed like the plane just glided down and disappeared into the trees. We didn't have far to go to the crash site, but the thick undergrowth slowed us down. When we got there, the fuselage was in a small clearing on top of a hill. The wings and top of the cockpit had been ripped off when the plane went through the trees. The pilot was still strapped in his seat, dead, and there were NVA sandal footprints all around the wreckage. We had to cut his harness to get him out and onto a medevac chopper that took him back." The pilot, Maj. Marion Reed, had become the first casualty of Operation Rich.

At dawn the next morning, the infantry companies moved out of their night defensive positions near the Ben Hai River. More enemy bunkers and caches of food and ammunition were found and destroyed.

C Company's Kit Carson scout translated a sign on one complex identifying it as an NVA battalion headquarters. The stakes had just gone up. Under observation by the NVA, the Americans came under long-range harassing fire from the far side of the Ben Hai River. Another Barkey spotted the enemy positions and called in air strikes and 5-inch fire from the cruiser USS *Boston.*

THE AAR RECORDS THE FOLLOWING: "At 241334, B/1-61 came under the heavy enemy fire from the Northern bank of the Ben Hai River. Air Strikes and Naval Gun Fire were initiated. A detailed search of the south bank of the Ben Hai River revealed extensive enemy fortifications and supplies."

By the time the sun slipped behind the mountains, an estimated forty NVA soldiers had been killed, but it was small consolation for the friends of Pfc's. Larry Martin and Lonnie Parker of Charlie Company, who had been lost to enemy fire. As the men of 1-61 pulled ponchos over their heads and settled into their night defensive positions near the abandoned village of Kinh Mon, it seemed the elusive enemy had no intention of closing with them.

Soon after midnight on the third day of Operation Rich, intelligence sources reported enemy movement near Trung Luong, an abandoned village two miles northeast of the American unit. When the information reached the Tactical Operations Center at Con Thien, the battalion duty officer checked his watch and made an entry in the log at 1:35 a.m.: "Con Thien Duty Officer's Log #5: 0135 From Bde G-2, en[emy] activity increased YD 199 785 believed moving south."

Those who managed to sleep awoke to the twin-engine growl of Barkey 1-6 overhead. The battleship USS *New Jersey,* steaming ten miles offshore in the South China Sea, advised the air force FAC that she was in position and ready to fire on the suspected enemy force near Trung Luong. Her big guns were about to be used for the first time in direct support of U.S. troops.

Joe Krawcykowski: When the FAC told us to get our people down, I told him that we were in the bottom of B-52 craters and digging already and how much farther could we go? He replied something along the line of, "You'll see." A spotting round landed in the rice paddies and seemed to burn a lot longer than a normal artillery round, then those 16-inch shells started coming in. They sounded like freight trains, and I remember the ground shaking and pieces of debris coming down like rain. The reaction from some of the troops was, "What the hell was *that*?" The FAC was on the radio and said, "That's the USS *New Jersey*, son." It made me feel good that we were getting help from a ship named after my home state.

A FEW HUNDRED METERS west of Ski and A Company, Recon Platoon was leading Capt. Jack Langston's B Company. Moving cautiously along a narrow trail that snaked through the elephant grass, they stumbled onto a camouflaged bunker complex. A small cooking fire flickered on a hearth. Hand signals from Lieutenant Merrell sent men to the left and right.

Jim Roffers: We spread out to search it. Even close-up the bunkers were very hard to see because of the thick vegetation around and over them. They were covered with logs and a foot or so of dirt, with ground-level firing slits about a foot high and two or three feet wide. Each had a sloping entry at the rear, and they were spaced about ten to fifteen yards apart around the small perimeter. There was a small Vietnamese pig running loose in the brush. Inside one camouflaged hooch within the perimeter we found freshly pressed NVA uniform shirts and a lot of papers. A metal washbasin filled with water had a catfish swimming around and around in it.

Wayne McKendree: Lieutenant Merrell told me we needed to get the documents back to intelligence, so I grabbed them and threw 'em into my poncho bag.

DONG HA DUTY OFFICER'S LOG #21 states: "0815 1-61 to TOC Spot Report A. B/1-61; B. 250811H; C. YD 154760 D. Found complete bunker complex. Hooch, furniture, documents. VN interpreter says it was Colonel's quarters through documents found."

Colonels in the People's Army of Vietnam had twenty years of combat experience against the French and Americans. They commanded regiments. Two days earlier, the marine-ARVN task force had killed more than one hundred North Vietnamese soldiers a few miles to the east of where 1-61 now was. Added to the sign identifying an NVA battalion headquarters, plus fresh intelligence on a large enemy force in the area, the documents can have left no doubt that 1-61 had entered the enemy's back yard. Alarm bells should have been ringing throughout northern I Corps.

Recon Platoon set off again ahead of B Company.

Jim Roffers: All of the streams that we crossed were running pretty high because of the heavy rain. Tom Coopey swam a rope across one and nearly drowned. When we got across, we could only get one cigarette lit, so we all shared it to burn the leeches off.

ALPHA COMPANY, STILL separated from Bravo, spotted a small group of NVA soldiers two hundred to three hundred meters east of them. Captain Haddigan dispatched a squad to make contact. Minutes later the company came under heavy mortar fire.

Joe Krawcykowski: We were about a klick from a railway embankment, advancing east through rice paddies, in the rain, when we started taking mortar fire. The squad was pulled back in, and we all started running through knee-deep water for the embankment. I was about tenth back in the column when we started and second when we made it to the west side of it. Mortars were landing on that side, so we ran over the tracks to the east side. As soon as we got to the other side of the embankment, the NVA opened up with machine guns—lots of them—from a wooded area about two hundred yards to our east.

We ran south along the embankment until reaching a river. Radio in one hand, rifle in the other, I don't remember swimming across the twelve-foot-deep river, but I got to the other side in record time. Captain Haddigan dropped his SOI codebook and started diving for it. The rounds were coming in very heavily, sounded like bees whizzing by. I shouted, "Leave the fuckin' thing!" but he finally got it and we continued south. The terrain the embankment followed rose just enough to make our run through the mud more difficult. The rain kept coming down, harder and harder.

FIRST LIEUTENANT DAVE PITTAM, battalion S3-air, was in command of the 1st Battalion, 61st Infantry Regiment's Tactical Operations Center at

Con Thien. He heard Ski on the company net, noted the time, and made an entry in the Duty Officer's Log: "0925 A Co on railroad track. Taking automatic weapons and mortar from N and E."

Jim Roffers: We were partway across some little abandoned paddies, leading Bravo when Lieutenant Merrell told us to fall back. We were the reserves, he said, "to be used only in dire need." Bravo moved past us toward the enemy mortars. Suddenly there was just a storm of firing on the left. Some was M16, and a lot was AK-47 and SKS. It had to be A Company being engaged and returning fire. Then there was a very fast buildup of firing to our front.

Joe Krawcykowski: My call sign was Baby Tides 6 Romeo. One of the air force Barkeys contacted me and asked where an air strike was needed. I replied to the east of the railroad track.

Con Thien Duty Officer's Log #32: "0847 A Co to FAC 18, mortar behind Hill 124."

Alpha Company was engaging the enemy positions with small-arms fire when Barkey 1-8 brought in a flight of Phantoms.

Joe Krawcykowski: There was still a lot of the company trying to get down the line under heavy fire when the planes dropped their loads and the 1st Platoon reported friendly casualties.

Two men with superficial wounds were treated by medics and returned to the fight. More mortars and machine guns opened up from across the Ben Hai River, and Barkey scrambled more flights of air to hit them. As yet unknown to anyone in 1-61, fresh intelligence was coming into the 3rd Marine Division Headquarters about NVA reinforcements moving down from North Vietnam. If they could cross the river, the American battalion would be in grave danger.

Con Thien Duty Officer's Log #58: "1007 CG 3RMAR (relay Bde) need to know if any fording sites or crossing points on the Ben Hai for foot troops. ASAP message received from COMUS MACV thru 3rd MARDIV."

Even without enemy reinforcements to face, the men of 1-61, tired, wet, and scattered, had already entered what was fast becoming a battle for survival.

Joe Krawcykowski: We'd gained some distance from the river and were still going uphill. I was a step or two behind Captain Haddigan, with Spec. 4th Class Jim Soriano and Sgt. Jim Wright running more or less abreast of each other a few feet in front of him. There was an explosion as a mortar round landed, and I hit the ground. I jumped up, saw no one moving, hit the ground again, and low-crawled over to check everyone out. I rolled Soriano over and saw that he was KIA. I next checked on Sergeant Wright, who was very badly wounded and dying. I heard a moan and went back to check the captain, who was bleeding from several wounds. I pulled him back to a bomb crater, then pulled Sergeant Wright back to it. I also believe I pulled Soriano's body back to the rim of the crater. There was a lot of small-arms fire in the area, but I saw no one else. Captain Haddigan gave me instructions on what he wanted done, then I got on the radio to the battalion CO, Colonel Wheeler.

CON THIEN DUTY OFFICER'S LOG #61: "1019 A Co to Bn CO my CO hit bad. Bad situation fire from three sides."

Bravo Company had completed the river crossing behind recon and was ordered to envelop the enemy force from the south and capture or destroy the enemy mortars. Still west of the railway embankment, they overran a company-sized bunker complex and came under intense automatic weapons fire from all sides.

Con Thien Duty Officer's Log #65: "1023 Bn CO to B Move fast [enemy] are closing in on [A Co]."

Con Thien Duty Officer's Log #66: "1024 Bn CO to A Co, anyway you can pull out? [No,] separated from one of my elements."

Joe Krawcykowski: The 1st Platoon was reorganizing after the airstrike, higher-ups wanted to know the status, and the firing was getting heavier and closer. I juggled things as best I could, relaying orders and giving a few of my own over the radio. When the battalion commander called again for an update, I told him to stand by until I called him. I had enough to do and didn't need him at that time. I yelled for "Top," First Sergeant Ledford, who had been behind us when we were working our way out of the paddies and running south on the track line.

We had only one radio because the mortar that killed Soriano and Wright had ruined the other one. That was the company push. I had the battalion push and converted over to company. We were spread out after running across the rice paddies to the railroad embankment, and I directed the platoon leaders to their right rear and left rear from the firing I heard. Captain Haddigan was in and out of it, so when they finally made it back to my location, I passed on what he had told me to tell them.

CON THIEN DUTY OFFICER'S LOG #68: "1033 Bn CO Bde CO need medevac with gunships within 30 minutes. Tides situation bad[,] pinned down with auto weapons and mortar. B Co trying to relieve pressure. A Co 6 WIA."

B Company attempted to reach A Company but was halted by the same overwhelming fire. At its rear, Recon Platoon was laying down suppressive fire when it was sent forward.

Jim Roffers: Word came down the line that Captain Langston had ordered Recon to attack the ridge top in support of A Company. My hair nearly stood on end. If they were pinned down, why were we going forward? Only four of us in the platoon had ever fought an infantry battle; the rest of the guys had been trained solely as recon men and had never been into anything like this. We were traveling light—I had ten mags and some only had seven. Our job, the one we had been trained for, was to slip up, find the enemy, and then turn them over to the rifle companies. Well, at that moment, we became the infantry and didn't have the ammo or trained people to do this.

SPECIALIST 4TH CLASS TOM COOPEY was a twenty-year-old Brooklyn, New York, native.

Tom Coopey: Recon reversed course back through B Company to bring relief to A Company. We made our way past the reinforced NVA bunkers, which had been searched and were about to be blown by the combat engineers when we came under intense enemy fire. The only way to advance was to lag several meters behind the man in front. I had to hit the dirt several times, as I could hear the rounds snapping very close to me. I managed to keep sight of Willie Williams, who ran like a deer. He dove into a bomb crater, and I was seconds behind him. We found Lieutenant Merrell, his radio operator Tommy Ray, and Wayne McKendree there. Barney Hyatt was on the ground, shot in the shoulder and in shock. At this point Dave Merrell had his back to the enemy and directed my squad to an empty enemy trench line to his left and another squad to his right.

As soon as my squad got to the trench line, we could hear automatic fire all around us, mostly big stuff, 12.7 crew-manned, some AK-47s. We couldn't see them because of their spider holes and the six- to seven-foot-high elephant grass. We began firing to our front, where the sounds of automatic fire were coming from. I had about fifteen magazines of M16 ammo and went through half of that in about five minutes. Some of the guys were standing up in the trench, with only elephant grass hiding their upper torsos, when, out of nowhere, Langston appeared and began berating us for firing on our own troops, presumably A Company. He was outside the trench line, oblivious to the risk he was taking, and I would almost swear he was alone and without a weapon.

SOMEWHERE JUST TO THE NORTH of them, Roffers' squad was advancing.

Jim Roffers: So here we are, going up a brush-covered little slope, in the rain, into battle. The rain made the grass slippery and had turned everything else to mud. The visibility was pretty bad, but the darkness helped to pick out the muzzle flashes. Heavy fire snapped all around us. We were running forward at a low crouch, crawling on hands and knees and bellies sometimes. I'm thinking, "Man! This is going to be bad!" I honestly didn't think I was going to come out of it alive. When we reached the end of the slope, there was firing all around us—360 degrees. All three companies were engaged, and recon as well. Charlie Company was on the right flank trying to hook around the enemy but was encountering heavy resistance. Alpha Company was being shot to shreds down by the abandoned railroad tracks to our east.

WITH LIEUTENANT MERRELL BETWEEN the two recon squads and most of the battalion now fixed by enemy fire, the rain slackened and the skies started to clear. The break in the weather would last only long enough to run one crucial air strike.

Wayne McKendree: The rain had stopped, but everything was wet and muddy. Lieutenant Merrell, Tommy Ray, and I were out ahead of B Company in a thick hedgerow when Captain Langston suddenly showed up, and he and Lieutenant Merrell moved away from us. I couldn't hear everything they were saying, but from the tone of their voices and their arm movements, I could tell that they were arguing. When the lieutenant got back to us, he was really mad, which was unusual for him.

He motioned for me and Ray to come on, and the three of us started moving forward through the elephant grass. We were under fire from an enemy machine gun nest, and I can remember the rounds whizzing by my ear. We kept on crawling until we got to a bomb crater. Ray was the first in, then the lieutenant. When I rolled into it, I ended up between them, elbow to elbow. The enemy machine gun was only about forty meters away, and when Ray rose up to look, I saw him get hit in the head. Just as I turned to my other side, to tell Lieutenant Merrell what had happened, I saw a round exiting his head. Ray was dead, but the lieutenant was still breathing. I needed to get a medevac for him.

I pulled the radio off Ray and tried to raise Sergeant Marzan. I kept calling, but I was on the wrong frequency, and there was no answer. Then I heard someone on the radio say he was a lieutenant colonel and that he could help. I looked up and saw this gray, twin-boom aircraft, with an engine in front and one in the back, and it was practically standing on one wing so the pilot could get a look. It was a Barkey, and he told me to throw a smoke to mark my position. The only smoke I had was white, and that was only used to mark enemy positions, but he told me to go ahead and throw it. Then he said, "I can see the machine gun."

I must have told him what had happened to Lieutenant Merrell, because he told me to get the lieutenant down into the crater. Then he brought in a jet that dropped a napalm. I can remember the heat and smoke. Then the jet came back again, firing his 20mm guns right over the top of me. An empty shell casing from the jet hit me on the helmet.

Barkey said the machine gun nest was destroyed and that I could move. I got the lieutenant on my back and crawled out of the bomb crater to find help. I was also dragging the radio. I must have crawled about a hundred meters when some other guys from recon found me. But Lieutenant Merrell was dead. He must have died on my back as I was carrying him.

THE BRIEF RESPITE FROM THE WEATHER ended. Ceilings again dropped to one hundred feet or less, and the rain returned, coming down in sheets. The Phantoms and Skyhawks circling above a thick and solid undercast broke off and returned to Da Nang or Chu Lai. Then the Barkey O-2s, already at the edge of their envelope for tight, slow, and low maneuvers, were forced to withdraw.

As the sound of the twin-engined Cessnas faded, Roffers remembers, "We were told that was it, we couldn't get any more air support because of the rain. I can only guess at the thoughts going through the heads of those who were running things. We didn't have things set up for this type or size of battle, no ammo ready to go, no resupply set up, nothing prearranged, or at least, it didn't appear that way to me. The top brass must have been scrambling around, wondering how it was going to look back home if an entire American battalion got annihilated up there."

The men of the 1st Battalion, 61st Infantry, were on their own and under attack by the seasoned 2nd Battalion of the 132nd Independent Regiment. On the other side of the Ben Hai River, more units of the People's Army of Vietnam were marching south to reinforce them.

Eleven miles southeast of 1-61 and unaware of the battle, Bill Hooper and new guy Rod Stewart were in the Dong Ha line shack, their early-morning, two-ship mission into North Vietnam scrubbed because of the weather. Stewart, twenty-two years old, from Westchester, California, had never flown with the other pilot who sat moodily at the end of the picnic table, watching the rain.

THE LINE SHACK'S telephone clattered.

Bill Hooper: A very worried operations officer from the other side of the airfield was on the phone. He told me that a battalion from the 1st of the 5th was fighting for its life in the DMZ and asked if we could lend support in any fashion. I looked out the door. The other side of the runway was barely visible four hundred feet away. There was a long pause. I was wondering what use a Bird Dog could possibly be under these conditions when he said very slowly and distinctly, "My people need help." Behind the words was a note of desperation. I gave the weather another long look. "Roger that, sir. If you'll send me an observer, we'll head out there, and whatever we can do, we will do."

Rod Stewart: I knew little about Hooper other than he was very enthusiastic about taking the fight to the enemy and had a bit of a John Wayne reputation within the company. When the phone calls started coming in that morning, the one side of the conversations I heard was alarming. My excitement was high, but Hooper became absolutely frothing to get to the fight. Switching our FM radio to a frequency used by the battalion in contact proved my feeling was valid: U.S. Army units in the DMZ . . . pinned down . . . medevacs requested . . . air strikes and artillery requested. Hooper hung up the phone, shouted instructions to the crew chief, and was out the door.

Bill Hooper: I was pulling on my flak vest, when the line chief came up and muttered, "There's no way you can help those guys." He pointed at the cloud base. "You're gonna get your ass shot off."

"Do we have any HEs?" I asked, trying to hide my nervousness. He shook his head and left to load Willie Petes. At the door of the line shack there were a few scraps of ceramic and steel armor plating. Grabbing one about the size of a frying pan, I ran through the rain to the airplane and started to place it under the back seat, then changed my mind and wedged it under mine. Soaked to the skin, I waited under the wing as the downpour drummed against it and ran in sheets off the trailing edge. The observer I'd been sent, an overweight and unhappy lieutenant, arrived and reluctantly crawled in. I taxied into position. "Dong Ha Tower, this is Catkiller 1-2 holding short, ready for take off. Over."

WITH THE CEILING AND VISIBILITY FAR below the minimums required by army regulations for flying, the controller was clearly not expecting any traffic this morning.

"Catkiller 1-2, this is Dong Ha Tower, you're ready for *what*?"

The controller's disbelief brought a brief smile to Hooper's face as he pushed the throttle forward. The Bird Dog started rolling, the tail came up, and the tiny Cessna disappeared into the rain.

Rod Stewart: I was the new guy, so I was to stay and monitor the radio and answer the phone. If this was as big as it sounded, we would be expecting orders from higher up. Our platoon commander, Captain Finch, was already on his way up from Phu Bai, and Hooper could call if he needed any help. I sat and listened to the radio. I could often only hear one side of a conversation. I did not know what units the various call signs represented. Locations and coordinates were not supposed to be given in the clear, but with map in hand and calls for strikes on such-and-such a target, I could piece together a confusing bit of the fight.

The phone rang again, and it was an officer at some command center. Instead of giving me instructions or orders, he wanted me to tell him what was going on up in the Z. My confusion only deepened. Why had we not been told of this operation before now? I radioed Hooper. He was not on our company frequency, but Captain Finch, trying to find Dong Ha in the rain, was, and I relayed all the information I could think of to him. Like Hooper, he sounded like he was grinning in anticipation.

HIS WINDSCREEN OPAQUE FROM the lashing rain, Hooper was skimming the underside of the clouds eighty to one hundred feet above Highway 1. When he reached the East-West Trace, the ceiling had lifted to almost 150 feet, allowing him to turn northwest toward Kinh Mon. "When I was within a couple of miles of the battalion's position, the weather started forcing me lower again, and I made my first call. The response was immediate. Given the heavy firing I could hear in the background, I was amazed at how calm the radio operator sounded."

"Roger, Catkiller 1-2, this is Baby Tides 6 Romeo. How do you read? Over."

"Tides 6 Romeo, this is Catkiller 1-2, I read you Lima Charlie. How me? Over."

"Roger, Catkiller, Lima Charlie. Do you have us in sight? Over."

"Negative, Tides 6 Romeo. I am an O-1 Bird Dog one hundred feet above the terrain. My heading is approximately 020. Do you have me in sight?"

"Negative, Catkiller, we don't see you, but we do hear you. We think you're to our southeast. Turn northwest. You should pick us up."

Down in a bomb crater, radio handset to his ear, Ski was peering into the rain. "Several of us were saying, 'Where the hell is that little plane, and how the hell can that guy fly in this soup?' We could hear a plane but not see him."

Bill Hooper: My vision was obscured in every direction by the weather. I brought the nose a little farther to the west, throttled back, and dropped some flaps, allowing the plane to sink. Punching through a wall of heavy rain, I was astonished by all the muzzle flashes in the low scrub and elephant grass. Smoke from a napalm strike was still rising just to the east. Tides 6 Romeo told me he was in a bomb crater about a quarter of a mile directly in front of me.

CON THIEN DUTY OFFICER'S LOG #73: "1056 A Co to Mar Fac* Loc 170 760 in bomb hole."

Bill Hooper: Through my open window I caught sight of a much bigger muzzle flash, and looked down. Just below me was a heavy machine gun in a trench filled with water, troops wearing helmets, light green uniforms, and back packs. At first I thought it was an American position. I passed over it and directly ahead saw a triangular pattern of three bomb craters, each filled with rainwater and more troops. I told Tides 6 Romeo I thought I had his position, but to give me a hand signal and tell me what it was. As I crossed over the crater, I saw someone on his back, waving and kicking his arms and legs. He rolled back to his stomach and said he'd given me a spread eagle sign. Another crater to the south was taking fire from the heavy machine gun I had just overflown, and I relayed its position to the radio operator.

---

*Never having worked with the Catkillers, and thinking Hooper was a Marine FAC, the troops used the generic "Mar Fac" when talking to him. This would complicate communications when the next Catkiller arrived.

Con Thien Duty Officer's Log #74: "1101 Mar Fac to A Co spotted machine gun and 10 men in bunker 400m[eters] from air strike[;] think it is unfriendly position check your position."

Flying within pistol shot of the enemy, Hooper soon learned that 1-61's companies and platoons were separated by strong NVA positions, which restricted return fire for fear of hitting their own people. And given the size of the enemy force, until they could consolidate, the scattered groups of young Americans were threatened with being destroyed piecemeal. Hooper made a wide orbit to familiarize himself with the area. Bordered by tree lines on three sides and covered with old bomb craters, the battlefield was crossed by a stream flowing north to the Ben Hai, a few hundred meters away. He located a second divided company in more bomb craters under fire from all sides. The rain, thick elephant grass, and darkened, rain-soaked uniforms made it difficult to distinguish between friend and foe. He asked for flares to pinpoint their positions.

Con Thien Duty Officer's Log #76: "1108 Bn CO to . . . B Co fired flare. Bn CO to A Co—shoot flare to help locate him . . ."

Bill Hooper: When I found the third company, they had their backs to a railway embankment and were under heavy mortar and automatic weapons fire from the eastern side of the battlefield. I advised the radio operator that the lightest enemy concentration appeared to be between him and the company just to the south. I reported a second machine gun and a mortar, and he said they had people moving forward to take it out.

Con Thien Spot Report # 77 [handwritten]: "A. Catkiller 12; B. 251110; C, b 171758; D. Enemy machine gun position & possible mortar position; E. Surrounding and taking under fire."

Jim Roffers: My squad received orders to pull back to the west. After only a minute or two of crawling on hands and knees, the word came to about-face and move easterly. Then a few minutes later, we were told to move directly south to hit an enemy 12.7 that was keeping everyone pinned down. My point man, Joe Shallcross, took the initiative and moved toward this heavy machine gun. I remember thinking, "Oh my God, Joe . . ."

I dropped my pack and rifle in the mud and got out the LAW rocket that I'd been carrying, and we all crawled forward to a large bomb crater.

HOOPER HAD REPORTED YET a third enemy machine gun when a desperate radio operator asked if he could put an air strike on the 12.7 that had them pinned down. It was wishful thinking. Even if there were fast-movers circling above the clouds, there was no way they could get through the low overcast without flying into the ground. One-six-one's only air support was an aging propeller-driven Cessna with four smoke rockets. It banked toward one of the most dangerous weapons in the enemy's arsenal and started closing to what, for the 12.7mm heavy machine gun, was literally point-blank range.

Bill Hooper: I eased my turn, reduced power, and waited until the gun appeared in front of me. It was difficult to see it clearly because of the rain against my windscreen, but the large muzzle flashes were very bright in the dark conditions. Tracers were going flat across the ground toward a crater somewhere to my right. I was about a hundred feet above the battle when I leveled the wings and went into a slow glide, fully aware that if they shifted their fire to me I'd never have time to evade.

Jim Roffers: The machine gun was just to the left and south of our crater. I moved to the edge, stood up with the LAW on my shoulder, and squeezed the trigger. Over all the shouting and gunfire, there was a loud *clack!* A misfire. The 12.7 gunner swung the weapon, and several heavy rounds struck the mud all around me. I ducked down, recocked the LAW, stood, and aimed again. There was another *clack!* It wasn't going to fire. Bullets were flying all around me.

Bill Hooper: I sighted down the crosshairs grease-penciled on the windscreen and, at a range of not more than 250 meters, fired my first rocket. I broke to the left and looked over my shoulder through the open side window and saw it explode just to the left and a little short of the gun emplacement, spraying white phosphorous over it.

Top / Some of 1st Platoon's pilots at Dong Ha. From left: Fred Willis, Terry Scruggs, Roger Bounds, Charlie Finch, Bill Hooper, Lee Harrison, and Dennis Dolan. *Rod Stewart*
Bottom / Bill Hooper flies toward Tally Ho, while his backseater talks to Dong Ha DASC. *Bill Hooper*

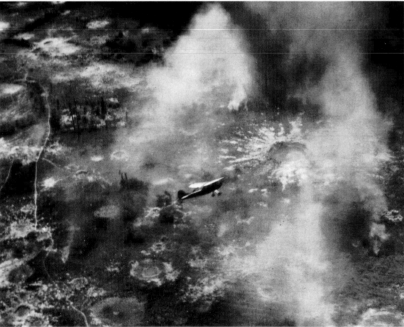

Top / Doc Clement in the front seat of his Bird Dog. *Charles Finch*
Bottom / A Bird Dog makes a low pass for a bomb damage assessment after an air strike in the DMZ. *Don Long*

Top / A hit from a 12.7mm heavy machine gun in a Bird Dog's horizontal stabilizer. *Charles Finch*
Middle / Captain Sarge Means (left) and Mac Byrd on the Phu Bai flight line. *Bill Hooper*
Bottom / Crew chiefs Dennis Jenkins (left) and Rich Buster at Dong Ha. *Charles Finch*

Top / Marine aerial observer Bob Happe and Doc Clement at Dong Ha after a mission along the DMZ. *Doc Clement*
Bottom / Crew chief Michael Donnick (holding a white phosphorus rocket) and Scott Goins. *Charles Finch*

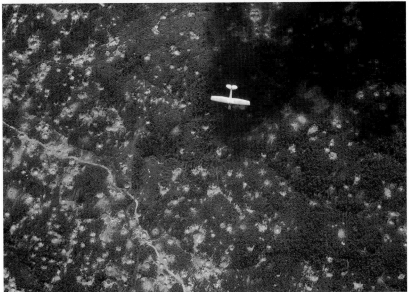

Top left / Jim Hudson before taking off on a mission to Tally Ho. *Jim Hudson*
Top right / Charlie Finch and one of his plane's many hits from small arms fire
(circled) during his year as a Catkiller. *Charles Finch*
Bottom / Finch takes the low position over Tally Ho, flying at about five hun-
dred feet. Taken from Bill Hooper's plane at about a thousand feet.
Charles Finch

Top left / Peter Van Haren, Bravo Company, 1st Battalion, 77th Armor. *Peter Van Haren*

Top right / Tom Coopey, Recon Platoon, HQ Company, 1st Bn, 61st Infantry (Mech). *Tom Coopey*

Middle left / Jim Roffers, Recon Platoon, HQ Company, 1st Bn, 61st Infantry (Mech). *Jim Roffers*

Middle right / Alan Ogawa, C Company, 1st Bn, 61st Infantry (Mech). *Alan Ogawa*

Bottom left / Wayne McKendree, Recon Platoon, HQ Company, 1st Bn, 61st Infantry (Mech). *Wayne McKendree*

Bottom right / Joe "Ski" Krawcykowski, A Company, 1st Bn, 61st Infantry (Mech). *Joe Krawcykowski*

Top left / Marine observer Mike LaFromboise. *Charles Finch*
Top right / Rod Stewart wears his Silver Star, awarded for leading an armored
force to Kinh Mon. *Rod Stewart*
Bottom / Charlie Finch and Bill Hooper after being presented with the Silver
Star for their actions over Kinh Mon. *Charles Finch*

Top / Aerial obsesrver Bill Norton, 108th Field Artillery Group (left), and Cat-killer Jack Bentley. *Charles Finch*
Bottom / Wearing a Velpeau cast, Bill Hooper plays Hamlet to poor Yorick at the Fort Gordon military hospital. *Bill Hooper*

Jim Roffers: I was half-turning to dive into the crater when I heard the raspy sound of a rocket go over me and an explosion. I peeked over the crater lip and saw the Willie Peter smoke, and then saw a FAC flying really low to my left. Where had he come from? There was no firing coming from the machine gun. I ran bent-over back up the trail to retrieve my rifle and pack and ran into Sergeant Marzan, who gave the word to pull back.

Recon was ordered a few hundred meters to the east. By the time we got there, we were scattered in small groups all over the hilltop. There were six or seven in my group, and we ran into someone who ordered us to move a little north to help guard a large crater filled with our wounded. A lieutenant from B Company kept going out to drag dead and wounded back into the crater. I witnessed three trips out and back. He was heading out again and asked if anyone had any hand grenades. I gave him my last two grenades, and he ducked up and over the rim and was gone.

Not long after hooper had taken off, Charlie Finch touched down at Dong Ha.

Charles Finch: The weather was so bad coming up from Phu Bai that I had to go feet wet and follow the beach north before turning west, but even then I got lost for a while. As soon as I'd refueled, I was met in the line shack by my marine observer, Capt. Russ Cedoz. Russ had already been fully briefed on the situation in the DMZ and reckoned the army was in a serious shit sandwich. Aggressive and motivated in the best marine mold, he had brought extra clips of M16 ammo and some grenades. Russ was ready for war as usual but much more wired than I had ever seen him. I usually carried five or six clips of ammo and could not really pack any more, so I stocked up on smoke grenades and filled the doors with them.

Rod Stewart had over-nighted at Dong Ha and had been monitoring the FM radio since Bill's departure. What he had heard indicated that the army had stepped into a giant hornet's nest. When he asked about coming up with me, I weighed the weather and his lack of experience with troops in contact and told him to stand by for the time being.

Russ and I lifted off about 0930. The rain was so heavy against my windscreen that I had to fly in a crab to see out the open right window. We could hear Hooper on the radio. It was clear that he was extremely busy and that very little separated him from the battle just below. He briefed me as much as he could. The picture Bill painted was that the army was not doing well. All three companies—as well as individual platoons—were separated, with enemy positions between them. That and the weather were making it impossible to give them the cover and support that we normally provided for troops in contact—support they needed desperately.

We came up on the eastern side of the battle, where there was a railroad bed that rose about ten feet above the paddies. There were NVA on top and on both sides. From the railroad tracks toward Con Thien, it looked like a shooting gallery. Muzzle flashes everywhere you looked. Russ and I were amazed at how close the NVA forces were to the American positions. We had seen this tactic of closing to within twenty meters of small marine units to prevent air strikes, but not a force of this size. At first glance, Russ said they would have to retreat.

I came across and we started firing our M16s and Russ was tossing out his grenades. Holding an M16 out the window against the air stream and firing on automatic while trying to fly below one hundred feet is not cool, but at that point it was about all we could do. Why the NVA did not shoot me down at such close range I will never know.

Jim Roffers: We'd been told that we couldn't get any support from the air because of the rain, yet now there was a second FAC overhead. It made three or four low passes—maybe twenty-five to fifty feet—over and in front of us, someone dropping grenades and firing an M16 out the window. The FAC was also taking fire, and a couple of times I saw green tracers going past him. They were all that we had, but it meant that we weren't up there all alone. With the craters, the rain, us and the NVA firing at each other, and the little planes silhouetted against the dark skies, it looked like something from *All Quiet on the Western Front.*

Charles Finch: I had the M16 braced against my chicken plate and got off some good, long bursts. We were running through magazines and empty shell casings were everywhere in that small cockpit. Every once in a while Russ would shout over the intercom, "I think I got one!" The radio traffic was very intense, very difficult at times to understand. The ground troops were giving us directions to where the guns were, but with two identical Bird Dogs low overhead, sometimes they thought they were talking to me when they were talking to Bill, or vice versa. Calling both of us "Mar Fac," they'd tell us to "turn right" or that "you are over our position," which sometimes had us making all sorts of unnecessary maneuvers. It was a classic example of the fog of war. Bill stayed west of the railroad, and I was east and south, and although we must have occasionally overlapped, because of the heavy rain and low clouds we never saw each other.

Jim Roffers: I saw two or three NVA running bent-over in single file toward our crater. Two of us opened up and they disappeared into some brush. The rest of the time I was shooting at muzzle flashes. The noise was unbelievable—the *crack*s of bullets, the firing from us and the enemy, explosions near and far, people screaming, radiomen yelling into handsets, the little airplanes overhead. . . .

Joe Krawcykowski: One of the guys in the crater with me thought we didn't have much time to live and lit up a Chesterfield. I didn't smoke, but I pulled it out of his mouth and sucked down half of it.

INSIDE THE TACTICAL OPERATIONS Center at Con Thien, 1st Lt. Dave Pittam was monitoring 1-61's company and battalion radios. He heard the voice of a rifle platoon leader pleading with a Catkiller to find and eliminate NVA mortars that were firing on his men.

Charles Finch: The first desperate call I recognized as definitely being for me was that the NVA mortars needed to be silenced quick. Russ and I could see NVA everywhere—at one point we saw twenty-five to forty uniformed troops lying on the east side of the railroad bed—but we had to ignore them and find those mortars. I lowered my flaps and got down to about sixty knots, and we immediately took a hit about two feet behind Russ. My slow pattern kept exposing us to more ground fire, but it was the only way to do the job. I knew that Hooper was taking heavy fire to my west. There was no safe place. Calls for medevacs increased, but the heavy rain and low ceiling were still preventing them from getting in.

Bill Hooper: With the three companies spread in a southwest to northeast arc and the company along the railroad tracks at the top, I orbited over the battlefield, advising on the disposition of the enemy troops. Tracers passed me and there was a *tic* as a round punched through the Bird Dog's skin. Slamming the throttle forward, I hauled back on the stick and escaped into the clouds, changed course, waited a few seconds, then descended into the open over the railroad embankment.

Joe Krawcykowski: I can't recall how long I was on the radio, but soon after the platoon leaders went back to their platoons, Top arrived, along with a Kit Carson scout named Thau. They helped out immensely when the NVA started to close in on our bomb crater. I directed Thau to cover the westerly side. An NVA soldier was about 150 feet away, coming toward us with a RPG. I yelled at Thau to shoot. Don't know if Thau hit him, but the guy with the RPG disappeared. The rain was still coming down heavily. Top Ledford helped to get more people to our location and then took over, relaying orders from Captain Haddigan and giving his own orders, until the designated platoon leader returned to take command.

SEPARATED BY THE SAME RIVER the rest of the battalion had already negotiated, Charlie Company was ordered across in support of Bravo Company.

Alan Ogawa: We had a rope stretching across the river, and the ones that couldn't swim held on for dear life. I took the loads off the nonswimmers and helped them across, and we kept on going, with Staff Sergeant Yonesaki as acting platoon leader. We came under fire in an old rice paddy. Myself and another guy made it across, but the rest of the platoon got pinned down on the other side, and the rest of the company ahead of us kept on going. Finally, after returning fire, the rest of the platoon was able to cross. We were going around a hill and, as soon as we reached the other side, Sergeant Yonesaki got hit bad. We went in an old B-52 hole and started to receive fire again.

AAR: "At 251130 October, C/1-61 completed the stream crossing at YD 155762 and was immediately committed to the east of B/1-61 in order to relieve pressure coming from a reinforced bunker complex on the eastern flank and to prevent the escape of the enemy forces to the south."

Tom Coopey: We'd been in the trench for what seemed a long time. We had no communications, were low on ammo and very, very thirsty. Then we heard friendlies approaching from our rear. One of them shouted that he heard movement to their front—us. Another voice said to throw grenades, and we all started shouting, "No, no! Friendlies!" A couple of our staff sergeants decided that we had to make a move. Much debate followed as to which direction we should use as our escape route. Finally someone jumped up and we followed. Moments later a figure came out of the elephant grass. He was shirtless and appeared to have a chest wound. He identified himself as a lieutenant, said he was policing up stragglers and that the NVA were popping up at random out of spider holes. He had two grenades, pins pulled, and advised us to follow him as fast as possible and that we should keep running if fired upon—his grenades would take care of the problem. He led us to an area pockmarked with 500-pound-bomb craters, and we jumped into the closest one. One of the adjoining craters was lined with the dead and wounded.

Joe Krawcykowski: Top Ledford was less than an arm's length away when I looked up and saw another NVA about 250 feet to our west fire a RPG at us. I yelled, "Duck!" and pulled Top down. The RPG went right over our heads and hit the next hole down, wounding several guys. The one whose cigarette I had swiped right out of his mouth earlier ended up paralyzed.

Charles Finch: Only on UHF was there some clear communication. Russ was all over the FM in response to the guys on the ground telling us to change frequencies between company and battalion. Underneath us there was a lot of vegetation for everyone to hide in. Our guys would pop out, and in the rain it was not always clear at first if they were friendlies. The weather was getting worse—the rain was unbelievably heavy—and it seemed the battle was intensifying. It appeared to a simple army pilot like me that the mission planners had never anticipated an engagement of this size and ferocity.

FINCH WAS NOT ALONE in his assessment. The battalion commander was desperate for helicopter gunships and a "demonstration," a diversionary attack by an armor company waiting at Con Thien. Their deployment had been part of the operational planning for Op Rich, yet only now, three hours into the battle, was the cavalry told to saddle up.

Dong Ha Duty Officer's Log #39: "1135 Bde CO to TOC: Est 1 NVA Bn is unit that A/1-61 is in contact with. Request 3rd MAR DIV launch gunships to contact area to support CO 1-61. B/1-77 (Rein) will execute contingency support plan and move southeast [*sic*] of A-4 to assist and reinforce 1-61."

Con Thien Duty Officer's Log #89: "1141 Bn CO to Bde CO 1. Need Gunships. 2. Start something out other way. 3. Captured two mortars here not down there. 4. Weather closing in. Demonstration. [Y]ou know what time it takes. Others I have requested."

Con Thien Duty Officer's Log # 90: "1148 Bde CO to Bn CO B1/77 plan from yesterday commencing now. Could get into trouble."

Bravo Company, 1st Battalion, 77th Armor Regiment was at Con Thien. Lieutenant Peter Van Haren, twenty-three years old, from Phoenix, Arizona, was 2nd Platoon leader.

Peter Van Haren: The first I heard of anything happening was over the tank radios when someone said to switch to battalion net. We heard that 1-61 had made contact north of us and that the enemy weren't running as they usually did, but deploying and attacking. I could tell from the background sounds and the excitement and fear in the radiomen's voices that they were in heavy contact.

I went over to the HQ bunker to listen to the radio traffic. My company commander, Capt. Art McGowan, was there and practically begging the colonel to let us get going *now*. But there was some kind of glitch in the operation plan, which HQ staff said meant we couldn't go yet: they weren't sure if the main route had been cleared or if the M88 [large-bodied tank retriever] was ready. Finally the old man said, "Screw it . . . *go*." Since I happened to be the only platoon leader standing there, I was assigned the point.

I ran back to the line yelling for my platoon sergeant, "Mac" McHenry. Thankfully, everyone was right around the area, and we were up and running in thirty minutes. I led my platoon off the firebase and onto the trail, heading northeast. I figured the other platoon and the two HQ company's tanks would join the column as I cleared the base—which would give us a total of ten tanks—but they had problems getting started, so we had to stop a few klicks down the road and wait.

Fuel gauges dropping steadily, Hooper and Finch were still over 1-61, looking for enemy concentrations and relaying the information to the rain-soaked troops in their bomb craters.

Charles Finch: We finally spotted the mortar positions, and Russ called in an artillery fire mission, but no one wanted to take charge of the target. Dong Ha and Camp Carroll were receiving incoming from north of the river, and the 155 and 8-inch batteries at various firebases were busy with counterbattery fire. We eventually got some 105s, but in order to adjust the fire I had to tighten my turns by lowering flaps, which obstructed Russ's vision out the windows. We finally destroyed the mortars, and I stopped the artillery so I could locate the automatic weapons firing on our guys. Right after that, the NVA over near the railroad bed came out of these holes and charged toward the friendlies. We could not believe our eyes. The number of enemy we saw going over the top toward our guys is burned deep in my memory.

Hooper came out of a low turn over the embankment to see fifteen to twenty NVA soldiers running down a trail not more than a hundred meters away.

Bill Hooper: Chopping power, I reversed the controls. I still wasn't coming around fast enough, and I shoved rudder and stick to the stops, forcing the nose farther down and to the right. Still descending, I squeezed the trigger. My snap shot sent the rocket straight down the path, but about ten feet over their heads, and I saw them hit the ground.

I was now very slow and less than thirty above the ground, so close I could see minute details of their muddy uniforms as they came to their feet. My eyes locked on one man not more than seventy-five feet away, firing on full automatic, and I could hear rounds hitting the airplane as

I flew through his fire pattern. I should have stayed low and kept going, which would have exposed me for far less time, but on the verge of panic I firewalled the throttle and went for the clouds in a desperate attempt to escape. Just before reaching them, I felt and heard a hard thud beneath me, and the cockpit instantly filled with white smoke. I was sure the engine had been hit.

Still under fire, we disappeared into the clouds. I rolled right, came back out of the clouds, pulled up again, broke off to the left, and emerged once more, anxiously scanning the gauges. Oil pressure was still good. A quick check of the wings confirmed the fuel tanks hadn't been punctured. I twisted around, expecting my observer to be dead or seriously wounded. He hadn't been touched, but wore a helpless deer-in-the-headlights stare and was begging me to return to Dong Ha. The smoke was sucked out the windows, and I turned back toward the battle.

Charles Finch: Cedoz was on the radio, switching back and forth between company, battalion, and brigade, and I was up on the guard frequency trying to get some gunships to help as I felt I could guide them into the area. Dong Ha DASC was also looking for us. We had fast movers on standby at Da Nang and Chu Lai, but the weather was still far too bad to get them onto the target.

Tom Coopey: Some E-7 rounded us up and said that we were to attack the enemy on his signal. We were out of the bomb crater and lying on flat ground with no cover. The sergeant blew his whistle, and we started to rise but got no more than ten inches off the ground before the NVA opened up with everything they had. We got down again, and there was no further mention of attacking.

Bill Hooper: The radio operator in the northernmost company reported they were in contact with the company south of them but needed help to link up. I circled to the west until I had their positions identified, then turned toward the gap occupied by NVA troops. Lining up on the target, I sent my third rocket into the gap, pulled the nose up slightly, and triggered the last. White phosphorus burst under the rain, and the NVA began scattering toward the east. Out of rockets, low on fuel, and thinking the worst of it was over, I advised Charlie Finch that I was returning to Dong Ha.

AAR: "WHILE ATTACKING TO the flank and rear of B/1-61, C/1-61 destroyed elements of an enemy platoon attempting to flank B/1-61 and the Battalion Command Group. Upon completion of the cordon, close Air Strikes and artillery were employed on the enemy forces to the north and east of the Battalion, resulting in the destruction of sizeable elements of the enemy force and driving small groups of NVA into the open where they were destroyed by the deployed Infantry forces."

When Hooper shut down at Dong Ha, a shaken observer crawled out of the back seat and slouched away without a word.

Bill Hooper: The line chief and I watched him go, then turned to examine the Bird Dog. Of the hits she'd taken, most were in or around the cockpit area. The "smoke" that I'd seen was the result of a bullet striking the slab of armor under my seat, pulverizing the ceramic layer and filling the cockpit with a cloud of fine ceramic dust.

THE LINE CHIEF STEPPED BACK and scolded him for being so careless with "his" airplane: "I told you that you were going to get your ass shot off, sir."

Rod Stewart: Hooper landed and I remember the holes in his plane—not just the holes, which were memorable—but him laughing and joking about it with the crew chiefs. I was ready to take my turn, but he suggested I wait until Captain Finch called for me. He refueled and took off for Phu Bai.

MINUTES AFTER HOOPER LIFTED off, Stewart got his chance. A call came into the Dong Ha line shack for someone to provide reconnaissance and air cover for the armored reaction force.

Rod Stewart: I was to fly out and find a column of tanks leaving Alpha 4. They were to be the knockout punch on the enemy's flank, and I was to lead them to the fight. An observer drove up, and we took off and flew out under the low overcast.

I dialed in the frequency for the battalion's operations center at Con Thien and learned that the tanks were moving too slowly, enemy strength was greater than anticipated, our infantry units were pinned down by heavy fire, and the enemy was sending reinforcements down from the north. Like a sand table problem at Fort Benning, an envelopment was shaping up. To make matters worse, the weather was holding out medevacs and resupply and making air strikes difficult or impossible so close to the spread-out friendly troops.

I followed an old road running northeast out of Con Thien, with battalion operations acting as the relay between me and the armor. When the radio operator in the TOC reported that the tanks could hear me but not see me through the rain, I asked him to tell the armor to pop a smoke grenade. Just about then, the lead tank hit a mine and started to burn. They were easy to find then. With battalion pressing them to move faster, the burning M48 was left. Minutes later, a second tank hit a mine.

Peter Van Haren: The entire column was moving as fast as the terrain would permit, just gritting our teeth and hoping that there were no mines or traps. We pushed hard for several klicks, then hit two mines. No one was seriously wounded, but both tanks were disabled so we pulled the guns and radios out, spread the crews among the other tanks, and kept going.

Rod Stewart: Battalion asked if I could find the tanks another route to hasten their advance and finally agreed to put me on the lead tank's frequency.

Peter Van Haren: We didn't know just where to go until a FAC flying overhead came on to our company net and began directing us. His call sign was Catkiller something, and he was outstanding in keeping us aware of the current situation, how far we had to go, and, most importantly, where the enemy were between us and our infantry. We were in high brush and trees by now, and we couldn't see any farther than the next bend in the trail. We had no choice but to go forward in column, because there was no room to spread out.

Charles Finch: At times the clouds came right down and, to keep from becoming completely disoriented, I had to cross the Ben Hai into North Vietnam, before reversing and coming back. The radio was going crazy. An NVA machine gun had pinned down some of the infantry. By sheer luck I passed right over two machine gun positions, flew out about thirty seconds, found my way back, armed two rockets, and punched them off no higher than one hundred feet and at about ninety knots. Couldn't see the result, but someone on the radio shouted, "Perfect! Keep it up."

We still could not get the medevacs because of ground fire, and I had to calm down Russ more than once, especially when it was a marine medevac that tried to get in and got blown off with automatic weapons. Russ figured that if *we* were in the same area and getting shot at the same way, *they* should be able to get in.

Con Thien Duty Officer's Log #111: "1242 A Co turned back medevac, too hot."

Joe Krawcykowski: Most of the 1st Platoon wounded were brought back down to us, but we could not get a medevac in. Too much fire. We were down to about twenty rounds per man. Because we figured that the wounded would be getting out soon, we took all their ammo. Those with chest or stomach wounds had their water taken, too.

Charles Finch: I ran into some clouds that were right on the deck, so I just headed east. The weather was the same in that direction. I turned south and eventually broke out south of Quang Tri. Very scary. Our low and slow flying with all the drag of flaps meant our fuel consumption had been higher than normal, so I headed for Dong Ha for fuel, but they were taking incoming, so I turned back to Quang Tri. It was only after we were on the ground that I realized a round had cut the chain connected to the rudder cables for tail wheel steering. Russ and I topped off the fuel tanks, the maintenance crew rewired the tail wheel, and we headed back to the DMZ.

Rod Stewart: Too many voices on too many frequencies, back seat talking on one FM radio and me on another, air-to-air on UHF, emergency traffic breaking in on guard, and the intercom back and forth between me and my observer. Suddenly an air force O-2 dove out of the clouds just to my left, and we banked sharply away from each other. Aside from Finch to the northeast, it was the first I knew of anyone else in the air. The Barkey pilot told me he had not been briefed about Catkillers being there, nor anything about the tanks. He pointed out a triple-A site. The thought of that big gun turning in my direction chilled and enraged me. I fired a rocket but the low angle made hitting it next to impossible. I asked the tanks if they could see the white phosphorous smoke. Too far away. Barkey flew off to the east. I saw a marine F-4 make one run but did not see any impacts, and weather caused his Dash 2 to abort. They disappeared into the scud.

By lowering flaps and using the O-1's ability to fly very slowly, I held a tight racetrack over the armor, giving steering directions around hidden obstacles like bomb craters and dropping smoke grenades to point out enemy locations—with my backseat watching out of one side and me out the other. The tanks were doing what armor was made for—fire and maneuver. I was on the radio to them—"Turn forty-five left . . . straight ahead . . . now more left . . . bunkers and troops to your ten o'clock, twenty meters . . ." We could see the NVA infantry falling back. Then a third tank hit a mine.

Peter Van Haren: My lead tank hit a big mine, and we got jammed up bad and had to leave the main road to get around him. I couldn't see what was ahead, but again the FAC steered us around the craters and obstacles like some kind of guardian angel.

I had a couple of seriously wounded now and had to deal with keeping them safe. Then Catkiller began to warn us that the NVA were massing on our flanks and moving toward the trail. I remember this part so well because (until we were overrun at night several months later) this was the most scared I ever got in Vietnam. Most of the time in combat, things are happening too fast or, if you're a leader, you're too busy to be that scared. But this time, as the FAC kept telling me how many, how well armed, and how close the enemy were, it was freaking me out!

We needed the info, but every tidbit made it harder for me to keep the pedal down.

And then they started shooting at him. Amazingly, he didn't peel off but hung right in there and kept directing us. As is true with many heroic actions in combat, he inspired us to keep hammering forward, even though the incoming fire was getting heavy now. That guy had some real guts!

We now had somewhere to direct our fire as well, and we began shooting up both sides of the route with machine guns and grape shot. The NVA continued to shoot at him, but not as much, and by now the brush had cleared enough for us to maneuver. I had my platoon turn left and move off in line-abreast. The rest of the company kept moving down the main trail, and we were now paralleling them. It had taken us several hours, but suddenly we were there, behind and to the side of the NVA, and we rolled right over them, killing many and scattering the rest. I think we also got a big .51-cal gun they were using to shoot at the planes.

AAR: "In the vicinity of coordinates YD 165745, B/1-77 encountered approximately an enemy platoon attempting to flank the Battalion (-), B/1-77 took this element under fire destroying two (2) squads and dispersing the remainder."

Rod Stewart: The remaining tracks spread into line-abreast and were rolling over the crest of the hill, past the antiaircraft pit, firing their main tubes into bunkers when my engine sputtered and started to quit. In all the excitement I had allowed one tank to run dry. I switched to the other, the engine roared back to life, and I told the armor and Con Thien that I had to leave immediately. It was a short flight back to Dong Ha, but weather made low-level navigation difficult. I could have flown east to pick up Highway 1 and followed it south, but I was terrified of running the remaining tank dry and going down anywhere near the DMZ.

Peter Van Haren: There was no real line of combat—with the enemy on one side and 1-61 on the other—but more like pockets of our infantry with NVA all around. We split up as a tank force and joined the infantry pockets individually, supporting them with machine gun and main gun fire. Some of the squads that had gotten separated used us as moving cover to rejoin their units.

Alan Ogawa: I remembered the tanks rolling into our perimeter. We were happy to see them!

AAR: ". . . B/1-77 CONTINUED THE ATTACK to the northeast, entering the right flank of the battalion cordon, eliminating the threat from the east and forcing pockets of NVA to flee into the open where they were destroyed in detail by elements of B/1-61 and C/1-61. B/1-77 continued its maneuver to the north and northwest, effectively sealing the eastern flank of the battalion and overrunning an antiaircraft machine gun position in the process."

Charles Finch: On the way back up, I heard Stewart talking about being low on fuel and needing to get back to Dong Ha. We made another call on guard for gunships as well as any fighters carrying snake and nape. Got a call from some Huey gunships south of Quang Tri. I gave them directions but they never made it up to us.

Just before we got back to the battle, a call came in from DASC. The armor had reached our guys, and now we had to find the NVA guns firing on Dong Ha and Camp Carroll. We headed straight across the Ben Hai into North Vietnam. The weather was marginally better up there and we found two active artillery positions fairly quickly. Russ was trying to get a marine or army battery to take the fire mission when we were advised that Onrush, the USS *New Jersey*, was ready to give support. Russ called in the coordinates and we cleared the area.

Everyone who fired this beast had his safety margin. We stayed parallel to the gun target line, because it was the short and long rounds that scared everyone, and at least two thousand meters from impact to avoid shrapnel from those one-ton shells. "Shot," then wait forever for "splash." Even from two klicks away we could hear them coming in. Because of the weather, I couldn't see the splash and told them to fire again. When I finally spotted a shell, it was way off target, and I had to adjust until we got them on target and took out the positions.

Still north of the river, I turned east and we flew over Highway 1. Our jaws dropped at the sight of trucks and fresh NVA troops heading south. They were in a loose formation, walking in front, alongside, and behind the vehicles. For the enemy to be on the road in those numbers meant their commanders were sure we wouldn't be flying that day. Russ got on the radio to his marine guns; I got on the *New Jersey* net.

As we were getting the coordinates established for the mission, I came around and flew straight up the road, both of us firing our M16s out the window at almost point-blank range. I broke to the east, came around again, and used one of my rockets. As we went by with our wheels almost touching the ground, Russ opened up again with his M16, and I can still see their faces. Given how slowly they reacted, they must have been inexperienced troops. They finally started shooting back, but it was all very inaccurate.

With the excitement of seeing so many NVA out in the open, writing on my windscreen and kneepad with grease pencil, getting a naval gunfire mission cranked up, staying out of the enemy's gunsights, trying to keep us below the weather and stay oriented, things were happening pretty fast for us. By now the *New Jersey* was ready. We broke away and those 16-inch shells started coming in. Once I had the *New Jersey* firing for effect, it stopped the column dead in its tracks.

Deck Log—Remarks Sheet USS *New Jersey* (BB-62): "25 October 1968 . . . 1433 Commenced fire Turret Three. 1526 ceased fire. Ammunition expended: 12 rounds 16"/50 Cal High Explosive Projectiles with 12 rounds Reduced Powder Charge Cartridges."

By the time Finch and Cedoz had returned to the battle, 1-61 and the tanks from 1-77 had been without air cover for an hour. But the rain was slacking off, the ceiling was lifting, and marine fighter-bombers were scrambling from Da Nang and Chu Lai. Catkiller 19 was waiting for them.

Charles Finch: All the marine pilots were familiar with the DMZ. We dry-rehearsed each flight using a west heading because of the weather, which meant they could not pull out feet wet like they were used to. As they orbited to the east, we could give them a pretty good idea of how they would do their run.

I ran a pair of Lovebug F-4s, a pair of Ringneck F-4s, and a pair of Hellborne A-4s. We had it timed so when one of them started to roll in above the clouds, I was beginning my roll in to mark the target. Fortunately, there was very little wind, so my smoke seemed to hang there forever. When one broke out of the overcast, all I had to say was where to hit relative to my smoke. They had confidence in us and themselves as long as they had enough time to see the target, release, and not hit the ground in their dive—and they were a lot lower to the ground that day than normal.

Tom Coopey: I remember napalm drops from an F-4, which were released to our rear and carried on over our heads. They hit a couple of hundred yards to our front, but close enough to dry my jungle fatigues.

Charles Finch: We did napalm first and frag bombs second. Running over friendly positions is a real no-no, but this time we did not have any choice. Because of the half-moon disposition of our troops and the enemy and the weather, the boundaries we always used to run air strikes had to be dramatically revised. Some napalm was close to the friendlies, and I was told later that we had warmed some soldiers with it. Then they came in with their 20mm guns.

Jim Roffers: I remember them coming in low and fast, spewing empty 20mm cases all over the place. A couple of us tried to shield the wounded from these empties. They hurt.

Alan Ogawa: When the spotter plane was flying low over our old B-52 hole, we were afraid it would take us for the NVA, so we flipped over on our backs and started to wave to make sure he knew we were friendlies. When the jets came we were happy to have them. We knew that they were taking out the NVA and had them on the run. The air strikes were closer than usual, but we didn't care or complain.

AAR: "AFTER EFFECTING LINK-UP with the right flank of C/l-61, B/1-77 and C/1-61 systematically destroyed elements of two (2) estimated enemy platoons located to their front area in conjunction with two (2) Air Strikes, which placed heavy ordnance within 30 meters of friendly troops and sent enemy bodies flying into the air. They effectively reduced the NVA threat from the right flank of the Battalion."

Charles Finch: When the jets pulled off, we went down low again. I still have a vivid image in my mind of the NVA running in circles, many with their uniforms torn off from the explosions or burned off from the nape. I felt sad in a way, as they had put up such a great fight. Russ never forgave me for waving to them to go north and get out of the way of the next artillery barrage. He wanted to stick around and kill them all.

After refueling again at Quang Tri and getting back to the fight, it seemed forever before we could get the medevacs. I guided several in from the east because of the weather. The marine pilots were unfamiliar with the area and took fire the whole way in, yet never wavered. The enemy was retreating but still kept firing at all of us in the air.

CON THIEN DUTY OFFICER'S LOG #122: "1633 send medevac with guns to A Co."

Joe Krawcykowski: It got eerily quiet. Really quiet. Then a Cobra gunship came up over the knoll behind us and unleashed a volley to the east. Staff Sgt. Jesus Fuentes jumped up and immediately aimed a pop flare at the chopper. When we asked why he'd done that, he said, "'Cause he scared the shit out of me." Everyone laughed like hell. Jesus was a helluva soldier and had been in the thick of things with A Company's 3rd Platoon before coming back to the command area. Their motto—"Jesus Saves"—was painted on the front of one of their tracks. The battalion chaplain thought it was very religious.

Jim Roffers: It was late in the day, and my squad had ended up with some guys from C Company. We were moving southeast and had just passed the trench and bunker area. A dust off was coming in when there was a heavy burst of enemy fire and we all hit the ground. A Cobra was behind it and opened up with his miniguns. Then the men on my left moved forward and dragged out four or five NVA bodies. With the arrival of the Huey Cobras, we knew that we would be okay. A tank from 1-77 was off to my right about one hundred yards, and the armor began crushing bunkers and caving in trenches. We kept watch, had a small firefight, and started loading the wounded onto the choppers.

Alan Ogawa: Sergeant Yonesaki was in bad shape with his stomach wound and a hip wound. When the first medevac arrived, I asked for help to carry him, but no one volunteered. Finally Frank Kaiser said, "Let's go." We borrowed two .45s and stuck them in our waist bands and carried Yonesaki in a poncho, sometimes in a low crouch and sometimes crawling. The rain was still coming down, and the poncho was full with blood and water.

When we arrived at the chopper, it was already full of wounded, and they told us they couldn't take Yonesaki. I pulled out my .45 and told the pilot the most seriously wounded must go first. He ordered someone with a flesh wound on his arm to get out, and we loaded Yonesaki. Frank thought I was crazy but I didn't care. Yonesaki was already in shock, and if we had to wait, he wasn't going to make it. When we got back to the platoon, Sergeant Morgan was already in charge, and we started returning fire at the NVA running through the tree line.

Peter Van Haren: Eventually, the combined firepower of us, the infantry, artillery, and air strikes forced the NVA to retreat. We tried chasing them, but they were really good at melting away.

AAR: "At 251730, B/1-61 continued the attack north to effect link-up with A/1-61 at 251800 October. Small groups of NVA and abandoned weapons were destroyed during this attack."

Tom Coopey: When we assembled, there were only about forty of us. At first we thought we were the only survivors. Night was approaching, and I thought to myself, "This is it. Charlie is going to overrun us at any moment." But as we moved out, more units began joining us, and I started to appreciate how dispersed the battalion had been during the battle.

Joe Krawcykowski: Suddenly, word circulated about gooks in the perimeter and I thought, "Oh, no! Not more of this bullshit!" Found out it was a wounded NVA medic who had been captured, and lots of people went to look at this guy. He was put on one of the medevacs. That night, we were cold, wet, nervous, worn out, and shot to shreds.

Peter Van Haren: That night it was cold and rainy, a damp cold that chilled you right through. The infantry troops were shivering badly and began standing right behind our back decks so they could get some warmth from the engine exhausts. After awhile, a couple of them keeled over, others started staggering around, and we realized they were being poisoned by the carbon monoxide in the exhaust. I remember feeling terrible that I had to order them away from the tanks. Some of them couldn't understand why and looked so miserable. We took a couple of the worst ones into the hulls for awhile. There were many more who couldn't get warm, so we let them back near the engines but made them move away every five minutes or so. They were hungry, too, and we threw them what we had, which wasn't much, as there had been no resupply.

Alan Ogawa: That night we were wet and cold, but they wouldn't let us stand behind the tanks to get warm. They mentioned the fight they'd had with the NVA on the way up from Con Thien. They threw us some cigarettes and cans of C-rations. So this guy Everett and I spent the night freezing in a muddy hole. We couldn't sleep knowing the NVA was still all around. His wife had just had a baby, and he asked me to contact her if he didn't make it.

Jim Roffers: I had always wanted to get a close look at a Russian 12.7, so I wandered over and found some soldiers dragging bodies and weapons from bunkers. The 12.7 that had been trying to kill me lay in the wet grass and was already rusting after being burned by the white phosphorus. The barrel was bent just in front of the action, where part of the rocket casing or tail fin must have hit it.

Joe Krawcykowski: The next day couldn't come soon enough. We loaded up our dead and extra equipment and started out for what we thought would be a straight walk back to A3, the closest base camp and

A Company's starting point for the operation. After some time walking, the word came that A Company was to walk down the track line through this little valley, with B and C companies flanking. Word was that the last people through this little valley had been the French. Column stopped. An undermanned company carrying our dead and all the rest . . . it seemed a dumb idea. The brigade commander wanted to know what the hold up was. Words were exchanged on the radio, and I seem to remember him landing and talking to Staff Sergeant Fuentes, then getting back into his chopper, and we veered off to the right for A3.

Alan Ogawa: While walking back from Kinh Mon to base camp, Gayatano, who was two men behind me, tripped a mine. A piece of shrapnel the size of a baseball tore through the radio on my back and ripped my flak jacket and knocked me off my feet. I had bad whiplash and my ears were ringing. Gayatano was badly injured, and acting platoon leader Morgan was hit in the legs. We loaded them on a medevac. I tossed in the busted radio and stayed with my platoon on the walk back.

Joe Krawcykowski: On the way out of the area, we went past some food cooking over a fire and a teapot on it, with plates surrounding the cooking area. It looked like the NVA had just left. Then we went through a hedgerow and there were news cameras. Really freaky thing. Fresh evidence of the NVA and then civilians taking pictures. The thought was that they were nuts for being out there when they didn't have to be. We didn't want to be there but had to be. The march back to A3 was pretty uneventful. When we arrived just before dark, the mess hall was open and had food, coffee, and fruit for us.

Jim Roffers: The usual method of having a memorial service is to take a man's rifle and bayonet, stick it into the ground, and place his helmet on the butt, but they used only four—one for each company and one for recon. After the memorial service, I turned Joe Shallcross in for the Bronze Star, which he was awarded. I tried several times to locate the FAC who had taken out the 12.7, just to say thanks, but he was always out flying missions, so I never got to do this until over thirty years later.

Joe Krawcykowski: Several days later, First Sergeant Ledford, and a young Shake and Bake buck sergeant and others went over to Con Thien to receive Bronze Stars from General Davis, 3rd Marine Division commander. Top Ledford left me in charge of the HQ section and gave me a case of cold beer and said my Bronze Star would be coming at the end of the month. Never did see it.

Low on fuel after shepherding Company B of the 77th Armor to the battle, Rod Stewart made it to Dong Ha.

Rod Stewart: When I landed, I taxied up to the platoon and got a new backseat, a stocky marine who climbed in. When I slid the seat back, he asked, "How do I get out of this thing?" I continued straight on down to the fuel pit. Incoming started landing just when I shut down, and we could not get fuel, so we tried to take off from there to the west. About the time the tail wheel came up, I ran out of gas and the engine quit. We went off the end of the wet runway and down that grassy slope and stopped with the left main in a hole. My backseat got out before I did, answering his own question.

The marines came out of their bunkers, our ground crews hurried over, and we manhandled the bird back onto the runway. The most amazing thing was that some of our ground crew drove over, climbed up on the wing, and poured gas from a jerry can into the bird while incoming was landing in the base. I have always regretted not finding out who did that. Those crew chiefs and mechanics should have gotten a medal, and I should have been grounded. I then took off for Quang Tri for fuel.

In the course of the battle, Charlie Finch had landed twice at Quang Tri for fuel, rockets, M16 ammunition, and smoke grenades. When he finally shut down after his third mission of the day, he had flown seven and a half hours, collected bullet holes in his door, wing strut, and fuselage, and twice received hits to his tail wheel. "At least they were not holes in Captain Finch or Captain Cedoz," he said.

Given the intensity of the close-quarter fighting, American losses were miraculously low, though each was a tragedy for the families and friends of those who died. They were: Tom Casey, Billie Long, Larry Martin, David Merrell, Lonnie Parker, Thomas Ray Jr., air force pilot Marion Reed, James Soriano, and James Wright. Another sixteen were wounded, some disabled for life.

When a search of the battlefield was completed, the bodies of 303 NVA soldiers were counted, each death a tragedy for a family in North Vietnam.

Lieutenant Joe Abernathy—who Jim Roffers thinks was the officer he gave his grenades to and Tom Coopey believes was the wounded, shirtless lieutenant who led his group to the bomb craters—was awarded the Distinguished Service Cross.

All three Catkillers were awarded the Silver Star.

> Life does not count by years. Some suffer a lifetime in a day,
> and so grow old between the rising and the setting of the sun.
> —Augusta Jane Evans (with thanks to Tom Coopey)

Chapter 8

Catkiller Down

"HEY, HOOP," HARRISON SAID AS HE ENTERED the club.

"Hiya, Lee. What's going on?"

"I just got my ass chewed by Gee Wisby."

"What for?"

"Some asshole lifer over at the 108th told him I never shaved when I was at Dong Ha, and Wisby gave me shit for it this morning," he fumed. "Listen, Hoop, do me a favor, okay?"

"If I can, sure."

"Everyone needs to tell Wisby that we can't shave there because the light's so bad in the latrine. Hell, we're likely to cut ourselves. And you know how easy cuts get infected in the tropics. What do you say?"

"Lemme think about it, Lee"

Charles Finch: Three days after our fight over Kinh Mon, I had a day off, so Fred Willis and I flew to Da Nang. After enjoying my first ice cream cone since leaving the States, we dropped off some paperwork at 212th Battalion headquarters. Everyone there had heard about the fight in the DMZ, right down to the number of bullet holes in my airplane and Hooper's. I was always surprised at how much they knew about the goings-on in the 1st Platoon, but with our unauthorized marine flight suits, low-level flying, and a reputation as mavericks, we regularly made good gossip fodder for the HQ noncombatants.

We flew back to Phu Bai, played some volleyball, and when I stepped out of the shower, the word was going round that a Catkiller had gone down north of the DMZ. I knew Hooper and Harrison were up there. I immediately headed over to operations and called Dong Ha.

Bill Hooper: At the end of my second Tally Ho mission that day, I'd been relieved by Lee and his high ship. My backseater and Lee's, Steve Bezold, exchanged good-natured insults as we traded places near Fingers

Lake and I returned to Dong Ha. Now, having refueled, dropped off my observer, and completed the debriefing report, I taxied out and opened the throttle for Phu Bai. I was clearing the pattern in a right turn out when a mayday call snapped me to attention. It was Lee's high ship, whose pilot was shouting that Lee had been shot down, then either asking for help or warning everyone away because of the heavy ground fire. I told him to get a fix on Lee's location and hold over it until I arrived, then banked hard to the north and pushed the preset button on my radio.

"Dong Ha DASC, this is Catkiller 1-2. I am off channel 109 at this time in aircraft 2646. I have no one in my back seat. I am northbound up Highway 1 to Tally Ho. I am responding to a mayday that Catkiller 4-9er has been shot down. I should be on station in twenty-five minutes. ETR to be advised. Over."

When DASC asked if a Jolly Green should be scrambled, I told him to stand by until I was there and could advise whether or not a rescue operation should be launched. Monitoring the guard frequency on the agonizingly slow flight, I listened to two air force Gunfighters that had responded to the mayday. They were already on the scene, making low passes in the face of very heavy ground fire. I crossed the Ben Hai River at 3,500 feet, still climbing. Scattered clouds earlier in the day had consolidated, and I was between layers when I spotted a Bird Dog silhouetted against a higher cloud layer. I caught movement in my peripheral vision and looked down to see a Phantom climbing hard out of the layer below, breaking left and then right as heavy streams of tracers pursued him.

The courage I was witnessing was incredible. Mountains reaching to three thousand feet lay just to the west, with the bottom of the lower cloud strata at two thousand feet. Orientating themselves as best they could, the air force Gunfighters were diving blind through it, then rolling inverted below eight hundred feet to look for Harrison as at least four 12.7mm or 14.5mm multi-barreled guns took them under fire. They'd escape to the safety of the cloud cover, and then go in again.

Because of the weather and evading ground fire, it would have been almost impossible for the high ship to provide more than an approximate location of Lee's Bird Dog. But he was so distraught that I recommended he head back to Dong Ha. Already low on fuel, the Gunfighter leader gave me what information he had before breaking off. It wasn't much to go on, but at least gave me some confidence that the Gaper had to be within a two-kilometer-square area. Sure that the white control surfaces of his Bird Dog would be fairly easy to spot in the low, scattered scrub, I didn't think the search would take long. My efforts to raise him on his emergency radio, however, were met with silence. The sun had already set behind the mountains, and visibility was fading rapidly.

Descending through the lower cloud layer, I alerted the rescue teams at Dong Ha and Quang Tri. If there was some way to continue the search, I had a good—and possibly last—chance of finding him before the North Vietnamese picked him up in the morning. But to do it I needed light. Switching to my FM radio, I explained the situation to the nearest artillery battery and asked for two guns in adjustment, advising that as soon as I found Lee, I would need two guns in effect to maintain a lighted umbrella for the rescue.

Orbiting just under two thousand feet, I saw the first two flares ignite inside the clouds, then emerge under their parachutes. It was now completely dark, and the ground fire had ceased. Staying three hundred to four hundred feet above the descending flares as I spiraled down gave me an excellent view of the terrain. When I reached six hundred feet above ground level, I began a slow climb back to altitude and gave the artillery a 250-meter easterly gun adjustment. By the time I reached the cloud base, two more rounds arrived and I began my next descent. It was a bit unnerving descending to six hundred feet where we normally flew no lower than three thousand. But after shifting my position twice without receiving any ground fire, I was confident that they couldn't track me in the darkness.

I'd just begun a third spiral and was at about 1,500 feet when at least two 12.7s opened fire. Short bursts of ten to fifteen tracers rose lazily toward me, seeming to accelerate the closer they got, and thudded past, much too close for comfort. At 1,500 feet the 12.7 is at optimum range, and the second and third bursts forced me into hard evasive maneuvers. I was bewildered by their ability to track me, until realizing that my anti-collision and navigation lights were on. While the lights hadn't provided very good range information, they made a very effective bull's eye. Cursing my stupidity, I hit the switch. Although the ground fire continued, they could no longer get a fix on me, and it became more a case of blind luck.

After the fourth set of flares, I shifted the search north by 250 meters and started incremental westerly adjustments of 250 meters. The thought of Lee and Steve on their own and possibly injured dug into my deepest fears. It could be me down there, praying that the circling pilot would see me under the next set of flares. An hour into the mission, I received a call from another Catkiller orbiting south of the Ben Hai as a radio relay station. He passed on the order from Major Wisby in Phu Bai that I terminate the search until the next morning. No way. I clicked my mike switch. "Say again, Catkiller, I'm having reception problems but will continue to transmit in the blind assuming you are receiving."

As my search of each sector was completed, I marked it off on my map and moved with the flares to the next. I continued searching for three hours, my last flares over a terrain feature I was sure I could find the next morning. Low on fuel and exhausted after almost nine hours in the air that day, I turned for home. Back on the ground, I received a landline call from Finch in Phu Bai.

Charles Finch: When I finally spoke to Bill, he had just landed and was still in his mission mode, controlled and self-contained. But underlying his calm, precise description of what had happened was a tone of deep-felt anguish. He kept going over the details of where he had been, his search pattern, what he had seen—as though somewhere in all that we could figure out just where Lee and Steve had crashed. He had been flying all day and was clearly fatigued, but the cool, calculating warrior and poker player I'd known for barely a month was revealing a human side that I'd not seen until now.

Unlike some of the other old-timers who'd rotated off the Z, this was the first time we were faced with a downed pilot. Neither of us wanted to hang up, and we kept going over all the details of that afternoon and evening. Hooper had done all he could, but not finding the aircraft was weighing very heavily on him. He seemed to be appealing for my assurance that we would find Lee and Steve.

After we hung up, I ran down to the 131st Surveillance Airplane Company. They had several OV-1 Mohawks scheduled for night missions, and I asked that one of them make some passes around the DMZ to see if they could pick up a beacon. They had already notified Seventh Air Force to be on the lookout for any emergency transmissions from the area.

When I got back, most of the unit was waiting beside the orderly room. I gave them a brief synopsis of what Hooper had told me and then ducked into operations, where I found Grayson Davis, marine Major Tank Meehan, Glenn Strange, Jim Hudson, and a couple of others. Major Wisby began by saying that he would be would be joining the search the next morning. Then he nodded at me and said that because of my familiarity with the area, I would be in charge of the search. As I walked to the map, more people crowded through the door.

With grease pencil in hand, I began by circling where we had recently taken AA fire around Fingers Lake, and the locations of enemy artillery pieces we had destroyed. The pilots who had never flown up north seemed shocked by the number of circles I'd drawn. If Lee and Steve had survived the crash, it was going to be very difficult for them to evade capture in an area controlled by the NVA.

I told the CO that I wanted Tank Meehan in my back seat and that Hooper and I would be the low ships. I also made it very clear that we would attract a lot of antiaircraft fire—.51-cal, 14.5mm ZPUs, 37mm, and possibly 57mm. Once we crossed the Ben Hai, constant changes in heading, altitude, and air speed would be essential. Although Wisby was overtly confident that we would find Lee's aircraft, talking about *when* rather than *if,* no one said anything about having a Jolly Green on station—as though overconfidence might jinx the mission. Wisby excused everyone from the room except Tank and me. He said there was a lot of anger among the other pilots, and he expected us to be a stabilizing influence.

Most of the pilots were in the officers club by the time I got there. I repeated what Hooper had told me and laid out the next day's plan. Then for the next half hour I listened as people started unloading. Normally, hate sessions were alcohol-fueled, but tonight there was a sober, cold fury at the stupidity of the mission, the stupidity of the military in giving us the mission, the stupidity of our politicians, the lack of support by the South Vietnamese, and on and on. No longer could the higher-ups deny the folly of sending a single-engine aircraft into North Vietnam.

Every criticism ever voiced about the DMZ mission had suddenly been validated with the downing of Lee Harrison and Steve Bezold. There was an "I told you so" right across the board. Enough was enough. People were going to different rooms, starting another hate session, then back to the club, then back to operations. I was in Donnelly's room when the drinking began in earnest, and all the old issues surfaced. Why did radar not pick up the aircraft on its way down? Did Lee and Steve have good survival radios, and were they tested recently? Why didn't we just say fuck it and invade the north? This was going on all over the compound. Then there were rumors that the Paris peace talks might result in a bombing halt of North Vietnam. What the hell was that about?

I slipped out to check if the 131st had heard a survival beeper. When they reported nothing had been picked up, I asked them to send a photo bird up at dawn and gave them a large grid area to photograph.

If anything, the night was becoming a vigil for Lee and Steve. Lee's classmates talked about him in flight school, the poker players about his ridiculous bluffs at the card table, all of us about his sense of humor, the grief we'd given him about his longer-than-regulation hair, the sloppy way he wore his uniform, his love of food, his loud laugh. Steve Bezold was the best of the 108th observers. Funny and bright, he had a great set of eyes, was good at flying the aircraft from the back seat, and added more to the mission than most backseaters. Many of us prayed together that they would be found. I finally went to bed at around midnight.

It was still dark at 0430 and I found no one in the latrine as I shaved. The company compound was equally deserted as I walked to the mess hall and found Tank Meehan and Major Wisby already there. Over a quick breakfast, I reminded them that enemy fire had been extremely heavy in the last week and many of us had taken hits. Wisby said he would be taking the photo bird. I was surprised at his choice; with a big camera pod on each wing, it was heavy, a gas-guzzler, and not good for maneuvering when the enemy was shooting at you. I told him that he'd need to get plenty of altitude or we'd end up looking for him, too. He didn't seem fazed, nor did Tank Meehan. With his ground-combat experience, Tank was someone you wanted with you in a bar fight or a foxhole.

Heading up Highway 1 in loose formation, I looked across at those camera pods on Wisby's airplane. As our CO, he was not expected to fly combat missions. Stepping in when only Jerry Bonning had volunteered said a great deal about his character. After landing and refueling, we taxied down to the 1st Platoon ramp, where a welcoming committee of pilots, observers, and crew chiefs was waiting. Bill Hooper looked like he hadn't slept and was wearing his I-am-not-happy look. At least I wasn't the reason for it this morning.

Bill Hooper: I woke before dawn to a cloudless sky and watched the three Bird Dogs touch down. Tank Meehan, the 12th Marines' S-2 liaison officer, was in Charlie's back seat, and three aerial observers from the 108th Field Artillery Group had been assigned to ride with me, Wisby, and Bonning. Colleagues of Steve Bezold, they said his one brief transmission was, "We've been hit. We're going down, and I don't think we're going to make it."

Charles Finch: When we heard that, Bill and I knew that if Steve had made that call, then Lee had probably been hit. But it also meant Steve was alive before impact and might have flown the aircraft to a reasonably safe landing. Images of what it must have been like in the cockpit when they were hit filled my mind and I could not erase them. I think Hooper also sensed the hopelessness. Finally Wisby said, "Let's go find Lee."

Tank and I did not talk on the way up north. I always preferred a broken or scattered cloud layer to provide some cover when flying Tally Ho, but today was as clear as it had been in a month, which meant the NVA would spot us and be ready long before we got there. Bill and I were between four thousand and six thousand feet and Wisby and Bonning two thousand feet higher when we crossed the Ben Hai. Bill started searching to the east and I went west, to just south of Fingers Lake. Behind me, Tank had binoculars to his eyes, and I was scanning from the side windows. The high ships came up on the frequency at regular intervals to let us know they had us in sight.

Bill Hooper: When we reached the terrain feature I'd marked the night before, Charlie began a westward search, while I hunted toward the east. Our arrival did not bring the immediate ground fire I had anticipated. In fact, it was so quiet that I was a little embarrassed for having given such dire warnings. Ten minutes after our arrival, I told Charlie that perhaps we weren't going to be engaged after all. Boy, was I wrong.

Charles Finch: Bill and I were talking about how quiet it was when suddenly the sky exploded around us. Every type of antiaircraft fire I had received in four months of flying the Z came racing up at us at one time. The sights and sounds of those shells had Tank and me flinching, ducking, and trying to find someplace to hide in that little aircraft. As puffs of gray and black smoke filled the air around us, the air inside was blue with our swearing. I was sure the NVA had found Lee's aircraft and then pulled in as many antiaircraft weapons as they could in the knowledge that we'd come looking for it.

Bill Hooper: The NVA normally used only 12.7mm and 14.5mm weapons to engage targets at our altitude, but this time we were also evading 37mm flak. I ducked when a shell detonated in front of me with a high-pitched *crack!*, and a second I later flew through a hail of shrapnel. It was the most intensive ground fire I'd ever experienced and must have taken the observers' minds off the nausea they usually suffered, for no one was complaining of airsickness. Thrown around by the violent maneuvers, they held on for dear life.

Charles Finch: I caught a glimpse of Hooper surrounded by exploding flak to my east. Rolling through sixty degrees in a diving turn to throw their aim off, I looked down and there were the white ailerons of Lee's aircraft directly below me. My call to say I had the aircraft in sight went unanswered; everyone was too busy dodging antiaircraft fire. There was a pause in the ground fire, and I made another circle, trying to spot any movement. I couldn't make out the tail or windscreen, but the wings were still attached to the fuselage, which was upright like it had been parked in the trees. Then they found my altitude and opened up again. It was terrifying.

Bill Hooper: Charlie announced that he had Harrison's Bird Dog in sight. It had crashed into a stand of trees, and all that could be seen were the white ailerons. Closing the four kilometers between us, I heard him trying to raise Lee on his portable emergency radio. I also tried to make contact. Given the possibility that the North Vietnamese might be too close for him to speak, we told him to key his mike three times, pause, and then repeat the signal, in which case we would wait until he could give us a verbal identification. Constantly changing altitude and heading, breaking hard one way or the other to evade the tracers and flak, we listened for any clicks or whispers on the frequency. *Talk to us, Lee! Talk to us!*

Charles Finch: With the sky filled with flak, ZPU rounds, and anything else the NVA could throw at us, all four aircraft scattered and headed south, just looking to survive. I dove and crossed the Ben Hai no higher than a thousand feet. The airplane had taken at least one hit, and Tank and I both were rattled. No one had gotten a grid reference. None of us wanted to face those guns again, but we had no choice. We were giving the NVA a free shot today. Were they going to get lucky again?

Bill Hooper: By now, cold logic told us that there was little chance of effecting a rescue. Even if Lee and Mike were alive and uninjured, the likelihood of evading capture in an area controlled by the NVA was remote. But again it came down to the question: What if it was me down there? What if I'd managed to stay hidden and my only salvation was the eyes of my fellow pilots? When we asked ourselves those questions, logic gave way to the brotherhood that only those who have shared combat can understand.

Charles Finch: I climbed back to altitude and we turned north. The ground fire started again and intensified the closer I got to Lee's aircraft. There was so much of it coming from so many different positions that I forgot about trying to locate them and concentrated on trying to stay alive. I dove down one more time, and we got a better look before having to break off and escape once again toward the DMZ, with Tank saying he'd managed to get a rough fix on it. Hooper and I tried flying toward the site at different altitudes and different headings and each time were driven back by a wall of steel.

After more futile attempts, I climbed to about nine thousand feet and tracked toward the site. From behind his binoculars, Tank said he couldn't find it. I pointed my left wing toward where we thought the airplane was and started a slow spiral. But it was gone, vanished. I was telling this to the others when we got lit up again, and I dove straight down for a closer look before the ground fire forced me back south again. We'd had a clear look at the site for probably thirty seconds, and either we were badly disoriented or the aircraft was gone. It was never seen again.

Bill Hooper: I couldn't believe it when Charlie rolled over and headed down in a tight spiral for a closer look. It took the North Vietnamese crews by surprise, and they failed to follow him down until he had passed through two thousand feet, at which point several of the guns shifted to him. Charlie made two tight turns over the site below a thousand feet and then dodged away to the south, miraculously untouched.

Charles Finch: By now we had been airborne for almost two hours—much of that under extremely intense fire—and Major Wisby felt we had done all we could do. Hooper and I were reluctant to leave, and we loitered on station for several minutes as Wisby and the other high ship turned toward Dong Ha.

When we landed, we taxied directly to the flight line and shut down next to Wisby's photo bird. A quick walk around revealed several shrapnel holes aft of the rear seat. Still hyped with adrenaline, we couldn't stop talking about the ferocity of the engagement. I had been shot at so much over the past four months that I accepted it as part of the job. But not today. Today was personal. I don't think any of us had ever been frightened so badly by ground fire. Our relief at surviving was dampened by knowing Lee and Steve were dead or facing brutal treatment at the hands of the North Vietnamese.

I flew two more missions that day. On the first one, I spotted muzzle flashes near Fingers Lake and ran two flights of F-4s that silenced the guns. When the fast-movers left, we started taking flak from a position farther to the north. Instead of risking another flight of fast-movers, I took up station over the northern edge of the DMZ and called in fire from the *New Jersey.* I am not sure what we destroyed, but the flak stopped.

After refueling again, I got another 108th observer and we headed across the Ben Hai toward the crash site. From three thousand feet I recognized the area but still couldn't see the aircraft. Then I noticed vehicle tracks leading away from it. Before the back seat could get a picture, the whole sky opened up again. I chopped power and dove to the ground so quickly that my high ship lost sight of me. He was calling in a very worried voice when I gave him my position on my way south.

When I landed two hours later, I learned that Westmoreland's boss, Gen. Ralph K Haines, and Brigadier General Pixton of XXIV Corps Artillery, were visiting. Although 50 percent of all U.S. casualties during the Vietnam War were suffered in I Corps, we seldom saw this much rank this far north. They were aware we had lost an airplane and crew and wanted an update on our efforts. Having just flown almost eight hours that day, giving a briefing was the last thing I wanted. But captains don't say no to that many stars.

I was trying to formulate something when there was the heavy *whump!* of incoming and the generals headed for cover. I jumped in my airplane and took off for Phu Bai as more landed on the base. It wasn't until I was a few minutes away from Dong Ha that I remembered I was on the board for the next day's early-morning mission. Then I decided to hell with it. I wanted to be in my own bed rather than spending the night in a hot, stinking bunker.

Still wearing my sweaty flight suit, I went from the ramp straight to the club to talk to the same bunch of angry pilots from the night before. I refused to address anything except the description of Lee's aircraft and how much fire we took. I slipped over to the Super Hooch. Hudson, Doc, and Glenn Strange were so angry about Lee that there was nothing I could say to make the facts less painful, so I headed to operations, where I found an exhausted Major Wisby. I thanked him for the confidence he had shown in me that day, then headed for my hooch. It had been a long, long day.

Two days later Finch was running air on NVA artillery positions near the coast. Ringneck 536 had just pulled off the target when he came up on guard to say he was hit and heading feet wet. Marine aviators George Libey and Lt. Bill Frizell ejected from their F-4 and landed off shore within sight of the beach.

Charles Finch: I flew out to orbit over them until they were picked up by the rescue chopper. I think they were mentioned in *Life* magazine or the *New York Times* for being the last Americans shot down over North Vietnam before the bombing halt came into effect.

AT 2000 HOURS THAT EVENING, it was official: no American aircraft—including the Catkillers—would henceforth cross the Ben Hai. The presidential order came forty-eight hours too late for Steve and the Gaper.*

---

*Steven Bezold and Donald Lee Harrison were declared killed in action in 1980.

Chapter 9
Bombing Halt

It was Halloween and somebody got the idea of using our bed sheets to dress up like ghosts and going over to trick-or-treat the CO. With those sheets draped over us, Hudson, Doc, myself, and someone else went over and knocked on Wisby's door. He got a real charge from it and tore the sheets off his bed so he could be a ghost, too, and we headed over to the XO's hooch to give him a scare. We weren't very quiet ghosts and Blanchard heard us coming. When he saw us in those sheets, he yanked us inside and squelched the frivolity by reminding Wisby of the racial problems the army was having and that we surely didn't need a complaint of KKK activity! With our Halloween fun cooled down, we all went back to the Super Hooch for wine and cheese.

—Glenn Strange, Catkiller 2

IN ORDER TO BRING NORTH VIETNAM to the negotiating table, 1 November 1968 saw the end of American bombing north of the Ben Hai River. It was a move that stunned the Catkillers.

Bill Hooper: If U.S. airpower couldn't take the war to the Communists by hitting their factories, roads, and supply depots, they would be free to marshal men and equipment along the border. Which meant it would be easier for them to infiltrate into South Vietnam and more Americans would die simply because we weren't allowed to stop them. We were hard-pressed to find and destroy those who were already getting through. When Major Wisby told us that Hanoi guaranteed to respect the so-called Demilitarized Zone, we shook our heads at the naiveté of our politicians. Lee's death had been in vain.

Our predictions that the NVA would cynically abuse the agreement were soon proved accurate. While the autumn weather remained good, the Communists began moving men and supplies into the DMZ under cover of darkness. Late-afternoon patrols returning at last light reported long columns of truck headlights moving south. In the first month of the bombing halt, we reported more than 1,500 NVA violations of the DMZ, yet our political leaders refused to unshackle us. With the arrival of the monsoons and the reduced threat of U.S. air strikes, the Communists gave up all pretense and brazenly began to operate during daylight hours.

Enemy troops and equipment soon appeared in the southern part of the DMZ in previously unseen numbers. Their lack of caution, however, opened a small window of opportunity for Finch, me, and one or two others. By launching patrols when weather conditions were well below minimums, the clouds that hid the enemy from us could also hide us from them, and we occasionally caught troops and equipment in the open. The downside to this was that we had to fly much lower than usual, which allowed little time to evade ground fire. Few of these low-altitude missions resulted in an engagement, but the fact that we were sitting ducks made them incredibly stressful.

I gazed morosely at the unrelenting rains. Finch and I hadn't flown in days, and we were both starting to get twitchy. I sat down heavily at the picnic table and picked up a tattered *Playboy*. But even the luscious playmate of the month failed to brighten my mood, and I tossed it back on the table. I hated not flying.

"What a bitch," Charlie said, but it was the rain he was maligning, not the playmate.

"You got that," I grumbled, standing and walking to the coffee urn for my tenth cup of the day. I carried it to the wall map and stared morosely at the black lines that registered roads and topographical features in North Vietnam. By now, I knew them well enough to picture the actual terrain, just like I knew the river that ran behind my family's home in Florida and the bays and sand flats along the coast where I'd spent so much time before the army grabbed me. The memory stirred something, and my eyes settled on the snaking blue line of the Ben Hai River. If there wasn't a war going on, it would be fun to take a boat up it. Sure would beat sitting on my ass in Dong Ha and watching the rain come down. A boat.

"Finch?"

"Yeah?"

"If you were a gook and you wanted to move shit across the river, when would you do it? I mean when would you prefer to do it? What would be the safest time?"

Charlie's eyes flicked from the map back to me, and he nodded. "You're right. I'd want to do it when I didn't have to worry about being spotted from the air. Like when the ceiling's on the ground and it's raining like a sunovabitch." He looked outside at the weather conditions he'd just described. "The only problem is, we can't do a fucking thing about it."

"Not today, maybe. But we will." And I picked up the *Playboy* with renewed enthusiasm.

A couple of days later, I awoke at Dong Ha to find a three-hundred-foot overcast with isolated showers and wisps of cloud dragging along the ground. It was ideal—bad enough to make the NVA think no one would be flying, but not bad enough to keep me on the ground. I lifted off without an observer at 0830 and followed Highway 1 north. About two klicks south of the Ben Hai the terrain flattened into long-abandoned rice paddies, and I turned east. At the mouth of the river, I reversed course, staying about fifty meters to the south side. Every now and then something would catch my eye—a bunker that looked like it had been used recently, a couple of dugout canoes dragged into low underbrush—and I'd haul the Bird Dog around in a tight 360 for a closer look. This was still rice paddy country, and aside from the heavy growth along the banks, there was very little cover. A little nervous about flying so close to the north bank, where the NVA often sited antiaircraft weapons, I crossed the controls to keep the airplane in a skid.

The weather had started to improve, but by the time I reached the Horseshoe an hour into the mission, it had deteriorated again, the ceiling dropping to 150 feet and oozing light rain. The rice paddies had dropped behind, replaced by thick jungle and forest. The Ben Hai River, which was a kilometer across at its mouth, had now narrowed to fifty meters. The weather continued to worsen, with heavier rain and solid stalactites of cloud reaching almost to the ground. Rain streaked across the windscreen. The conditions were ideal for concealing my approach and muffling the sound of the engine. And if I started taking fire, I could duck straight into the clouds. I was concentrating on the north bank when my view ahead was obstructed by one of the stalactites. When I came out the other side, I found what I'd been looking for.

A small barge lay in the middle of the river. On it were two rain-soaked NVA soldiers hauling themselves toward the south bank with a rope and pulley system. When I came out of the clouds, they were almost underneath me, too close to get a shot off. Giving no indication I'd seen them, I flew straight on until I disappeared into the next low-hanging cloud. The easiest and most effective way of destroying the target would have been with artillery, but my altitude meant there was too great a risk of being hit with friendly shrapnel from an off-target round.

With the barge's position and details of both sides of the river fixed in my mind, I banked sharply south and then made a tight 270-degree turn to the right until I was over the river again and retracing my flight path. I'd received no ground fire, but experience told me the barge had to be a defended target. Well constructed, with at least three feet of free-board and loaded with supplies, it was probably a link in a regular supply route used only at night or when the weather had us grounded.

I reached up and armed the left outboard tube and advanced the throttle slightly. The landmarks I'd memorized slipped past. I knew that there was going to be very little time to line them up and shoot. I dropped the nose slightly and had descended less than thirty feet when they came into view. To my surprise, they were still in the middle of the river, staring in my direction as though wondering if I'd seen them or not. They saw me, and both began pulling frantically toward the north bank. At a slant range of just under six hundred feet, I fired. The rocket hit a few feet short of the waterline, blowing one soldier over the side and knocking the other off his feet.

I pulled up and right, trying to assess my next move, when three or four light weapons opened up from the north bank. Turning away to present the smallest target, I eased into the clouds and broke to the east, arming the right outboard and left inboard tubes and bringing in more power. When I broke out of the clouds, the barge was at least a thousand feet away. I dropped the nose to build up my airspeed, but when the ground fire picked me up, I launched both rockets. They dipped slightly coming out of the tubes and exploded against the opposite bank, sending the riflemen to cover and allowing me to break to the south again and increase the range. In the few seconds between firing and turning away, I'd seen something floating in the water, but hadn't been able to identify it as a body or a supply crate.

I'd been in the air for three hours by now and decided to make one more attack. This time I came in from the south, picking up the target and ground fire at about eight hundred feet. There were no tracers, but I could hear the distinctive crackle of small-arms fire passing me. There was a *tic* when one hit the right wing. Realizing that if they got lucky and brought me down there would be no chance of rescue, I took another long, flat shot that went over the barge again and into the far bank. Disappointed, I broke to the east and headed for home.

Unknown to me at the time, Charlie Finch had arrived at Dong Ha at midday and gone over to DASC to follow my progress. When he couldn't stand it any longer, he jumped in his Bird Dog and headed my way to join in the fun. I was ten minutes away from the engagement when he came up on the radio. I gave him the map coordinates and a risk assessment, and we passed each other. He found the target but also failed to score a hit.

Ed Miler: Among the battalion CO's pet peeves was firing the M16 rifles out of the windows of the aircraft. He correctly maintained that the empty shell casings could get caught up in the pulleys and cables to the control surfaces and could cause a malfunction or short-circuit the electronics. More than once he found a shell casing in one of my aircraft and let me know about it. On my last day of command of the 220th, after the change-of-command ceremony, Colonel Mullen was boarding his helicopter to return to Marble Mountain when he turned to me and said, "Oh, by the way, Ed, here's a souvenir for you," and handed me three empty M16 shell casings.

Bill Hooper: Mike LaFromboise and I had cleared the traffic pattern when I heard a call from one of our new guys. An armored patrol he was covering about four miles northwest of Dong Ha had just been ambushed and, fresh out of experience, he was asking for help. Telling him to climb and hold a position over the armor, I turned toward the coordinates as

Mike cranked in the patrol's radio frequency. He had comms with them immediately and learned that two M113 armored personnel carriers and one M48 tank were under attack by a sizeable Viet Cong force. One of the APCs had already been disabled by an RPG. The crew had retreated to the second M113, but it and the tank were unable to withdraw without exposing themselves to more RPGs. I immediately raised DASC to report troops in contact.

When we got there, the enemy had seized the disabled APC and were preparing satchel charges for the other tracks. There was no time to wait for the arrival of the air; if we didn't act now, there might not be anything left to defend. "You up for taking them on, Mike?"

A marine to his fingertips, Mike knew I meant breaking orders. "You sure you want to do that, Skipper?"

"If we fuck around and just watch, we're gonna lose those tracks!"

"Okay, let's do it."

Holding a tight right-hand turn 150 feet above the ground, I pushed my M16 out the window. Mike was the first to open fire, and hot shell casings rattled inside the cockpit. We both concentrated on the figures atop the damaged track, our tracers kicking up dust and ricocheting in all directions off the light armor plate. They jumped to the ground and scattered. Because the cover was mostly tall, defoliated trees, I saw them run less than a hundred feet before stopping in a huddle. Occasionally glancing up at us, a tight group of six or eight men conferred urgently.

"They want that armor," Mike said, loading a fresh magazine.

"Can you see the rest of them?"

"Negative, but they're down there somewh—there they go! Four o'clock!"

I looked over my right shoulder and saw men running to positions north and south of the APC. They stopped, turned in our direction, and raised their weapons. Blue-green tracers from AK-47s rose toward us as three more men with satchel charges zigzagged toward the M113. We were at a dangerously low altitude but, save for the brief moments we were directly over them, the enemy had no clear line of fire through the trees. Ignoring those who were firing at us, we concentrated on the advancing sappers. I don't think we hit any of them, but our M16s slowed and then once more forced them to pull back. I thumbed the release ahead of the pistol grip, dropped the empty magazine in my lap, and snapped a full one into place. Shell casings littered the floor under our feet. Our ammunition was rapidly diminishing, which meant we weren't going to hold them off for long. Where was the air support?

My biggest tactical problem was selecting the correct altitude. Too high and our M16s wouldn't be effective; too low and we'd lose sight of the armor during part of each orbit. This is what I loved about the game. Both sides looking for the advantage, both sides equally determined to succeed, both sides playing for the ultimate stakes. A third rush carried them to the cover of the abandoned APC. Rather than withdrawing again, they rolled under it and disappeared. We had them pinned down, but they were only yards from the other tracks. It was then that our air reported in somewhere above the clouds.

"Catkiller 1-2, this is Hellborne 412"—I pulled in the M16 and turned my attention to the fast movers—"a flight of two Alpha-4s, with two Delta-9s and six Delta-2-Alphas on board, play time three-five minutes. Over." Although the visibility was very good, we had a ceiling of only 1,500 feet or so. Because of the mountains to our west and the danger of hitting them, Hellborne advised they were going feet wet before making their descent. A few minutes later, I saw two dots approaching us below the cloud cover. I gave them their target brief and a north-to-south run-in heading. Extending my pattern, I told Mike to tell the tank commander that I was laying a down a Willie Peter and to button up. I turned in and fired to one side of the tank, the rocket hitting within ten meters of it. Hellborne said he had the mark and was turning final. I had completed my turn and was flying toward him.

"Roger, Dash 1, be advised your target: one Delta-9, three o'clock from the mark, fifteen meters."

"Roger, Catkiller, one Delta-9, three o'clock, one-five meters."

"Roger, Dash 1, I have you, you're cleared hot."

Mike had told the patrol commander that the A-4s were about to engage the target, emphasizing that napalm would be dropped within fifty feet of his position. This caused him more than casual concern, but at that point he was far more interested in us stopping an enemy determined to blow him up. The first A-4 passed underneath us off my left wing and released a napalm, the teardrop canister tumbling end over end to hit precisely where I wanted it. The flood of oily, orange fire surged through the trees, and I caught a glimpse of men running away from the flames and the armor.

"Dash 2, from Dash 1's hit, your target: nine o'clock, fifty meters. I say again: nine o'clock, five-zero meters."

Dash 2 had just dropped his nape and pulled off when I saw a group of men about fifty meters north of the target preparing to withdraw across the area blackened by the first napalm. With less than forty meters of fairly smooth ground between themselves and the thick cover of the stream bed, they could have covered the distance in no more than ten seconds and escaped before Hellborne was in a position to engage them. There must have been some indecision on their part, for they waited a good ten or fifteen seconds, which gave Dash 1 time to turn final. At this point, about twenty men broke cover and went running downslope toward the creek. I immediately hit my mike button:

"Dash 1, we have troops in the open, forty or fifty meters, four o'clock from your first hit. Do you have them? Over."

"Roger, roger, Catkiller, I have them in sight."

"Dash 1, you're cleared hot with two snakes." I kept my eyes on the enemy troops, wondering why they had delayed, and if they knew their attempt to escape was now utterly futile. The Skyhawk again passed underneath and a little to my west and released a pair of 500-pound bombs that landed right in the middle of them. When the smoke and dust cleared, there was virtually no trace of them. Mike reported muzzle flashes coming from the streambed, where I directed Dash 2 to drop his ordnance. The ground fire ceased, but because of the thick cover, we weren't sure if we had inflicted any casualties.

While the action was taking place, a relief force had been dispatched from Dong Ha. It arrived twenty minutes after the engagement was over. Because the NVA often used small-unit actions to draw American forces into much bigger ambushes, Mike and I remained overhead for the next two hours, flying long figure eights as we searched for any signs of enemy troops. We found nothing and the armor's withdrawal was uneventful.

Back in Dong Ha, we began writing up our reports, noting that for one U.S. wounded, we'd killed eighteen or twenty Viet Cong and wounded an undetermined number of others. I was halfway through the report when Mike spoke up. "You're not going to say anything about using our 16s out the window, are you?"

"Hell, yes. That's the way it happened."

Mike shook his head. "You'll get your ass in a sling if you tell them, Skipper. Better if you just leave it out." I chose not to take his advice, though I did state that as the aircraft commander, I'd ordered Mike to use his weapon. A few days later we heard that the 1/5 had put us in for a DFC. When the paperwork reached our headquarters at Da Nang, it was reviewed by a garrison officer and passed to someone farther up the chain of command, who, after reading my report, concurred with the flunky's opinion. "I suppose if they'd been shot down we could've given them something," he was reported to have said, disapproving the recommendation. By breaking regulations to save American lives, we'd forfeited the right to any recognition for our actions. I had to wonder where our commanders' priorities lay.

I think it started when we were still flying north. It didn't happen every day, maybe not even once a week, but I remember the first time vividly. I'd come back from Dong Ha to Phu Bai, showered, and was in my hooch getting dressed when I started feeling a little funny. I sat on my cot and suddenly was shaking uncontrollably. I remember looking at my hands and wondering what was wrong, not for a second thinking it might be combat related. It lasted for maybe half a minute and then stopped. I finished dressing and headed for the club and the poker table.

Although some men seemed to thrive on the danger—Finch was the best example—others who had performed superbly for months might come back from a mission and admit they just couldn't hack it anymore; they had finally depleted their reserves of courage and had no more to give. Captain Neil Tanger had been flying in the DMZ for some time when I arrived. His combat record was solid, with scores of missions into North Vietnam and Laos. The cumulative effect of them, however, began to show up in small ways a few months after I joined the unit. Pilots on Tally Ho missions with Neil noted that if they received any fire at all, he would simply drift out of range and find some reason not to engage the target with his smoke rockets. Then he started arriving late for his missions, or sometimes not at all, leaving his observers waiting on the flight line. His preflight checks became long, drawn-out affairs where minor deficiencies that in no way affected the operational readiness of the aircraft were sufficient for him to "red line" his airplane and scrub the flight. When he did fly, he stayed just above the reach of the 12.7s or, with increasing frequency, returned soon after takeoff due to claimed radio or other problems.

It was quietly accepted by everyone that Neil had come too close to death too often and rationally decided he had done enough. No one held it against him. There was just so much some people could take. When the position of section commander opened up in the 1st platoon, Neil, whose date of rank made him senior to me, would have been the logical choice. As a consequence of his declining performance, however, I was given the job. With my new responsibilities, I had to make a decision about him. It was obvious I couldn't rely on him to complete assigned missions over the DMZ. Transferring him to another unit and finding an experienced replacement was not a possibility. So in order to get some use out of him and at the same time keep him away from the more hazardous work, I began giving him scouting missions to the south and southwest of Dong Ha.

This worked well for a while, until Neil began experiencing chronic radio problems again. Though they never prevented him flying a mission, he would regularly be out of contact for two or three hours at a stretch. This was completely contrary to our standard operating procedures, which stipulated regular comms with the appropriate controlling agency. When I asked him about it, he would show me his notations on the airplane's "gripe sheet" as proof of the problems, which the maintenance section could never discover.

His debriefing reports indicated there was now no VC or NVA activity in areas where it had previously been noted and expected to increase. Analyses of his reports painted a potentially alarming picture, however. Given the amount of known NVA activity along the DMZ, there was a growing suspicion that the apparent lack of enemy movement in Neil's patrol areas indicated exactly the opposite. Clearly, the intelligence experts told us, the enemy were making every effort to camouflage a major troop buildup. We all nodded wisely at this contradiction. Those North Vietnamese were slippery characters alright.

Neil took off one morning and soon lost radio contact. About an hour later a UH-34 "Murray" spotted a Bird Dog sitting on the end of an abandoned airstrip about fifteen miles southwest of Dong Ha. The pilot reported it to Dong Ha DASC, which immediately diverted a Seaworthy gunship, whose pilot confirmed the sighting. Getting no response on the guard frequency, he made a low fly by and saw a body under one wing. He reported his discovery and warned that the pilot could have been left as bait. The report was relayed to a marine rescue team at Quang Tri, which immediately launched four Huey gunships and two UH-34s loaded with marines. Less than twenty minutes after the alarm had been sounded, they were racing for the old French airstrip.

The Seaworthy pilot advised the rescue team that the airstrip sat atop a low ridgeline and was surrounded by low scrub. While the surrounding undergrowth wasn't tall or thick enough to hide heavy weapons, it could easily conceal an ambush. When the rescue team arrived overhead, a pair of gunships rolled in with their miniguns to chew up the edges of the strip, while the marines followed in their UH-34s, leaping out before their choppers had come to a complete stop and racing the last fifteen meters to the Bird Dog. As they came around it, there sat Neil propped against the right wheel and holding an enormous joint. He was so stoned all he could do was look up at the panting, grim faced marines and giggle. The team leader wasted no time in throwing a limp Neil Tanger into one of the choppers, while one of the UH-34 pilots turned his ship over to the copilot, jumped into the Bird Dog, and took off for Quang Tri with the rest of the force following.

When Neil was returned to Phu Bai, he admitted that he just couldn't handle the pressure any longer. His nerves long since shattered, he would land on the abandoned airstrip, smoke pot for a couple of hours, and then fly back. Because of his combat record, he was simply reassigned to nonflying duties, and nothing more was ever said. Neil had fought two wars: one against the NVA and another against his own fear and common sense. How long the second one lasted before he decided that facing those guns was insane, only he could say, but in between it had taken enormous courage. Perhaps at the end of the day, justice was served after all.

Doc Clement: One day I had to take a full-bull army colonel out to watch an Arc Light. We were on station, and I held an orbit a few klicks from the target. The B-52s came in so high you couldn't see them. Suddenly, hundreds of tons of bombs landed and a few square kilometers of jungle disappeared. As soon as it settled, this guy wanted me to fly over the site to take a look. It wasn't the first one I'd seen, and I knew that sometimes there would be a second wave. I refused, and we had something of a confrontation over the intercom. Sure enough, ten or fifteen minutes later another load of bombs whistled in, and there wasn't another word out of him. I later found out he put himself in for a DFC and got it for being in my back seat and watching a bunch of bombs explode.

Bill Hooper: I was waiting for my observer in the Dong Ha line shack, when one of our crew chiefs came in shaking his head. "Sir, you know that new pilot we got in?" I nodded. Captain Baker had come to us on temporary duty from battalion headquarters in Da Nang. An abrasive academy graduate, his constant harping on the glories of a military career and the superiority of West Pointers had not endeared him to the 1st Platoon of the 220th. Even this could have been more or less overlooked if he had been a team player. What was particularly grating was his sole purpose for spending time with us.

"You people are here by sheer accident," he explained in the club soon after his arrival. We loved being called "you people." "If you were career-minded, it would be ideal. Well, ideal if you didn't have to spend a complete tour here. There's not a better O-1 platoon in Vietnam for seeing action and getting decorations. If you were like me, you'd appreciate that. Without a combat assignment and a couple of good citations in your 201 file, getting promoted in the first zone is tough."

"Let me get this straight," I said. "You're here just to get a medal?"

"Sure. As soon as I get my DFC, I'm heading back to Da Nang. I got other tickets to punch."

"Who says you're going to get a DFC?" someone asked.

"Hey, I know people," he winked. "There are ways, and there are ways. You people help me out and maybe I can put in a good word when I get back to Da Nang. You really don't need a good medal, but you might want one to show your kiddies someday."

Baker's comments were like dragging fingernails across a blackboard.

We were flying some of the most hazardous Bird Dog missions in the entire theater on a daily basis. It was a job we believed in and took pride in doing well. The thanks we received from those on the ground, and the respect earned from each other was the currency we dealt in. For Baker to drop in on our war just long enough to further his career, and then tell us what a bunch of shmucks we were for taking our job seriously, was deeply offensive and brought him dangerously close to physical damage. As it was, we simply ostracized him.

Our ground crews also developed a cordial loathing for the man. We knew that our lives depended on their keeping our aging Bird Dogs airworthy, and they often worked impossible hours to ensure that we didn't go down because of mechanical failure. Their dedication was complete, and for us they were part of the family. For Baker they were no more than tools, and he treated them with cold indifference.

Sadly, Baker was but one minor example of the declining professionalism of the American officer corps in Vietnam and its systematic abuse of the awards system. For those wanting to make a career of being in uniform, it was more important to have a postgraduate degree than extended combat duty, a little experience in a wide range of assignments rather than mastering what they'd joined to do, and a chest full of medals, whether they were deserved or not. It all went toward ensuring that the promotion boards—made up of career officers with the same mindset—agreed that he was qualified to advance in rank. Never mind that Baker's leadership skills, as indicated by the way he treated the enlisted troops, were almost nonexistent, or that war, the ultimate reason for donning the uniform, was an inconvenience once the requisite ribbons were safely in hand. This wasn't to say they were all like that. We all knew first-class career soldiers and pilots who loved the uniform and all it stood for, men we were proud to serve with, but they were depressingly rare.

"So what's the news on Captain Baker?" I asked our oil-stained and weary crew chief.

"Sir, you know that gook tank you took out a few weeks ago?"

"Well, it was a tank retriever that Lieutenant Byrd found. He hit it first and I just sort of polished it off the next day."

"Whatever," Sergeant Benson shrugged. "Well, Captain Baker told me before he took off that it was a hot target and he was going to hit it."

"Really?" I mused. "Not much left to finish off."

"That's what I tried to tell him, sir, but he told me he wasn't interested in an NCO's opinions."

"You wouldn't be criticizing Captain Baker, would you?"

"Oh no, sir, I wouldn't do that. I think he's outstanding."

"Just like all of us, sergeant. Any sign of my observer?"

I'd already returned from my first mission of the day when Baker landed, ordered the crew chief to refuel his aircraft, and ran excitedly into the line shack. Filling out his after-action report, he announced he'd run two flights of high-delivery ordnance against an undamaged tank retriever. By an odd coincidence its location was the same as the one Byrd had destroyed.

"There wasn't anything left when I finished with it," he exclaimed, refusing to meet our silent stares. "Christ, you should have seen the ground fire! Accurate as hell. Shot the shit out of me."

When we followed him to the aircraft, we saw two 12.7mm holes in the Bird Dog's tail. Someone started to ask Baker about the details, but he had no more career time to spend with amateurs and opened the throttle for Phu Bai. He was there only long enough to refuel, before flying back to his Da Nang headquarters. He wrote himself up for his DFC, had one of his career buddies endorse it, and fed the paperwork into the system. Three weeks later he had it and we never saw him again. For the professionals like Baker, it really was a Sears & Roebuck war.

Chapter 10

Air to Air

DOC CLEMENT: MARINE CAPT. TOM JONES was enjoying the hospitality of the Catkiller Club when one of his troops ran in looking for him and said, "Sir, you need to get down to DASC fast, we got bogies in the DMZ." We hauled ass down to their underground bunker, where the radio operators were receiving reports from three fire-support bases along the East-West Trace about unidentified helicopters. A couple of guys were plotting positions and writing furiously on the other side of a transparent Plexiglas map. DASC had already confirmed there were no friendly air-assault operations in progress, and when Tom asked about the terrain, I told him the area had good LZs for off-loading troops and supplies. He scrambled several flights of F-4s and a tanker to refuel them. When the fighter jocks got on station, they could see the landing lights of up to a dozen helicopters landing, heading back into North Vietnam, and returning. Tom was giving a general in Saigon a minute-by-minute account of what was happening but was told that unless they could positively identify the bogies as Russian helicopters, then no one could fire on them. For almost three hours, we listened to the firebases and the F-4 pilots pleading for permission to engage. The last of the landing lights finally flew back into North Vietnam, and a bunch of pissed off pilots returned to base. Although there were later sightings of single helicopters coming down, that was the only time they crossed the border en masse. We never did find out what it was all about.

Carl Drechsel: The weather that day was intermittent rain, cold, and cloudy, when I departed Dong Ha and headed directly to the tri-border area. I spotted hundreds of fifty-five-gallon drums floating down a river, over a waterfall, and continuing down the river. I flew about three miles so they could hear the sound of my engine growing fainter, climbed to two thousand feet, and then glided back to the waterfall to get a better look. There were at least a dozen VC in the open, some smoking ciga-rettes, and when they saw me they hauled ass. Couldn't get any air in, so I climbed back to two thousand feet and headed for Dong Ha. About five minutes later I saw something heading right for me. At first I thought it was something on the windscreen but then it went right by me very fast. It was a MiG-19. It turned and came back at me. He was either just curious, or his guns were jammed, because he shot right past heading north. I called for air support, and as soon as I mentioned "MiG" it was like the war had just begun. Within one minute I was talking to a flight of two Phantoms scrambled from Da Nang. They wanted info like altitude, last known direction, color, and markings. As quickly as they arrived, they must have been in max-afterburner all the way, giving a wing wave as they passed me to go MiG hunting. Never heard anything more about it.

Bill Hooper: A mile-thick layer of monsoon cloud turned early after-noon into twilight, and rain spattered my windscreen as I patrolled south of the Ben Hai River. I pulled the heater knob out a little farther to fight the damp chill. With the prospect of two more dreary hours of routine patrolling, I yawned and shifted in the seat.

"Catkiller 1-2, Catkiller 1-2, this is Hillsboro Control. Over." Hillsboro handled air north of the river. Puzzled, I answered the call. Hillsboro told me that they were tracking a bogey west of me and that if it maintained its heading it would cross the western end of the DMZ into Laos. This was interesting, but I couldn't imagine what it had to do with me. The explanation was not long in coming. "Catkiller 1-2, request you divert to intercept and identify bogey. Over." Thinking that Hillsboro must have confused me with a different aircraft, I asked if he understood that I was an O-1 Bird Dog capable of a max cruise of a little over one hun-dred knots and armed with nothing more than four white phosphorus marking rockets. The controller confirmed that he was well aware that I was an O-1 Bird Dog and how I was armed—and then gave me an intercept course.

The bogey's reported airspeed suggested a Russian helicopter, the presence of which was the subject of much rumor and speculation. They were heavily armed and considerably faster than a Bird Dog. Unless I could pop out of a cloud and ambush it with a first-pass hit, my chances of success were less than zero. The only thing that chopper crew was likely to die from that day would be laughter at the sight of my under-powered Bird Dog chugging resolutely toward them.

The vector I was given led toward the proposed intercept position north of Khe Sanh. I throttled up to one hundred knots, eased a little farther south to get on course, and climbed to clear the mountains and have the advantage of altitude. If we crossed paths, I planned to identify and then dive on the Russian chopper, firing both pairs of rockets. If I missed—as was likely—I'd run like hell into the nearest cloud. I continued to receive regular updates until, much to my relief, Hillsboro lost contact with the bogey and terminated my mission.

The most coveted badge of honor for those of us in the 1st Platoon was a metal pin bearing the image of Snoopy flying his Sopwith Camel doghouse. Although it was worn by pilots who had completed at least fifty missions over North Vietnam, Snoopy's eternal dogfight with the Red Baron appealed to the frustrated fighter pilot in all of us. Our frustration was alleviated now and then by mixing it up with other Bird Dogs, but this paled against the challenge of fighting marine UH-34s. These chunky, piston-engined helicopters, call sign "Murray," bore neither resemblance nor comparison with the sleek, turbine-powered Hueys that became one of the hallmarks of the Vietnam War, and though already phased out by the army, were still used by the marines for "ash-and-trash" runs throughout I Corps.

While one might assume that we had the edge, the opposite was true. The UH-34 was not only more maneuverable than a Bird Dog but slightly faster, too, so our only hope lay in ambushing them. The game was always played the same way over the same area with the same results. We lost.

Coming back from a mission, we'd tune into their tactical net to learn if a Murray was airborne along the West Trace, then climb above a large expanse of rice paddies dotted with stands of tall trees. Once a victim was spotted, we maneuvered for a head-on attack that would give us the chance to escape before the marines knew what hit them. Rolling over and diving out of the sun in the best tradition of Snoopy and the Red Baron, we riddled them from nose to tail with imaginary bullets. Flashing past, we'd shout, "Rata-tat-tat, rata-tat-tat, jarhead, you're dead!" and head for the trees, adding pointed comments about the ancestry and incestuous relationships pertinent to marines in general and these in particular.

But marines are unblushing cheaters. In spite of being shot to pieces and going down in flames, they'd shout back, "You missed!" and haul their UH-34s around in hot pursuit. Twenty feet off the ground, we'd try to lose them in a game of hide-and-seek in the trees. With their speed advantage, they'd soon be closing on us, and then it was their turn to shout, "Rata-tat-tat, dogface, I got your ass!" We were never cheaters, but we knew they'd missed, and we'd scoot around another clump of trees, shouting, "Yer shooting blanks just like all marines!" It was little boys' fun, but before long they were on our tails, and we had to admit defeat. Climbing out of the trees in formation, army and marine pilots exchanged grins and waves, then broke off and returned to the war.

We had fought the marines a few times when Major Wisby called the 1st Platoon together in the mess hall for a briefing. At the end of it he walked to the door, then stopped and looked back at us. "Oh, by the way, gentlemen, if I hear any more of this 'rata-tat-tat-you're-dead' shit, I'm gonna have somebody's ass"—he paused and looked straight at me— "Captain Hooper." I gave him my most innocent look. . . .

My experiences as a fighter pilot were given a completely different perspective one dreary day in late 1968. At that time a company of army OV-1 Mohawks shared the Phu Bai airfield with us. These twin-turboprop aircraft carried side-looking airborne radar and flew recon missions deep into North Vietnam.

Patrolling south of the Ben Hai River, I received a call from another Catkiller. "Go to Waterboy's push," he said. When I tuned in the radar station at Phu Bai, the controller was speaking to a Mohawk somewhere over North Vietnam. "—hawk, Nighthawk, this is Waterboy. Two bogeys now bearing 347 degrees, forty miles and closing."

"Roger, Waterboy," a flat Midwestern voice answered.

There could be little doubt that the pursuers were MiGs. Three to four times faster than the unarmed Mohawk, they carried cannon and heat-seeking air-to-air missiles that could home on the Mohawk's hot engine exhausts. The surreal drama unfolded through the remarkably calm voices of Waterboy and Nighthawk. "Nighthawk, this is Waterboy, bogeys now bearing 350 degrees, twenty-two nautical miles and closing."

"Roger, copy."

Under better weather conditions, the Mohawk would have dived toward the mountains to hide from the North Vietnamese radar controllers directing the MiGs. Even if the interceptors spotted him, his lower airspeed and superior maneuverability would have allowed him to snake through narrow valleys no MiG pilot in his right mind would enter. But the weather had canceled that escape route. Hitting a mountain in the clouds would be as final as a burst of 30mm cannon fire. His only hope was to reach South Vietnam before the MiGs saw him. "Nighthawk, Nighthawk, this is Waterboy. Bogeys bearing 010 degrees, ten miles and closing."

"Roger, copy."

There was usually a substantial American air presence in this area, and I kept expecting to hear that our own fighters were racing in to give him cover. Then I realized that if the MiGs had been vectored this far south, it could only mean that the North Vietnamese radar controllers knew no American fighters were in range. "Nighthawk, this is Waterboy. Bogeys at your nine o'clock, three miles."

"Roger, Waterboy, we see one, we—" The transmission cut off.

"They're taking evasive action," I thought. I imagined the Mohawk going through violent maneuvers to avoid a burst of cannon fire. They'll start talking any second now. I waited. "Nighthawk, Nighthawk, this is Waterboy, how do you copy? Over."

"Nighthawk, Nighthawk, this is Waterboy, how do you copy? Over." I was picturing a pall of black smoke rising from a rice paddy when—

"Roger, Waterboy, this is Nighthawk. We saw them, then lost visual contact. Do you still have them? Over."

"Roger, Nighthawk. Bogeys are withdrawing."

I automatically scanned the instruments and brought the nose a little farther to the west. There were still two hours to go as I continued my quiet patrol above the Ben Hai. . . .

Wind and rain beat against the walls of the line shack. "God, not ham and lima beans again," Byrd complained from the opposite side of the picnic table. "What did you get?"

I opened my C ration pack and picked through it. "Beef stew."

"Want to swap?"

"Nope." I unfolded the P38 can opener and began cutting the top off. "Ham and lima beans are good for you, Byrd. Didn't your mother ever tell you that?"

"Yeah, but she said that about everything I didn't like. Man, I'd kill for a pizza right now. There's no justice in the world. Hey, you've got fruit cocktail. I'll swap you my canned peaches for it."

"Nope."

"Anyone ever tell you what a selfish motherfucker you are, Hooper?"

"Yep. But you can have my Lucky Strikes. How about that?"

"I don't smoke. You know I don't smoke."

"Hey, I'm just trying to be a good guy," I said, digging into the cold meat and potatoes. "So don't say I never offered you anything."

The door of the line shack opened to a gust of wind and spray followed by a marine in a glistening poncho. He shut it quickly behind him and pushed the hood of the poncho back to reveal a wet face under a cap bearing the oak leaf insignia of a lieutenant colonel. I recognized him as the executive officer of one of the marine battalions headquartered on the other side of the Dong Ha base. Byrd and I stood.

"We've lost one of our companies," he said without preamble. He opened his map case to show us their last known position. It lay about ten miles southwest of Dong Ha. He explained that their last helicopter resupply had been over two weeks earlier, after which the weather closed in. Radio batteries had died one by one until contact was lost.

Byrd and I knew the area. Cut with narrow mountain valleys and overgrown with double canopied jungle, it was extremely difficult terrain. Because of the heavy rains, the rivers were in flood, which would force the marines to hump back and forth looking for fords. This made it impossible to guess in which direction or how far they might have moved since their last transmission. With no food and daytime temperatures in the low sixties, they'd be half starved and shivering. If they stumbled into a firefight, their physical condition and lack of communications placed them at great risk.

"We'll start by reconning these two valleys," I said, tapping the map. "Both are near their last known position and both lead down to the coastal plain. If they've reached either one, they'll know they lead east." I checked my watch. "We still have almost three hours of daylight, sir, so we'll go ahead and saddle up now. Why don't you put your extraction team on standby so they're ready to go in case we find them today."

He pulled the hood over his cap and stepped to the door. "Thank you," he nodded, and disappeared into the rain.

Still early afternoon, the day was already dark as we flew through steady rain. Under an eight-hundred-foot ceiling, our ground clearance shrank as the terrain rose on our approach to the mountains. Visibility decreased steadily. This, at least, would make it difficult for the enemy to see, much less track us. Byrd rogered my "Good Luck" as we split up and I turned west into the first narrow valley. Mist swirled along nearly vertical walls that rose into the clouds. For the first couple of miles it ran fairly straight, then narrowed in a series of tight S turns that offered no room to turn around. The rising floor of the valley would eventually meet the clouds; without room to maneuver, I'd soon be forced to climb blind out of the funnel and hope I missed the peaks. The twisting course eased for a moment and then swung hard to the right. Hugged on both sides by the steep valley walls, the foaming river below me formed almost a perfect horseshoe. Turning hard over it, I looked directly down to see men waving wildly from rain-filled foxholes.

Continuing up the valley until it unexpectedly widened and the clouds thinned to admit a brief ray of sunshine, I reversed course and passed over the marines again, rocking my wings to confirm that I had seen them. A few minutes later I was orbiting at the mouth of the valley and reporting their position. I waited until two Chatterbox CH-46s and an escort of Seaworthy gunships arrived and then led the rescue choppers back up the valley. Passing the horseshoe, I climbed slowly through the clouds and looked over my shoulder to see the helicopters already breaking into the clear. Rarely did rescue operations end so quickly or successfully. Byrd was back on the ground by the time I landed at Dong Ha. We dug into another pack of C rations, bullshitted for a while, and crawled into our clammy bunks for the night.

I awoke at dawn to more steady, chilling rain. Draping a poncho over my head, I squished miserably through the mud to the latrine and then to the line shack. The smell of full ashtrays and last night's beer hung in the damp air, the same dog-eared copies of *Playboy* and *Reader's Digest* lay scattered on the table and chairs, and clumps of red mud left by our jungle boots covered the floor.

It was going to be another day of acute boredom when the hands on our wristwatches seemed to move with the greatest reluctance. Where previously we'd logged upward of 150 hours a month, we were now flying less than 20. If there were a time for a combat pilot to learn the virtue of patience, it was during the monsoon, but few of us saw any value in quiet meditation.

I propped myself in the doorway and stared despondently at the rain. I knew that somewhere out there, marines and army troops were humping seventy-pound rucksacks through the same miserable weather. Those guys had an incredibly tough job at the best of times. Out in the boondocks on ten- to fourteen-day patrols, they were never dry, had lousy food, little or no sleep and, except for resupply choppers and sporadic radio messages, were on their own. And that was the good part. While they were hunting the enemy, the enemy was hunting them, and in the event of a hard contact there was little chance of close air support in these conditions. They either fought their way out or died cold and wet. I yawned and stretched out on some storage boxes to slip into one of those fitful naps that mercifully passed the time.

I awoke about midmorning to find the same low overcast, but the rain had stopped and visibility had increased to a mile or better. There were no missions scheduled because the ceiling was still well below what the army considered safe minimums even for combat. The hell with it. There was a target out there somewhere and enough visibility to get off the ground. It was time to go to work.

I found the crew chief and told him to arm whichever Bird Dog was available. He looked at the weather, shook his head, and trudged off to ready the aircraft. Although there were a few others who disregarded the regulations on minimums, at the time I think Finch and I were the principal offenders. It wasn't that we went out of our way to ignore them, rather that there simply came a point when we could no longer tolerate sitting on the ground. Strapping on my survival gear, I enjoyed the thought of Charlie Finch back at Phu Bai. Just as frustrated as myself by the lack of action, he was going to be seriously pissed off if I found something and he wasn't there to share it.

I slung the balance of my gear over one shoulder and headed for my aircraft, which had already been pushed out of its revetment by the line crew. That old 2646 had seen her share of combat was attested to by the many riveted patches over new and old bullet holes. Strapping myself into the cold seat, I plugged in the helmet jack and pumped in a couple of shots of prime, before catching sight of the concerned NCO standing under the wing tip, a sad and bewildered look on his face. He never did understand me or Charlie. I'm not sure we did either.

"Don't worry!" I grinned, slamming the door and calling, "Clear!"

The propeller spun through a few revolutions, and the six-cylinder Continental caught with a satisfying roar. When the instruments had settled in the green, I pushed hard against the right rudder pedal and throttled up to swing the tail around with a burst of power and taxied out. No military pilot knows real freedom of action unless he has the fortune to fly combat missions out of a place like Dong Ha, and when it's all over, will never know it again.

"Dong Ha Tower, this is Catkiller 1-2. Over."

"Roger, 1-2, this is Dong Ha Tower. Go ahead."

"Ah, roger, Tower, this is 1-2 holding short number one, run-up complete and ready for takeoff. Over." From the stuttered request to repeat myself, I knew he wasn't expecting any traffic this morning.

Off the ground, I set up a skid and tracked straight up Highway 1. The terrain dropped off immediately north of Dong Ha, rose again near the East-West Trace, and began sloping gently down toward the Ben Hai. My altimeter read barely over a hundred feet and I was in and out of whirling vapor and occasional showers. I turned west on my approach to the river and began a slow decent over thicker and taller ground cover.

Despite the cold, damp air swirling through the cockpit, I began to sweat. My eyes moved constantly, flicking back and forth for muzzle flashes. I'd been patrolling for less than thirty minutes when DASC called. A recon platoon needed help to rendezvous with an armored patrol that was en route to recover them. Scribbling their frequency on the windscreen, I swung south and headed for their approximate position. "Hard Tack 6, Hard Tack 6, this is Catkiller 1-2. Over." A surprised and relieved voice answered.

I had descended well below the cloud cover but they still couldn't see me. I flicked on my landing light. Flying slow S-turns, I watched tensely for muzzle flashes. The marines saw the light and directed me toward them. The rain had started again and ran in rivulets up the windscreen. Leaning out the right window, I soon spotted half a dozen men in a waterlogged bomb crater and several others in the sodden undergrowth around it. Hard Tack Actual explained that they had one wounded grunt as the result of a contact that morning. The enemy unit had almost immediately broken contact, but the lieutenant was worried that they might be following him. He needed help in getting his wounded man to a rendezvous point as quickly as possible

Very familiar with the area, I knew of a nearby road that intersected the East-West Trace. When I suggested they wait until I reconned a route for them, Hard Tack made it clear that he didn't like the idea of losing me even for a few minutes. He said they'd be ready to move in another ten, if I could just hang on.

Sixty feet above the ground, I began flying flat lazy eights. My first leg took me about five hundred meters to the south, where the terrain opened to scattered bush and elephant grass. I came back, crossed over the marines, then made a wide right turn over forest and thick undergrowth and headed toward them again. I had drifted about seventy-five meters north of their position, where the terrain dropped a few feet to a long-abandoned and overgrown rice paddy. Examining the higher ground, I saw three crouching, camouflaged figures. A second pass revealed what appeared to be a least a squad. One looked up at me. Their position covered Hard Tack's northern flank, and my first thought was that it made a prudent and logical defensive position. Then I wondered why an experienced combat leader would place that many men so far from his command post. "Hard Tack, this is 1-2. Over."

"Roger, 1-2, this is Actual. Over."

"Roger, Hard Tack. From your position, how far north is your perimeter?"

"Not more than twenty meters. Over."

Shit.

"Ambush!" My transmission was lost to the simultaneous *thunk, thunk* of two mortar rounds being lobbed almost straight up. My warning was late, but the distinctive sound of the charges had already sent the marines rolling into the closest craters. Dammit! How could I have been so stupid not to check there first!

Too close to the enemy to fire, I kicked hard left rudder and pulled the stick to my belly. The NVA were walking the mortar shells through the position. In a forty-five-degree bank, horizon spinning past the nose, I could see two trees coming up. The target had to be behind one of them, and I had only a couple of seconds more before I'd be lined up on them.

There was no more time to decide, and I snapped the wings level and flew into a swarm of small-arms fire. I aimed at the closest tree and fired the first rocket, lifted the nose, fired the second, a little right rudder, and fired a third, before breaking hard left. By a stroke of luck the second hit high in one tree and exploded like an air burst, blanketing the enemy mortar position with white phosphorus.

Hard Tack said that none of his marines had been hit, but we both agreed he had to withdraw. I watched them hoist their wounded man in a makeshift litter and head south. I turned west, then doubled back along the edge of the old paddy. A pair of NVA soldiers suddenly emerged from the underbrush, running down a trail twenty meters ahead and to my right. Again too close to engage, I turned hard over them and saw one dive into the underbrush and the other slide to a stop on one knee. I held the turn and looked over my right shoulder to see him lift his AK-47, rest an elbow on his raised knee, and take careful aim. Now it was his turn.

I could have firewalled the throttle and disappeared into the clouds a few feet above me. Instead, I found myself engrossed in watching his very deliberate moves. By reflex I was in a skid to the outside of the turn when he opened fire from about fifty meters. My eyes followed the tracers with clinical detachment as they passed under the Bird Dog. My only emotion was curiosity. Satisfied, I returned to the marines.

I told Hard Tack that if the enemy was regrouping, they were not far behind him. Less burdened and better rested, they were going to catch up quickly.

With only one rocket, I wasn't going to be much help. We needed another asset and we needed it now. Estimating we were about three klicks from the Ben Hai, I switched to our artillery net, explained the need for immediate indirect fire, and gave them coordinates that would place the first rounds on the Ben Hai River. It would be a risk firing over friendlies, but I wanted to make the enemy unit more worried about the artillery walking in behind them than coming after my marines. Knowing Hard Tack would not want to risk the possibility of a short round landing on his men, I chose not to tell him.

I heard the faint detonation of the first rounds, but their point of impact was hidden by the weather. Thinking it was NVA artillery, a very concerned Hard Tack asked if I had observed the impacts. "Negative, Hard Tack, that is friendly covering fire." I ordered the artillery to drop five hundred meters and repeat. The second set of explosions was louder, but the impacts were still masked by mist and rain. I brought it down another five hundred meters, but the rounds again detonated out of sight. Estimating the visibility to be around half a mile, I took a deep breath and brought it down five hundred meters more.

I saw the shells impact a good six hundred meters north of us, brought it down another one hundred meters, and called for battery, three rounds in effect. The ambush site was ripped apart by the high-explosive shells. Ordering them to retain the last coordinate in case I needed more help, I headed back to look for the enemy. My search revealed nothing. If they weren't dead, they'd certainly been discouraged. It took the marines an hour to move about a kilometer, and when they had less than another klick to the road, I gave Hard Tack 6 his most direct course and headed through the rain to find the column.

A few minutes later I saw two M48 tanks and three APCs approaching the trace and about to turn east. That good news was followed by better news that a Chatterbox was heading for us. I waited over the armor until the CH-46 arrived and then led it back to the marines. The wounded grunt was put on board and it lifted off for the hospital at Quang Tri. I continued covering the marines until the armor arrived and scooped up the rest of the exhausted platoon. Hard Tack signed off the net without a word of thanks, and I headed for Dong Ha.

After shutting down and helping the line crew push the airplane into the revetment, I did a slow walk around to inspect the old girl for bullet holes. To my surprise, she'd taken only a single hit through the right elevator. Just one more for her collection.

Chapter 11

Thanksgiving and Christmas

GLENN STRANGE: THEY MAKE A BIG DEAL OUT of Thanksgiving dinner in the army, and the 1968 Phu Bai version was no exception. We had voluminous amounts of the traditional turkey, dressing, potatoes, pumpkin pie, and all the other trimmings. At each place on the table was a card with a syrupy message from General Abrams, the USARV CG [U.S. Army, Vietnam, commanding general], about Thanksgiving, peace and good will, yah, yah, yah.

The Catkillers contributed to an orphanage over in Tri Bac, a little settlement not too far from Phu Bai, and the CO sent troops over to get the nuns and little children to share in our Thanksgiving feast. It was an incredibly absurd sight—a big deuce-and-a-half with a bunch of soldiers wearing steel pots and flak jackets and carrying M16s in the back of that truck with a bunch of nuns and orphans.

I doubt that they enjoyed the food we had, but there were treats for the children, and they were given lots of food to take home. I was helping to load them and their loot on the truck back to Tri Bac and picked up one little girl. I don't have big hands, but when I picked up that child, my hands completely encircled her waist—she was tiny! When I stood her on the truck, she looked at me with the saddest eyes I'd ever seen and said, "Thank you, Dai Uy."

That afternoon I had a mission to direct naval rocket fire into a little village that was not too far from the coast. "Intelligence" had determined that enemy activity had risen to such a level in the village (not really a village, just a bunch of huts) that destruction was justified. Salvo after salvo went into that little "cherry ville" until there was nothing left but smoldering rubble. When I went down lower for a BDA, I saw several bodies, but one caught my attention and I came back to take a picture. It was just a kid.

I didn't need to see that just after my encounter with the sad little orphan I'd put on the truck. I flew out over the South China Sea, my mind full of the ugly images of the afternoon and confusing thoughts about who I was, where I was, and what I was doing. I couldn't make any sense of it, so I said, "The hell with it!", went back to Phu Bai, and got a beer.

When I got back to Georgia, I sorted through my stuff and found that Thanksgiving Day message from General Abrams and the picture of that kid we killed, and showed them to my wife in an attempt to explain the paradoxical character of the Vietnam enterprise. She got visibly ill, went into a tirade, and really berated me for showing her that picture. I knew then that my experiences and memories of Vietnam were mine and she didn't want to hear anything about it.

Charles Finch: Of the many Catkillers in the 220th RAC, Stanford graduate Roger "Outa" Bounds was certainly one of the most meticulous, organized, and best connected. A couple of days before Christmas we were at Dong Ha, watching the rain. I wasn't complaining about the break. In the last week I'd taken eight hits, four of them when I'd been down low chasing a tiger. Out of the blue, Bounds mentioned that he had a relative on the USS *New Jersey* and we might fly out there the next day. In Vietnam there were always helicopters going somewhere and, knowing Roger, I figured it just might happen.

The next morning we flew a two-ship mission, but after less than two hours and no targets, we landed. Half an hour later, Roger's helicopter arrived. I was 1st Platoon leader, the responsible officer, but figured what the hell, and without a pass or permission we climbed on board and lifted off for the *New Jersey* for what I thought might be a two-hour visit. Roger had his fatigues, I was in my marine flight suit, both of us with two days' growth of beard when we stepped onto the deck and were escorted down to the captain's mess by the *New Jersey*'s skipper.

I couldn't believe the spread. A few hours earlier we'd been pawing through our collection of C-rations. Suddenly we were in heaven, with real china, real linen napkins, real cooks, and about twenty spic-and-span naval officers watching us like we were aliens from Mars. The perfect host, Captain Snyder said, "You will stay for the Bob Hope show tomorrow, won't you?" Roger smirked at me. No one in Phu Bai knew where we were, and this ship was steaming south. I smiled, "Yes, sir," and dived back into the food.

We were given quarters near the Bull Halsey Memorial Suite, and after a shower, shave, and a change into fresh navy khakis, toured the ship. We spent most of it in the ultra-sophisticated fire-control center, amazed that we were allowed to direct such a weapon from our Bird Dog cockpits.

On Christmas Day I was up at 0630 to see the Bob Hope entourage arrive. Ann-Margret and the Golddiggers stepped off the chopper with him. She and her husband stayed in the stateroom next to ours. She was young and stunning, but Roger Smith never left her side. Before the show, I sat beside Hope while he rehearsed his cue cards as Bounds was eyeing all the gorgeous girls and making deposits in his fantasy bank. That night we were up till 0200 with Captain Snyder, discussing the *New Jersey*'s role in the DMZ and North Vietnam and listening to tapes they'd made of us firing her big guns.

After breakfast we briefed part of the ship's company on our mission in the DMZ and the effect of their guns on NVA targets. Their eyes were like saucers by the time we finished. We finally boarded a navy helicopter to Tua Hoa and then a C-130 to Cam Ranh Bay, where we went to a floorshow at the officers club. We had nurses as escorts: Roger's was fat; mine was a size four who dated an F-4 mechanic. I told her I did not do charity work. I'm sure she cried herself to sleep.

Next day we had to fly to Bien Hoa to get a hop up to Phu Bai. When we arrived we were not very popular, as someone—I think it was Bud Bruton, who had replaced Doc in the 1st Platoon—had to fly our missions. Our punishment was flying the DMZ on New Year's Eve.

Bud Bruton remembered Christmas '68 a little differently.

Bud Bruton: If you are far away in a foreign land, homesick, being shot at, and have the chance to see the Bob Hope Show aboard the USS *New Jersey*, you will not want to miss it. Because we were the "Eyes of the *New Jersey*" (on account of being most likely to direct her guns when she was off the coast of northern I Corps), word was that the entire 1st Platoon was invited for Christmas Day. According to Finch and Bounds, all we had to do was be at Dong Ha the evening of the twenty-fourth to catch a Huey out to the ship.

I was the last to land after the late-afternoon mission, only to discover that our ride had long-since departed. *What?* Worse, I was the only pilot still at Dong Ha. Which meant I would have to fly early the next morning to make sure the NVA didn't violate the Christmas truce. If I was feeling abandoned and screwed by my friends, my marine GIB (guy in the back) observer, whom I had invited, was devastated. Nightfall found us on top of a bunker, morosely watching the firepower display and complaining about being left behind. Two NCOs walked up and asked if they could share our spot. Since each of them had a bottle of VO, we welcomed their company. It was a chance to drown our sorrows.

The firepower demonstration was dramatic, an endless series of explosions, tracers, and color, and totally against regulations. The longer it went on, the drunker we got. Praise the Lord, Good Will to Men, and pass the bottle. A quart of VO and many stories later, I learned that one of our benefactors was from my home town area and had taught at Valley Forge Military Academy. He even knew one of my best friends.

By the time the pyrotechnic display was over and the second bottle was empty, we were stone drunk, and I had to carry my backseater to the transit-overnight tent for a couple hours' sleep. I was awakened at dawn by the charge of quarters NCO. Through my stupor I saw he was wearing a Santa Claus hat and holding two red bags—"Merry Christmas! Ho, Ho, Ho!"—each containing toothpaste, razor, nail clippers, pocket knife, and a New Testament. To this day, I can see him walking away in the morning fog as I tried to clear my head. (I still have that pocket knife and New Testament from Santa Claus.)

When I woke up my GIB, he said he wanted to be allowed to die right there. But duty called, and the jeep took us to the flight line. Nearly comatose, he was begging me not to make him fly. Sorry, buddy. With the help of two crew chiefs, I got him into the aircraft. When they realized how bad I was, they tried to talk me out of the mission. I shook my head. We had to fly. I may have been drunk and my GIB puking drunk, but the fear of not being in the air should anything happen made me bite the bullet and strap myself in. (I still don't know what happened to all the other pilots, as only Finch and Bounds had made it to the *New Jersey*.) I got the Bird Dog started and taxied out, thinking maybe this wouldn't be as bad as I feared. When there was no answer from the tower—I think *everyone* in Dong Ha was drunk that morning—I cleared myself to the active runway.

My confidence was premature. Head reeling and stomach heaving, the second I lifted off I was hit with vertigo. I was in real trouble, made worse by my GIB puking all over the back seat and pleading with me to land. With all that going on behind me, I kept telling myself to climb straight ahead and not move anything. *Lock your legs, don't reduce the power, and get as far away from the ground as possible*—nothing else, because if the wings tilted even a little, it felt like the aircraft was going on its back.

The distractions from the back seat weren't helping. When I screamed that we were going to die if he didn't just calm down and be quiet, he finally shut up and passed out. Eyes on the horizon, I headed due east over the South China Sea and climbed to about six thousand feet; no turns, no looking down, not moving the stick, nothing to aggravate my vertigo. No one knows if the NVA had plans to break the truce, but the Lord knows that on Christmas Day 1968, I would not have been able to do anything about it if they had; Catkiller 18 was just trying to keep the aircraft straight and level.

Flying drunk is a sobering experience, especially with an even drunker GIB in the back seat. We may have been young and brave and the best of the best, but my God, sometimes we were really stupid. Fortunately, however hard I tried to make it happen, it was not my day to die. Three hours after taking off, I'd sobered up enough to attempt a landing. When I shut down, the relief pilots were there to fly the rest of the day's missions. When we complained about being left behind the day before, they told us that Bounds and Finch were AWOL, and that we would have been AWOL too, if we had caught that Huey. But you know what?—given the chance, I still would have gone with them. Bob Hope on the USS *New Jersey* only comes once in a lifetime, and from the pictures Bounds and Finch showed us, it would have been worth it. I mean, what was the army going to do if we'd been on that chopper—send us to Vietnam?

Ed Miler: I was personnel officer for the 212th Combat Support Aviation Battalion at Marble Mountain, when the CO, Lt. Col. Bernard Bruns, asked if I would like to take over the 220th RAC when Jim Wisby left. I was well aware of the Catkillers' combat record and its collection of brash, flamboyant, and irreverent young pilots. It was a cocky outfit that "Gee" Wisby had at Phu Bai, full of real characters who exuded self-confidence. Wisby's visits to battalion headquarters, in a blue nonregulation flight suit and a "What, me worry?" air, seemed to underscore the Catkillers' reputation as mavericks.

At the end of January 1969, I assumed command and, with the able assistance of my XO, Russ Blanchard, was introduced to the officers and men of the 220th. Blanchard, a senior captain with a previous combat tour in Bird Dogs, was a levelheaded and steady man whose advice and counsel were invaluable. He took me on a tour of the mess hall, officer and enlisted billets, company motor pool, maintenance hangar, flight line, and the ramp where the aircraft were parked. Looking a little uncomfortable, he said he needed to show me something else and led me into the area of the 131st Surveillance Airplane Company, a Mohawk unit commanded by Maj. Gary Alton. Inside a large building fronting the ramp were a bunch of my men and a huge assortment of jeeps, other vehicles, spare parts, and all kinds of other contraband, none of which belonged to the 220th. Blanchard explained that everything there had been "borrowed" from other units, mostly the ARVNs, who had made the mistake of parking in front of the PX. I immediately ordered that all the "midnight requisitions" be gotten rid of. (Which they did, but at their own pace. To my knowledge, Alton never knew the stuff was there, nor, fortunately, did the battalion commander. I sweated blood during an inspection by the 1st Aviation Brigade, the parent unit of the 212th CSAB, but they did not find the now much-depleted stash, and no one ratted on me. Jim Wisby had chosen not to brief me on this treasure trove, and I chose to do the same with my successor.)

We finally reached the officers club, where Blanchard took me first to see Catkiller Beach. On a concrete slab at the rear of the building lay three or four of the 220th RAC's finest, sunning themselves and being served liquid refreshments by a pretty Vietnamese girl who tended the bar. When Blanchard announced my presence, they jumped up and stood at attention. If they weren't a sight, standing there dripping sweat, with virtually no clothes on. I could hardly contain my laughter as I told them to carry on. That was my introduction to Charlie Finch, Sarge Means, and, I think, Bill Hooper.

When they weren't flying, the pilots gathered in the officers club to have a beer or two (or more), tell war stories, read, shoot darts, and play cards. There was always a poker game going on with serious money changing hands. (After he rotated back to the States, Finch bought a Mercedes convertible with his winnings.) There was also taped music, which got louder as the evening progressed. The two songs I remember most vividly were "Young Girl" and "Lady Madonna" and my mind goes back to those times whenever I hear them today. We even had our own company hypnotist, Quinton "Andy" Anderson, a reluctant but excellent performer whose real talent was that of 1st Platoon Leader for the Myth Makers. The club was also where we held discussions on matters affecting all of the officers, and the scene of a classic clash of wills between me and them.

Because enemy rocket and mortar attacks were frequent at Phu Bai, I had directed the first sergeant to have the men build sand-filled revetments around their quarters. The idea was to stop shrapnel from penetrating the walls of their hooches as they scrambled for the bunkers. When the officers discovered that I expected them to build their own revetments, there were loud protests. *Their* job, they stated forcefully, was to fly the missions and find and destroy the enemy; manual labor was for enlisted men. Holding my temper, I sat them down at the poker table and explained that it was the enlisted men whom they trusted to maintain the aircraft and vehicles, prepare our meals, pull guard duty on the perimeter, and all of the other unglamorous work that kept the 220th running smoothly. They had more than enough to do. I don't know what the pilots talked about after I left, or what the XO added on my behalf, but the next day all of the officers, led by Jim Hudson and Blanchard, were building retaining walls and shoveling sand. Nothing more was ever said of the incident, and except for Glenn Strange chewing out the battalion commander, and a little grumbling when I directed that amyl nitrate ampoules be put in their aircraft, I never had any more trouble from them.

Charles Finch: If any of the 1st Platoon pilots deserved being described as fearless it was Bobby Goodspeed. Not long after he arrived, I decided to see what he was made of and challenged him to fly under some of the bridges around Quang Tri. After the third or fourth pass, Bobby wanted to fly formation with me under one of the larger spans. We got right on the water, and he pulled ahead to take the lead. As soon as we passed under it, he went into max climb, wrapped it around, and went back the opposite way.

Bobby would borrow money from me at the poker table a lot, and the next morning he would come into my room with brand new MPCs [military payment certificates] and pay me back. He always had a lot of money stashed. When we were playing, everyone would try to buy him out of a pot—it never worked. He had the money or would come up with it somehow. He would get in these horrible losing streaks but would not fold under any circumstances, getting madder all the time but sure that the cards would turn. About the time we were feeling sorry for him, he would get a great hand, and then we'd all fold. That made him even angrier. I loved Bobby Goodspeed as much as any officer in that unit. There was not a truer friend, a more loyal officer, a more obnoxious loser at cards, or a more caring Catkiller about saving the lives of the guys on the ground.

Bobby would get up early to steal my observer so he could go get in the fight and be the first one to call in the fighters. One morning we flew up from Phu Bai to Dong Ha for our 0900 missions, his for the 108th mission, while I had marine hop with one of his favorite observers. Close to Quang Tri, he challenged me to go under a bridge with him. Because we always worried that the Viet Cong might hang a concrete block from a wire and ruin our day, he said he'd make a pass over the top to make sure it was clear. When he confirmed everything was okay, I went under it and came out looking for him, but he was already on his way to Dong Ha to steal my marine backseat. He refueled quickly and was back to the ramp to pick up the backseater as I landed.

I was right behind him when he took off. He came up on the push and said neither he nor his back seat had ever been to Khe Sanh, so off we went. About halfway there, we got a call from DASC that a marine recon team was under mortar fire west of Con Thien. We immediately turned toward their position, with me scrambling air and Bobby getting some artillery ready. When we got there, the marines were boxed in on the north and west by NVA troops and blocked on the south by rising terrain. Their only escape route lay to the east.

Because of the terrain, arty was not an option, and fast movers were nowhere close, so we decided to attack the bad guys from two directions. I explained to the recon team that we'd keep the gooks' heads down while they started their withdrawal. I rolled in first and put the 2.75-inch rocket right beside one of the mortar positions. White phosphorus scattered the crew. Although I took no fire, when Goodspeed rolled in he got hosed pretty bad. He pulled off and turned east, did a 180, put the nose down to build the speed necessary to climb over the rising terrain west of the target, and got lit up again by ground fire. I could see and hear AK-47s and machine guns unloading on him.

My next pass was north to south and I again took no ground fire. Goodspeed was not amused by this, so he told me to take another run east to west. About this time the marines told us the NVA were closing in. I went in, punched off a rocket, and took a hit in my right wing. When I told Bobby, he laughed happily over the radio.

With a couple of more passes and the rest of our rockets, we stopped the advance just as a flight of Gunfighter F-4s came on station. Bobby was adamant about running them, but he was missing one thing. In his hurry to steal my backseater and get airborne, he had forgotten to grab any smoke grenades, so he had no way to mark his target. I told him I would mark and he could adjust the air. I came over the target and managed to drop the smoke grenade and took another hit, this time through the fuselage, which pleased Bobby even more. With him directing them, the Gunfighters finished the mission in about four runs with snake and nape. As Bobby gave them and DASC the BDA, he gave me the air strike credit. That was how Bobby was. He would push everyone until they wanted to hit him, and the next minute he would laugh and hug the person. We rushed back to Dong Ha to rearm and refuel and spent the rest of the day going back to Khe Sanh and just sightseeing.

That night the 108th invited us to a poker game. I didn't have any money, so Bobby loaned me $100. It was one of those games where Goodspeed could not get a hand, and he ran out of money in the first hour. I won over $150, but it took me all night to do it. I'd been asleep for maybe two hours when Bobby woke me up. He said he heard I was the big winner and wanted his $100 back. He bugged me all the way to the flight line. I finally said we would have a rocket contest in the DMZ. We flew out toward the mouth of the Ben Hai, and I told him to pick a target. He said we would shoot from a thousand feet at an old antiaircraft site near the beach on the North Vietnamese side.

I agreed and off we went. I shot first and my rocket went into the ocean. Bobby was a lot closer and he won. When he asked why I was laughing, I told him he should have asked for double or nothing, because all he won was the $100 dollars I already owed him. It was fun seeing him get pissed off again.

Chapter 12
Gypsy Rose Lee

BILL HOOPER: IN EARLY JANUARY I WAS AT Dong Ha gathering up my gear for the flight back to Phu Bai when Byrd handed me the landline phone. It was Russ Blanchard asking if I was interested in a two-week temporary-duty assignment. Saigon had just sent a USO request for a bachelor over six feet tall and with a solid combat record to serve as escort officer for the Gypsy Rose Lee show.

My mind raced through the opportunities this offered. Having seen the film *Gypsy*, I knew she had risen to fame as a stripper and then a Hollywood actress before World War II, which put her in her mid-fifties—too old for me. But Finch and Bounds had driven us nuts with their stories of the Bob Hope show and Ann-Margret's Golddiggers, so I knew she'd be accompanied by a bevy of young beauties to remind the boys of what they were fighting for.

"You have to be in Saigon toni—," he was saying when I shouted, "I'll do it!" and bolted for my airplane. At Phu Bai I crammed wash bag, starched jungle fatigues, khakis, and .45 pistol and holster into an AWOL bag and sprinted back to the flightline. Andy Anderson flew me to Da Nang, where I hopped a C-123 that got me to Tan Son Nhut Air Base just before midnight. A major from the VIP office briefed me on my responsibilities, which included arranging transportation and serving as Gypsy's bodyguard. I was also to ensure that Miss Lee's visit be "as pleasant as possible."

Scrubbed, polished, and starched, I was in the arrivals lounge the next afternoon when her flight landed. I patted down my hair, hastily cleaned my fingernails, and gave my shoes an unneeded buffing in anticipation of all those beautiful, hero-worshipping young ladies. They were mine for fifteen glorious days and nights. Vietnam was about to become heaven on earth. There was an explosion of flashbulbs, and Gypsy Rose Lee, a slim and strikingly attractive woman of fifty-four, entered and was immediately pounced on by a USO representative and a *Stars & Stripes* reporter. I stepped forward with only a slight swagger. "Miss Lee? I'm Captain Hooper. Welcome to Vietnam. I have the privilege of being your escort officer during your stay. If you'll follow me, I'll arrange for your bags to be collected and brought to your accommodation."

In the course of this well-rehearsed greeting I kept glancing over her shoulder for the first sight of my private harem. "Captain, I assume you're looking for others," she said, undoubtedly aware of what I was looking for. "Sorry, but I do a solo act." Visions of sweet nights evaporated on the hot tarmac. "Disappointed, Captain Hooper?"

"Uh, oh, no, Miss Lee," I lied. "I mean, with travel so difficult inside the country and not always the easiest or most comfortable, I'm sure it will be far more pleasant with just the two of us."

"Fine. By the way, captain, I want you to personally take charge of my luggage."

Now, military pilots are walking, talking egos, so being told immediately after one of the greatest disappointments of my young life that I was someone's personal baggage boy did nothing to win my undying affection. Recalling the briefing officer's final order, I gave her my most plastic smile. "I'll see to it, Miss Lee."

From that moment on, what was supposed to have been two weeks of bliss became an unremitting battle of wills. Knocking on her door in the Continental Palace Hotel at 0630 each morning, I'd wait resentfully by the jeep until she emerged an hour later for our daily routine of visiting hospitals, major bases, and R&R locations. She had a taste for fresh fruit, and would insist on stopping whenever she saw a market. Given that some were in areas considered insecure, I always tried to dissuade her. Gypsy's response was that she was unhappy if she didn't have fresh fruit every day. She was unfazed when I told her the army would be pretty unhappy with me if she was killed.

For the first few days, we based out of Saigon, returning each afternoon to the hotel, where Gypsy showered, changed, and was whisked away for cocktails and dinner by one more general and his staff. Coming from eight months of combat flying, I was stunned by the luxury enjoyed by American officers assigned to Saigon. Seeing them at sidewalk cafes, often in the company of their beautiful Vietnamese mistresses, and knowing their records would show they had served in a combat zone, was infuriating. I was equally unimpressed by the number of senior officers who seemed to spend a significant portion of their time at Le Cercle Sportif, the most exclusive club in Saigon. Its most famous member, of course, was Gen. William Westmoreland, commander in chief of all U.S. forces in Vietnam.

After seeing Gypsy to her room one afternoon, I wandered into the bar, where another USO tour, this one made up of professional football players, was relaxing over cold beers. Among them was one of my heroes, Billy Ray Smith of the Baltimore Colts. We struck up a conversation, and after a few beers he decided he wanted to arm wrestle. Though he exceeded my six feet one inch, and 160 pounds by at least two inches and another 100 pounds, I propped my elbow on the bar and told him he didn't have a chance. On "Go!" I found myself forcing his forearm steadily downward. I was gleefully contemplating telling the Catkillers how I whipped Billy Ray Smith at arm wrestling when my downward progress abruptly stopped. A quick glance showed a good inch of daylight under his hand. I frowned and put everything into it. Billy Ray picked up a beer with his other hand, popped the top off with his index finger and, between sips, nonchalantly chatted with the other players. Pop-eyed with strain, I decided that if I couldn't win fairly, the best option was to cheat. Jumping up, I fell chest-first on his forearm and was rewarded by the crack of his watch hitting the bar.

Thinking I'd broken his new, duty-free Rolex, Billy Ray responded with a roar and heave that almost sent me over the bar. As soon as he determined that it was still working, he thought it was the funniest thing he'd seen all day. Turning to his teammates, Billy Ray threw an enormous arm over my shoulders and told them how I'd just beaten him "fair and square."

At the height of the guffaws, Sebastian Cabot, a British film actor and star of a popular comedy series on American television, entered. The players greeted him with profane comments about Brits, which he countered with equally rude comments about Yanks as he opened the freezer behind the bar. Billy Ray repeated the story of my arm-wrestling prowess. Cabot suggested that if I was truly desirous of being a man among men, I should abandon beer for a more fitting elixir, at which point he lovingly brandished a bottle of ice-cold gin. Anyone who drank gin, I said, would drink anything.

"My dear chap, anyone who doesn't drink gin wouldn't know the difference." He took the beer from my hand and gave me a glass with three fingers of tooth-achingly cold gin. Not wanting to appear unmanly in front of Billy Ray, I downed it in one gulp. Between gasps for air and the raucous approval of the pro players, Sebastian gave me a cherubic smile. "Tastes like shit, doesn't it, old boy? Don't worry, the second is better, and by the third it's quite delightful."

When I returned the next afternoon, the bar was empty. I was washing the dust from my throat with the first beer when Sebastian appeared. Diplomacy required that I immediately switch to gin. We depleted half of the bottle, and Cabot decided it was time for dinner and more gin. We found a restaurant and ate, drank, and talked for hours, the world becoming an increasingly cheerful place. With life so pleasant, he said, the night would be incomplete without a little companionship. I agreed, and we set out for an up-market cathouse recommended to him. Drink having muddled his memory, the location of this fine emporium was somewhat obscure. In the course of our blind-drunk search along Tudo Street, Sebastian halted at regular intervals to ask for directions in colorful English. Given that I could barely stand upright, I was very impressed with his lucidity.

The evening's glow was dimmed by the appearance of two stone-faced MPs, who informed us that we were in violation of the curfew. Undaunted, Sebastian implored them to transport us to the fabled house of pleasure forthwith, or to at least give us proper directions and send us on our way. They countered by suggesting that they escort him back to the hotel and "the captain here" to the stockade.

Swaying mutely, I wondered how an arrest was going to look on my records and who was going to replace me as Gypsy's escort. Sebastian propped me up and in his best Shakespearean voice, dramatically detailed how I'd just received my first R&R after months of frightfully hazardous missions over North Vietnam and was soon to return to my unit. A minor transgression such as this, surely, should not be considered so calamitous a sin as to put me behind bars. As he warmed to his role of defender of this errant knight of the air, his language and gestures became ever more expansive. It was an inspired performance. The two MPs exchanged a wink, and one held up his hand for a word. When Sebastian paused, the sergeant asked me where my duty station was. I slurred through my story, and the sergeant interrupted to say he would consider letting us off this time. After our repeated and humble promises not to stray again, we were loaded into their jeep and delivered to the hotel.

I didn't see Sebastian again, but the hangover lasted two long, miserable days, during which Gypsy asked repeatedly what was wrong with me. I finally admitted that Sebastian Cabot and I had gotten knee-crawling drunk and been picked up by the MPs on our way to a whore house. Far from being amused, Gypsy further endeared herself by letting me know just how much she disapproved of such behavior.

Her increasing moodiness, exacerbated by confusing me with one of her stage hands, placed considerable strain on my poorly developed social skills. This was intensified by feelings of guilt for being with her while the section I was supposed to be leading was facing enemy fire over the DMZ. Particularly galling were the disdainful looks from combat veterans which labeled me a garrison officer enjoying the good life while others did the fighting. My response was a sullen silence broken only when necessary, and then with such cold politeness that she sarcastically dubbed me "The Prussian."

Though our relationship hovered a knife's edge from open hostility, it was fascinating to see how others responded to her. At the beginning of the tour, most of her audiences comprised troops my age or younger, few of whom knew her name. However, as word of her presence spread, those old enough to remember her as one of America's great sex symbols began to pack the open-air shows. She loved performing for her lusty, shouting fans but never shirked from visiting the wounded awaiting evacuation back to the States.

A week into the tour, we were in a ward reserved for senior NCOs. She went from bed to bed, greeting each soldier with a few light words until she reached one who must have been in his late forties. Badly wounded, he started to cry as soon as she touched him, whispering that he'd been in love with her since World War II. The feeling that we were intruding on something very personal saw everyone back away to give Gypsy and this scarred veteran their privacy. She stayed with him a long time, leaning close, stroking his hair. I couldn't hear what she said, but the look that came over his face said that a lifelong dream had come true.

What truly impressed me was how gentle and sincere Gypsy was when she met these long-standing fans who had been wounded. It was difficult for her, but I think she accepted that they had voluntarily chosen this path. Yet, while she was by turns warm, caring, and flirtatious with them, her entire persona changed when she visited wards filled with very young draftees with terrible injuries. She once said that every time she spoke with these boys all she could think was, "That could have been my son," and how grateful she was that he hadn't had to serve. There were times traveling from one hospital to the next when, if no one could see, she would weep quietly.

Passing through an amputee's ward one day, she heard a teenager snarl that she was "an old has-been trying to get publicity." Afterward, she said she understood his anger and might well have said the same thing if she'd been in his place. Regardless of the horror she saw, she maintained her composure, treating them all with a dignity untainted by pity. Only once, while talking to a youngster who'd just come out of surgery, did she almost break down. Most of this boy's face was gone, yet even in his pain he smiled as she spoke with him. When we emerged from the hospital, she suddenly turned and clung to me, sobbing heartbrokenly.

Dinner invitations from senior officers were a nightly affair. As might be expected, Gypsy always enjoyed the place of honor, whereas I was invariably placed well below the salt. One such dinner was hosted by a marine brigade commander whose beefy visage might have been the model for the U.S. Marine Corps' bulldog mascot. With his staff arranged at the table in descending order of rank, he regaled Gypsy with tales of fighting in World War II, Korea, and the success of his command in Vietnam. His quoting the brigade's "body count" of enemy dead, without a mention of the casualties his own young marines had suffered, saw her grow uncharacteristically quiet. Over coffee, he nodded to his adjutant, who stepped out of the dining room and returned with a present, which he proudly handed to her. When she had removed the camouflage wrapping, she was staring at a framed and autographed photo of our host.

Deadpan, she looked up as though to compare the image in her hands with the jowly, beaming face next to her. She mumbled her thanks and cleared her throat, the hint of a smile playing at the corners of her mouth. The smile spread and she tried to camouflage the first chuckle with a cough, but it slipped out. She checked it, made another comparison, and her shriek of laughter brought conversation at the table to a halt. It didn't stop, and the general cast bewildered looks at his staff. His quick-thinking aide stepped out of the room, reappeared almost immediately, and informed his boss that there was a "situation developing" and he was needed in the operations room "ASAP." Jaws like pebbles, the general growled his apologies and escaped through the open door as quickly as his short legs could carry him.

Another dinner had been arranged by a dozen army colonels, all so eager to sit as close to her as possible that they had fallen back on their respective dates of rank to determine who was more senior. When we arrived, the host's adjutant met us at the door. He greeted Gypsy with oily charm, then looked down his nose to inform me that if I wanted to eat I could do so in the kitchen "with the rest of the help." This was a young captain about my own age, who always wore clean fatigues, whose hot food was always hot, whose cold drinks were always cold, who slept between clean sheets in the comfort of an air-conditioned billet, and who was never shot at. My lips and fists tightened. Shocked by his rudeness, Gypsy turned at his comment, read my body language, and quickly put a hand on my forearm. She had probably just saved me from a court-martial. I gave her a blank look and told her to send for me when she was finished, then abruptly walked away.

As we were returning to the hotel, she asked me to stop by her room for a chat. Given our bristly relationship so far, I knew we were heading for a showdown. When I got to her room, she was taking off her makeup with cold cream and cotton. After a few minutes of small talk, Gypsy sat back and frowned. "Why the hell are you so hard to get along with?"

"I'm not hard to get along with, I just don't appreciate being ordered around like some baggage boy. You need to understand what I do, so let me explain. The bottom line is that almost every day I fly, I'm doing my best to kill someone who's trying his best to kill me. Given that kind of reality, being your transportation officer, bodyguard, and tagging along to ensure your every whim is gratified is very difficult for me. So if you're not satisfied with the way I'm handling it, then I suggest you ask for a new escort officer first thing tomorrow morning."

"Do you think I'm too demanding?"

"You are what made you successful in Hollywood."

"But this isn't Hollywood."

"Guess what? You're right!"

This stopped her, and she looked at me for a moment, before nodding slowly. "Have I been bitchy?"

"Goddamn right!"

Nobody talked to Gypsy like that, and I waited for the explosion. Which was fine by me. One eyebrow lifted. "Mind if I say something?"

"Help yourself."

"Well, if you'll admit you've been acting like a goddamned Prussian, I'll admit I've been a bitch. Then, if it's okay by you, I'd kind of like to kiss and make up," she smiled, leaning over to tug my ear and give me a peck on the cheek. It was, in part, Gypsy performing, but there was also an apology there, and my anger faded. There was no question that she could be difficult, but so could I. Just turned twenty-three years old, I didn't understand how close to the surface my nerves were from the stress of almost daily combat, nor how deeply affected I was by seeing scores of men my age and younger who'd been maimed for life. Nor did I comprehend how deeply distressed Gypsy was by the same thing. It simply hadn't occurred to me that her moods might be the result of that horror, and that I was the nearest person on whom she could vent her anger.

With a truce in place, we talked about her son and how relieved she was he didn't have to serve. She admitted how confused she was by briefings from senior officers which bore little resemblance to what she heard from the young men she met in the hospitals. I agreed, adding that one day America would realize that the officer corps in Vietnam represented the worst our country had ever seen.

"Then what keeps you going, Bill?"

"I guess because every time I do a good job, maybe more American soldiers will go home alive rather than in a casket."

She gave me a long, quizzical look, before bidding me good night. When I closed the door, I understood that our confrontation was over. From that moment on, I relished my time with her. Wherever we went there were still senior officers lining up to invite her to dinner, but each day saw her distancing herself from them and spending more and more time with the wounded.

With only a day remaining, she insisted I dine with her in her Tan Son Nhut VIP suite. That last evening, we spoke of the war, of my life before the army and my plans for the future, of her days in Hollywood and her reasons for coming to Vietnam. We talked and laughed and learned from each other, though her own wealth of experience and wisdom taught me far more than I could offer in return. That said, she honored me by listening quietly, commenting when comment was called for, and questioning when she didn't understand or wanted to know more. It was a pity, she said as we bid each other good night, that we hadn't become friends earlier, because there was so much to talk about.

The next morning, I picked her up at 0900 and accompanied her to the gate. We stood there for a long, awkward moment, neither of us ready to say good-bye. Finally she gave me a little hug and whispered, "Be safe." Hoping she was looking from her window seat, I waved good-bye as the 707 taxied out. I waited until it took off, straining to keep it in sight until it faded to a pinpoint and disappeared. By that night I was back in Phu Bai preparing for the next day's mission.

Two days later, Gypsy called my mother to let her know that her boy was safe.

When I got back to Phu Bai, the first news I heard was that Mac Byrd was missing in action. He'd been returning from a mission along the Laotian border when he was diverted to support a marine recon team. With North Vietnamese soldiers swarming throughout the area, the six-man team had been cut off and forced to take up a defensive position on a heavily forested hill west of Khe Sanh. It gave them excellent cover, but they were vastly outnumbered and low on ammunition. Mac was within a mile or two of them when he got the call. Already low on fuel, he refused to abandon them. He remained on station long enough to run two flights of air in the fading light, which allowed the team to break contact and escape. By now his fuel condition was critical and the weather had closed in. Mac advised Dong Ha DASC that he didn't think he had the fuel to make it over the mountains. Letting down through the clouds to find a place to land, he must have hit a mountain. Despite a desperate search by the bulk of the 220th's pilots, no trace of his aircraft was ever found.

Jack Bentley: I was Mac Byrd's replacement in the 1st Platoon, something that didn't please everyone because of my inexperience, but Finch had recommended me, and I was determined to prove myself. My first time over the DMZ was on a three-ship mission with him and Hooper. I didn't have a clue what was going on at that time but decided that these two guys had enough knowledge to keep me alive.

Charles, Bill, Sarge, and Len Bumgardner became my professors. Sarge was like a mother hen and made his expertise readily available, as did Len. Finch, Bill, and Doc were much harder to get close to. If I had to rank the three of them, Finch was easiest, Bill second, and "The Doctor" third. Finch was a bullshitter, but he knew what he was doing. There was no bullshit from Bill. You had to prove yourself with him, but he'd readily give his advice if asked.

Doc was the most difficult. I had spent my high school years in a car club whose members thought Saturday night was for fighting. I knew I could whip Finch, was certain I could give Bill a run for his money, but I just didn't want to fuck with Doc. Barrel-chested and with arms as big as my thighs, he moved like a pro football player and could be very intimidating. I swear if my wife said today that Doc Clement was on the phone, I would pick it up and timidly say, "Hello?"

DOC READ THROUGH HIS MISSION ORDERS. A marine helicopter assault was going in near Con Thien that morning, and his first job was to register artillery on their landing zone. As part of his pre-mission preparation, he called the DASC bunker and spoke to the duty officer, Capt. Tom Jones. Doc explained that he would spend the first half an hour zeroing the guns, after which he wanted air support on station. Jones assured Doc that he would tend to it himself. Satisfied that everything was ready, he and Corky—call sign Klondike Sierra—climbed into his Bird Dog and lifted off from Dong Ha for the fifteen-minute flight.

Arriving over the LZ—a flat, almost treeless area pocked with old bomb craters and bordered by a ridgeline to the north—they quickly identified a complex of enemy bunkers. Trails leading to the entrances indicated recent use, and Corky used them to register the artillery. Thirty minutes later, Doc's requested air, a pair of F-4s with 500-pound snakes, arrived overhead. Corky shut down the arty. As soon as the last round impacted, Doc sent a rocket down as a mark for the Phantoms. Dash 1 and Dash 2 were right on target with their first runs, and Doc came around again to mark a second complex of bunkers for the rest of their bombs. Smoke and dust from the last of the explosions were still drifting across the terrain as the F-4s headed home, pleased with the bomb-damage assessment the little Bird Dog had given them.

Still holding an orbit over the LZ, Doc checked the sky. The day had started clear, but now clouds were forming as the ground heated and thermals carried the humid air aloft. The bottoms of the clouds were starting to consolidate at around 2,500 feet, and Doc knew they would settle lower as the day progressed, which meant that the grunts would probably lose their air support by early afternoon. Corky received the call they had been waiting for.

"Klondike Sierra," radioed the leader of four marine CH-46 helicopters inbound with the first wave of marine infantry, "this is Chatterbox 1-1. Over."

As Corky was briefing Chatterbox, Doc got a call from the next flight of air. "Catkiller 1-8, this is Lovebug 312."

"Lovebug 312, this 1-8. Go." The two F-4 Phantoms reported their weapons load and position. Doc acknowledged, giving them his position and a weather report. "Roger, Catkiller, understand 350 from Channel 109 at twelve nautical miles, cloud bottoms at 2500."

Lovebug arrived overhead just as the choppers were circling for their first drops. Doc kept the F-4s just below the clouds in an east-west pattern over the landing zone while the twin-rotor CH-46s descended. As soon as their wheels touched, marines spilled off the tailgates. The first Chatterbox flight lifted off and the second, Chatterbox 1-5, came in right behind him. More men hit the ground and were fanning out when mortar shells started detonating among the still-disembarking troops. Corky was trying to break into the excited radio traffic, and Doc was searching for the source of the fire, when Chatterbox 1-5 exploded and rolled on its side. Rotors still spinning, the blades dug into the ground, shattering into lethal shrapnel until the engines stopped and the helicopter came to a rest. A cloud of dust hung over it. Chatterbox 1-3 was ordering his flight to pull pitch and get out when Doc saw a puff of smoke from a mortar tube. He switched to Lovebug's push.

"Lovebug 312, this is Catkiller 1-8. Our target is three hundred meters north of the downed helicopter. Let's set up a run-in heading of 280 with a left-hand pull."

"Roger, Catkiller, 280 with a left break, awaiting your mark. You copy Dash 2?"

"Dash 2 copies."

"Catkiller, Dash 1 is on downwind."

"Roger, Dash 1, I am going in for my mark." Doc reached up to flip the arming switch on the third rocket and nosed over in the direction of the mortar. He squeezed the trigger, and the white phosphorus warhead exploded just west of the pit.

"Dash 1 is turning final, I have your smoke."

"Roger, Dash 1. From my mark let's go fifty meters at six o'clock with two napes. I have you, you are cleared hot." Doc watched the F-4 as it released and climbed away. The napes exploded wide of the pit.

"Dash 2, from Dash 1's hit let's go twenty meters at nine o'clock with two napes."

"Roger, Catkiller, Dash 2 on base at this time."

"Roger, Dash 2, I have you in sight." Doc saw muzzle flashes from small arms in the tree line. He turned toward the mortar pit and saw the NVA crew dropping mortar shells down the tube as fast as they could. A glance to the right showed Dash 2 coming down the pipe and looking good. He cleared him hot and saw the teardrop canisters hit thirty meters short, the napalm surging across the ground, over the lip of the pit and beyond. Mortar shells began exploding off in the flames.

"Beautiful, Dash 2, great hit! Dash 1, from Dash 2's hit, let's go seventy-five meters at eleven o'clock with your last napes." That next run set the tree line alight. Doc circled over the blackened mortar and three charred bodies. He ran the two Phantoms on where he suspected more of the enemy might be. With nothing left to drop, Lovebug made a last call.

"Catkiller, Lovebug is Winchester. Be advised we are down to a two-thousand-foot ceiling now and it looks like it's dropping fast. You may not have much longer to run fixed wing." It was not what Doc wanted to hear.

Chatterbox 1-5 was again settling into the LZ, this time to pick up the wounded. Behind him, another four CH-46s were on short final. Suddenly, more mortar shells shrieked out of the sky. Corky was calling for artillery as Doc turned west and hit his mike button. "Dong Ha DASC, this is Catkiller 1-8, do you have any air in the area? Anything. Over."

"Roger, Catkiller 1-8, Seaworthy 4-4 is inbound your position and he is up this push. Over."

Gunships.

"Roger, DASC. Break, break. Seaworthy 4-4, this is Catkiller 1-8. Over."

"Catkiller 1-8, Seaworthy 4-4."

"Okay, Seaworthy 4-4, we have mortar fire coming from just to the northwest of Alpha 3. How soon will you be on station?" The helicopter gunships were still ten minutes out, which could be all the time left for some of the grunts on the ground. The Bird Dog was over the still-smoking first target when Corky spotted the flash and smoke from another mortar tube 150 meters to the south. He called for more artillery. Doc broke away to watch the 155mm shells exploding just as Seaworthy reported in again, closer now.

"Corky, shut down the arty, I'm putting a Willie Pete in!" He lined up at a thousand feet and pushed the nose down. At five hundred feet Doc's eyes went wide as a .51-cal opened up on them, its big tracers flashing past the Bird Dog. He punched off his last rocket, pulled hard left, and dove for the trees. As Doc leveled out he felt the engine beginning to lose power.

"Catkiller 1-8, Seaworthy 4-4 is over the LZ."

"Roger, 4-4, I have you. Come west of the LZ about three hundred meters and you should see my white smoke coming up." Seaworthy rogered. "OK, 4-4, we have a mortar firing on the LZ and we are firing artillery on that position and a .51-cal position about fifty meters due south of it. Over."

Seaworthy advised that they would come in from the north to line up both targets on the same pass. As soon as Corky shut down the artillery, the Hueys rolled in, line astern. The heavy machine gun swung toward them, and orange tracers reached toward Dash 1, who loosed a swarm of HE rockets directly into them. He pulled off and Dash 2, flying into more tracers, sent his rockets toward the machine gun pit before announcing he was hit and breaking off. Too badly damaged to make it to Dong Ha, he descended into the LZ to land near the destroyed CH-46. Before he'd touched down, Dash 3 came in, rockets rippling from his pods, and wolfed it around to follow Dash 1 for another run. Circling out of their way, Doc watched the lead Huey salvo his remaining rockets into the .51 position. Right behind him, Dash 3 thudded through the lighter ground fire once more to blanket the mortar pit with the last of his ordnance. Guns and pods empty, they formed up and headed back to base.

Three hours into the mission, Doc was low on fuel, and the engine was running rougher and rougher from fouled plugs. They had killed two mortar pits and a heavy machine gun, and it was time to head home. He was on final approach to Dong Ha when he heard the marines reporting more mortar fire. *Dammit!*

He shut down next to the fuel bladder, and he and Corky sprinted to another Bird Dog and were airborne again, leaving their M16s behind in the rush. Back over the battlefield, Doc spotted the third mortar position on a small knoll west of the grunts. When he called for air support, DASC said nothing was available. Corky was talking to the artillery, but it would need a direct hit to knock out the pit, and that could take a long time to talk in. Meanwhile, mortar shells were still exploding across the LZ, and the marines were taking casualties.

Corky's voice came through Doc's earphones. "Doc, I got six CS grenades back here! Let's see if we can get one in the pit!" It was a desperate measure to save the marines.

Doc cut power, leveled out above the trees, and passed over the pit at fifty feet. Corky's first tear gas grenade went wide. He came around again, this time from the west.

Doc Clement: The secret to staying alive on this trick was hanging right on the treetops till the last possible moment so the bad guys couldn't see us coming. Corky was leaning out of the window, a grenade in each hand as I turned in. A treetop rose above the scrub just ahead. I threw the Bird Dog hard left to avoid the tree, then kicked it back right, thinking we had probably lost our heading. But as we broke out over the edge of the tree line, there was the mortar directly below us. Corky opened his hands and the grenades whistled directly into the pit.

I pushed the throttle to the stop and headed for the trees on the other side of the clearing. The NVA only had time for a couple of wild shots in our direction before we were gone from their horizon. We scraped the trees until a safe distance away, then climbed and circled back. The NVA crew had abandoned the weapon and a squad of marines was maneuvering toward it. I don't know to this day if it was the gas that ran the crew off, or if they thought those were explosive grenades and bailed out.

About then, another Catkiller arrived to relieve us. I brought him up to speed on the situation, and then clicked the intercom to Corky. "You ready to go home?"

"Bet your ass!"*

---

*On the recommendation of the marine battalion commander, Clement was awarded his second Distinguished Flying Cross.

Chapter 13

Night Contact

I ran one of the few night air strikes a few miles south of Dong Ha, to extract a marine recon team that was in heavy contact. I had already run air and shot artillery that afternoon to get the same team extracted only to have their CO send them right back to the same spot, telling them not to come back without a POW. Needless to say, they found themselves in heavy contact again, only this time it was dark. Basketball 214, a marine C-130, was dropping flares while I ran several flights of air on the bad guys. The team didn't get extracted but was able to break off the contact. They later acknowledged our help and gave us a big thank-you. That was probably one of my most satisfying moments, when I could see that I had helped some of our guys.

—Grayson Davis, Catkiller 45/3

BILL HOOPER: ABOUT TWO HOURS AFTER SUNDOWN I was reading in the transient overnight tent at Dong Ha when the charge of quarters NCO stuck his head in. "Captain, there's an emergency landline for you." Puzzled that anyone would call us at this time of night, I pulled on my jungle boots and followed him to the line shack. I sat on the picnic table and lifted the telephone.

"This is Captain Hooper."

The marine operations officer on the other end didn't hesitate. One of their companies had collided with a large enemy force in the foothills about ten miles south-southwest of Dong Ha. On unfamiliar ground and unable to maneuver in the dark without the risk of being split up, they were calling for immediate air support. I jotted down the grid references, which he admitted were approximate, and the call sign and frequency of the company's tactical net and ran back to the tent to get my gear. By the time I was dressed, the crew chief had rolled my Bird Dog out of its revetment, and we gave it a quick preflight. I asked him to hold a flashlight over my tactical map while I plotted the position and drew a line between it and Dong Ha. What got my immediate attention were the three-thousand-foot mountains just a couple of minutes' flying time to their west. They ran roughly northwest-southeast, which meant that my course and theirs would rapidly converge the closer I got to the marines; the problem was that, to give myself the best chance of finding the battle, I'd have to be below one thousand feet.

Climbing into the cockpit, I knew this was going to be a challenging mission. The only lights available to orientate myself were those marking the runway. Once I took off, there would be no visual references anywhere, not even the stars, which were blocked by a solid overcast at about four thousand feet. Aside from a magnetic compass, the only navigational aid in the Bird Dog was an ADF, which was of questionable reliability due to signal reflection from the mountains. Nor could I count on Waterboy, the radar site at Phu Bai, to provide a safe vector. A combination of the same signal reflection, the small size of a Bird Dog, and my low altitude made radar undependable. I would have to rely on dead reckoning—course, airspeed, and elapsed time—to find my way there. And if I made an error in navigation, I'd never see the mountain I ran into.

I lifted off just before 2100 hours and contacted Dong Ha DASC to scramble two flights with snake and nape, then leveled off at about eight hundred feet and concentrated on tracking outbound from Channel 109. I keyed the mike and made my first call to Hammer 3-4 on the FM radio. The only sound in my earphones was static. I waited a few minutes before trying again. More static. Nighttime atmospherics and the mountains were undoubtedly interfering with my transmission. With the map case open on my lap, I examined the chart under the red map light. My course looked correct, but I had been outbound for six or seven minutes by now, and at 85 knots, I should have been a little more than halfway there. I called again.

"Hammer 3-4, Hammer 3-4, this is Catkiller 1-2, an O-1 Bird Dog. Do you copy? Over."

"Catkiller 1-2! This is Hammer 3-4! I have you Lima Charlie! How me? Over!" The noise that accompanied that transmission reaffirmed my preference for flying. The roar of AK-47 and M16 assault rifles, M60 machine guns, and outgoing and incoming mortar shells filled the background. Men screamed instructions and obscenities. *Fire right! Fire right!*

"Hammer 3-4, this is Catkiller 1-2. I have you Lima Charlie. Be advised, I am approaching you from the northeast. Do you have me in sight? Over." I was counting on them spotting the rotating anti-collision light on the Bird Dog's belly.

"Negative!" Behind the hard, staccato crackles of automatic weapons there was the shout of "Ammo! I need fucking ammo!" "Negative, Catkiller! I do not have you! Over!"

"Roger, Hammer. Stand by."

I glanced at my watch: twelve minutes since liftoff. Christ, I should be there, or real close. I checked my outbound track again. Plenty worried about those mountains and unsure if the upper winds might be pushing me toward them, I had made a couple of cautious easterly course corrections. I opened my right window and strained to see something in the black. Having flown over these foothills on many daytime missions, I knew they were covered with thick bush and tall trees, but nothing was visible. I also knew that if I flew another five minutes—unless they were way off—I would have overflown them and would have to turn around and try again. And somewhere just ahead was a solid barrier rising two thousand feet above me.

"Catkiller, Catkiller!" He was almost screaming to be overheard above the battle. "This is Hammer 3-4! We do not see you! We are turning on a red light, a red light!"

"Stand by, Hammer. Negative on the light!" I knew that as soon as they turned it on to give me a beacon, they'd make themselves an even better target for the enemy. I had to give them something to look for. From my outboard left wing a white beam stabbed into the night. "Hammer, this is Catkiller 1-2. I have my landing light on. Do you have a visual? Over."

"Roger, roger, Catkiller!" *Corpsman! Get the corpsman up here!* "We have you in sight! You are directly to our east! Maybe one-half mile! Over!"

Airborne dust particles illuminated by the bright beam were distracting. I flipped it off and turned a little nervously to the west. It was impossible not to think about those mountains.

"Catkiller, this is Hammer! We have lost you, we have lost you!"

"Roger, Hammer." I hit the switch again. "I have my landing light on."

"Roger, Catkiller, we have you in sight! We're a few degrees to your right! A few degrees to your right, and you're almost over us!" I looked down. Without telling me, they'd turned on the red light, and I banked hard to keep it in sight. The command element must have been in a small clearing, because I could see it during most of my orbit.

"Roger, Hammer, I have your position. Over." Five hundred feet above the target, I was surprised at how little light from the muzzle flashes and the mortar explosions penetrated the vegetation in front and to either side of Hammer 3-4. But there was enough to hold my position, and I turned off the landing light. This was as difficult a situation as I'd ever faced with troops in contact. Even more worrisome than the proximity of mountains was the possibility of casualties inflicted by friendly fire. The slightest error on the part of anyone involved—be it the grunts on the ground, me, or the fast movers—could have tragic results. I had to be absolutely sure of their location. "Hammer, Hammer, this is Catkiller. Give me the position of your lines relative to your beacon. Over."

"Catkiller, we are on a line approximately northeast to southwest, northeast to southwest! Our front faces the northwest! Over!"

"Roger, Hammer. Stand by."

Dong Ha DASC had confirmed a few minutes earlier that the first flight of A-4s was wheels-up out of Chu Lai and would be over my position pretty quickly. Waiting for their arrival, I tried to figure out how I was going to run them when my only point of reference was a faint red light in the middle of nowhere. If it were daytime, I'd have the fast-movers set up a rectangular holding pattern northwest of the target and bring them in parallel with the line of contact. That way they would not fly over our guys on the ground. But at night those mountains made that impossible—the A-4 pilots wouldn't be able to see them any better than I could. There was only one other option, an orbit to the northeast side that partially straddled the line of contact. This meant giving the pilots the more difficult and potentially dangerous task of making their crosswind and base legs over friendly positions, which violated one of the cardinal rules of close air support. But I couldn't see any other way. An equally critical factor was the elevation of the terrain below them. Their altimeters were set at Chu Lai, which was just a little above sea level. The terrain here was notably higher. Misjudging their altitude above the ground by as little as one hundred feet could be fatal when making target runs in total blackness. Looking at the map again, I narrowed my location as close as possible and counted the contour lines. Then the UHF radio was talking and it was game time.

"Catkiller 1-2, this is Hellborne 252, flight of two Alpha-4s with eight Delta-2-Alphas and two Delta-9s onboard and twenty-five minutes play time. Over."

Given what I'd been hearing on Hammer's net, Hellborne's calm, professional voice seemed out of place. "Roger, 252, this is Catkiller 1-2. I'm an O-1 Bird Dog orbiting at eight hundred indicated on the 220 radial out of channel 109 at thirteen nautical miles. Over."

"Roger, Catkiller. We are at angels one and a half. We do not have you in sight. We should be within two miles of you. Over." I hit the landing light switch again and told Hellborne that I was in a left-hand turn over the target. "We have you in sight, Catkiller. Please advise target. Over."

"Roger, Hellborne. We have troops in contact. Line of engagement runs northeast-southwest. Terrain is approximately 320 feet. Look for a red beacon, a red beacon. That is the friendlies. We have three-thousand-foot mountains a mile and a half to two miles west of the target. Please set up a left-hand pattern with your crosswind leg breaking to the east. Dash 1, you need to make a dry pass, I say again, you need to make a dry pass over my position on a heading of 210 degrees. Over."

"Roger, Catkiller. Dry pass on a two-one-zero with a left break. Dash 2, you copy?"

"Dash 2 copies."

This guy knew what he was doing and had already turned to the northeast to give himself plenty of room to come in on the proper heading. I was holding tight over the target as he passed two hundred feet below me to get a fix on the beacon. As the second Skyhawk maneuvered for his dry run, I advised Hammer 3-4 that we'd come in with nape first, dropping seventy-five meters west of his position.

"Catkiller, this is Hammer! That's too far! Too far! We've got them thirty to forty meters to our front! Bring it in closer!"

Closer? At night? Okay, they were the men on the ground. They knew the situation. But if seventy-five meters was too far, then thirty meters was way too close under these conditions. Did I risk their lives by splitting the difference? Marine aviators were the best in the world at this business, but the decision on where Hellborne put his first nape—and the responsibility for its aftermath—would be mine alone. Dash 2 passed beneath me on his dry run, and I turned off the landing light, relying on my anti-collision lights to keep the A-4s oriented to me and the target. I had a solid fix on the beacon and knew it was the one thing I couldn't lose.

"Dash 1, this is Catkiller. Be advised: on your run-in heading, your target, three o'clock"—I took a deep breath—"five-zero meters. I say again: three o'clock at five-zero meters from the beacon. Nape first, nape first. Over."

"Roger, Catkiller, Dash 1 turning base. Target from the beacon three o'clock, five-zero meters, nape first." The Skyhawk pilot had no room for error. It was a difficult enough job during the day; at night, the pressure on him would be at the top of the scale. He had to keep his eye on that small red beacon to make sure he was far enough to the right of it that his ordnance killed the enemy and not Americans. At the same time, he'd be monitoring his instruments—air speed, artificial horizon, rate of descent, and altitude. In a shallow dive at 350 knots—covering more than six miles a minute—he had to calculate where to release the Delta-9, at which point he'd have less than three seconds to recover; any hesitation would put him and his A-4 into the ground. And always in the back of his mind were those invisible mountains.

Twenty seconds from engagement the marine aviator broke the tension by muttering into his mike, "It's times like these that make me wish

I'd gone into the hardware business with my old man." Waiting anxiously in my dimly lit cockpit, I couldn't help laughing aloud as somewhere out there in the dark he was setting up his approach.

"Catkiller, Dash 1 turning final."

I was already on a reciprocal course, heading toward the light on the ground. "Roger, Dash 1. Tell me when you see the red beacon."

"Catkiller, I have the beacon."

Peering through my windscreen, I could make out the green and red wingtip lights coming toward me just to my left. "Dash 1, I have you, you're looking good,"—the moment of truth—"you're cleared hot." As he went under my left wing, all I could see were those nav lights and the dorsal anti-collision light. The lights begin to climb, and then the napalm impacted behind him, illuminating his departure with red-orange flame surging through the trees. The aviator with a dad in the hardware business announced he was clear and climbing through one thousand feet. I held my breath. The next two seconds seemed an eternity.

"Catkiller, this is Hammer! Good hit! Good hit! We need the next one to our right! Over!"

I started breathing again. So far, so good, everyone was okay. Dash 2 radioed that he was turning base. I had completed a 360 to the left and was again on a reverse bearing of thirty degrees. With the napalm and burning trees, there was neither lack of light nor any question about the location of the target.

"Dash 2, this Catkiller. From Dash 1's impact: six o'clock, one hundred meters. I say again: six o'clock, one hundred meters. Over."

"Roger, Catkiller, six o'clock, one hundred meters. Dash 2 on final."

"Roger, Dash 2, you are cleared hot."

When he passed under me, the stubby A-4 was suddenly silhouetted against the fire and just as suddenly disappeared again. Behind him another gush of flame erupted, and two brightly burning magnesium igniters came out of it to score diverging arcs over the ground. An ecstatic Hammer came up on the FM to say the nape had landed right where it was needed. Two more runs left walls of flame west of his company's line. Outboard racks bare of napalm canisters, bombs were next.

"Hammer, this is Catkiller. We're coming in with the snakes. How much cover do you have? Over."

"Catkiller, we have plenty of cover! Give us one hundred meters! Over!"

"Roger, Hammer. Stand by." Back to Hellborne on the UHF radio. "Dash 1, Dash 1, this is Catkiller. From your original impact, three o'clock, fifty meters, with all your snakes. Over."

"Roger, Catkiller, three o'clock, five-zero meters. Dash 1 is in hot."

Each Skyhawk pilot strung out his 500-pounds bombs about 120 meters outside their original contact line. At that point the second Hellborne flight reported in. The surviving North Vietnamese had already disengaged, and I used the new arrivals to saturate the area out to about five hundred meters to inflict as many casualties as possible as they withdrew. The second flight broke off to return to Chu Lai, and I stayed over Hammer until he released me with a heartfelt thanks. Two hours after taking the call, I returned to Dong Ha and collapsed into my dusty cot. Before falling asleep, I reran the action in my mind, analyzing each decision and looking for where I might have made a better one. This was the job I was being paid to do. I loved it.

With our area of operations reduced after the bombing halt, we began including the extreme western end of the DMZ in our patrols. Unmarred by the bomb craters that defined the eastern part of the DMZ, it was easily the most beautiful and dramatic terrain I saw in Vietnam, with knife edged ridges thrusting out of deep, jungled valleys cut by clear, fast-flowing rivers. Where vegetation could find a home on the sheer walls, it gave the impression of baskets of orchids and ferns clinging to rock faces that plunged far into double and triple canopy rain forest.

If we had been shown an old map with the notation "Here be dragons," we would not have been surprised. It was so wild and pristine that we logically assumed it must be honeycombed with well camouflaged NVA logistics and infiltration routes. In fact, of the seventy-eight thousand enemy troops believed to be in the area of I Corps, intelligence reports placed a large percentage of them here.

Some of us also surmised that its very remoteness made it perfect for North Vietnamese Army supply depots, hospitals, and R&R camps (if they had such things). Once, when following a mountain stream tumbling out of Laos, I surprised four NVA soldiers swimming in a deep pool. By the time I came around again, they'd disappeared into the jungle. They were in there, all right, but no one knew exactly where or how many.

Another day, another mission, I was droning over this astonishing topography, when a voice from Dong Ha DASC alerted me that a Chatterbox CH-46 had been hit by ground fire and forced to auto-rotate into a small mountain meadow a few miles way. Rescue helicopters were already en route, and I was diverted to provide air cover. I was over them less than ten minutes later. Two UH-34s had already landed with a reaction force, while a second CH-46 was settling into the meadow. Just large enough for the helicopters, the LZ was surrounded on three sides by almost vertical walls climbing to over a thousand feet and capped with thick vegetation. The forth side rose some seven hundred feet to a razorback ridge that sprouted a few gnarled trees. When I established radio contact with the marines, they advised that the damage could be repaired in less than an hour and asked me to remain overhead for the duration. I settled into a lazy orbit along the three more densely covered areas, looking for signs of the enemy.

Half an hour later the marines radioed that they'd spotted movement at the top of the razorback. I made a tight 180 degree turn and followed the edge of the bowl back toward the reported position, descending until I was level with the top of the narrow ridge. As it filled my ten o'clock, I suddenly saw the back of someone. Dressed in black and carrying no webbing, he was partially obscured by branches and sitting with his shoulder against a tree.

I applied power and brought the nose up to protect me if he opened fire. As I passed over the position I looked straight down and grinned widely. At least four feet tall, the biggest monkey I'd ever seen was squatting with elbows on knees like a sports fan watching the game far below him. He glanced up at me unconcernedly, then returned his gaze to the activity in the meadow. I continued to the other side of the bowl, but each time I looked toward the razorback I could see him still engrossed with the marines and their helicopters. The last chopper was lifting off when I made one more pass over my friend. With the show now over, he stirred, stretched, and ambled slowly away.

* * *

One of the recurring stories in the *Stars & Stripes* was the deployment of the USS *New Jersey*. It seemed that hardly a week went by without a few more column inches appearing about the refurbished World War II battleship. There was no denying it was an impressive fighting machine. For connoisseurs of firepower, her armament was mind-boggling. Just for close-in defense, the *New Jersey* bristled with 130 20mm and 40mm antiaircraft weapons. If tasked with short- and medium-range bombardments, she relied on twenty 5-inch guns that were bigger than the 105mm howitzers we often used in support of ground troops. But the most awesome examples of naval artillery were her nine 16-inch guns. Utilizing the latest computer technology for pinpoint accuracy, they fired a shell weighing more than a ton at incredible distances. As one of her gunnery officers was quoted in the *Stars & Stripes*: "We can hit a moving car at over twenty miles."

Finch was the only Catkiller pilot who had fired her, and I was fed up listening to him talk about it. And I was even more fed up hearing about the two days he and Bounds had spent on her, ogling Ann-Margret and the luscious Golddiggers. When he started with the *New Jersey*-this and the *New Jersey*-that, some of us wanted to strangle him, even if secretly we were green with envy.

It was a quiet day as I turned over the beach near the mouth of the Ben Hai River. Head swivelling from one side to the other in my eagerness to find a target, I spotted some old bunkers that looked like they might be under repair. "Not worth the effort," I thought, when Hillsboro contacted me to say that Onrush was requesting a fire mission. Onrush? Then I remembered it was the call sign for the *New Jersey*. Great! I twisted in my seat until I spotted her about fifteen miles to my southeast. She really was a magnificent sight, nine hundred feet and forty-five thousand tons of steel dragging a foaming wake across the South China Sea. If she could hit a moving car twenty miles way, then a stationary bunker at this range would be a dead cinch. I took a quick look at my list of frequencies and switched to her push.

"Onrush, Onrush, this is Catkiller 1-2. Fire mission. Over." The fire control officer rogered my call and I provided a target description and eight-figure grid reference. He acknowledged and told me to stand by. Remembering Finch's descriptions, I could visualize the data was fed into the computer in the ship's super-sophisticated fire-control center.

"Catkiller 1-2, this is Onrush. Shot. Over." Even from this distance, the muzzle blast of a 16-inch gun was something to see. "Catkiller 1-2, this is Onrush. Ten seconds to splash." The navy terminologies of shot and splash seemed a little exotic.

"Roger, Onrush." Not only did they know the shell's exact flight time, there wasn't going to be any of this business of giving one-hundred meter adjustments to an army battery in order to get the rounds on target. Hell, sometimes a first round from a 155mm or 175mm gun might be as much as two hundred or three hundred meters off target. But this was modern warfare.

"Five seconds."

I stared at the target, counting down the seconds . . . and . . . now! But there was no satisfying ball of fire, earth, and smoke. Hell, I must have counted too fast. I waited confidently, counting up, but the target sat there undisturbed. A dreadful possibility crossed my mind. Oh shit, I've given them the wrong coordinates. A bit worried, I rechecked them. Yep, they were the right ones. Even if the shell had been a dud, a ton of steel slamming into the ground at supersonic speed would have raised a hell of a geyser. But a dud had to be the only explanation.

"Onrush, this is Catkiller 1-2. Over."

"Roger, Catkiller." The coolest, smuggest army pilot in the world could have taken lessons from this guy.

"Onrush, this is Catkiller. Lost round. Over"

"Say again, Catkiller?" The tone was not only disbelieving, but somehow managed to imply that I was at fault. God, maybe I had screwed up somehow.

"Roger, Onrush, this is Catkiller 1-2. I say again: lost round. I suspect you had a dud. Repeat. Over."

"Roger, Catkiller. Repeat. Wait." The muzzle blast from the next round completely hid the turret. "Catkiller 1-2, this is Onrush. Shot. Over."

I acknowledged and watched the bunker. Onrush advised ten seconds to splash, and then five seconds. The five seconds passed and I scanned north, east, and west of the target, before kicking right rudder to the south. Nearly three miles away, a cloud of debris was rising alongside the Ben Hai River. This was not what I'd expected from reading the *Stars & Stripes*. "Onrush, I have splash. Stand by."

"Roger, Catkiller."

I ran my finger carefully along the north-south and east-west grid lines on my map to check the coordinates again. I looked at the figures I'd given to the *New Jersey*'s fire-control center. The same. I'd never heard of anyone having to give adjustments on this scale before. I closed one eye and calculated a bagful of Kentucky windage.

"Onrush, this is Catkiller 1-2. From the gun target line: right two kilometers, add eight kilometers. Over."

There was a tiny pause. Then, incredulously, "Say again, Catkiller?"

Feeling better now, I tried to keep the grin out of my voice. "Roger, Onrush. Right two kilometers, add eight kilometers. Over."

The fire control officer seemed to be suffering a major sense of humor failure. He tersely read back the original coordinates. I confirmed them cheerfully. He rogered, but I could tell that his cool was fraying at the edges. "Catkiller 1-2. Shot. Over."

"Roger, Onrush. Shot. Wait."

A little nervously: "Ten seconds to splash . . . five." My very rough corrections were better than I'd hoped, the third shot raising an enormous flash and cloud of earth less than six hundred meters from the target. The next shot brought him within seventy-five meters, after which I directed him to fire for effect. Two 16-inch guns opened up with a total of six shells. When the smoke and dust settled, the bunker complex no longer existed.

A couple of weeks later, I opened the latest edition of the *Stars & Stripes.* My attention was drawn to a story about the USS *New Jersey*. According to the article, she had attacked a major bunker complex a few kilometers south of the DMZ. Aside from the location, the balance of the piece was utterly fanciful. "We can hit a moving car at twenty miles," the fire control officer was quoted yet again.

"Did you read this latest shit about the good ol' *New Jersey?*" I asked Finch.

Charlie picked up the paper and read intently. He looked over at me. "So?"

"If the NVA read that, they'll be laughing their asses off."

"Of course they read it, Hooper, and that was the problem. Don't you know you never give the enemy information that can be useful to them? Soon as they learned the *New Jersey* could hit a moving car twenty miles away, the little bastards cheated."

"What do you mean 'cheated'? How the hell did they cheat?"

"Easy. They just made sure that bunker didn't move an inch."

Chapter 14

Taking the Edge Off

CHARLES FINCH: AFTER MY LAST MISSION OF the day, I refueled and taxied back to the flight line. When I finished my debriefing report, the crew chief asked me to take another ship back to Phu Bai. The weather was worsening, so I jumped in and took off, assuming the tanks were full. On the way I decided to go under my favorite three bridges. On the second one near Quang Tri, I ducked down late to get as much airspeed as possible for a good pull up. Coming out the other side, I brought the stick back and began a steep climb. Just then the engine sputtered and quit. I immediately pushed the nose down and switched tanks, but the engine did not catch, and I turned for shore and the only road I could see. It finally roared to life, but I was a lot lower than I wanted to be.

Doc Clement: I spotted a VC running down a trail. I was scraping treetops chasing him and didn't see a leafless tree taller than the rest. *Wham!*—and suddenly we were heading in another direction. I looked out at the right wing, and there was a V-shaped dent all the way back to the spar. As I got us straightened up, the ARVN observer in back was going crazy, screaming in Vietnamese and English to land on the nearest road. I got him settled down and radioed John Kovach, who was the maintenance officer by then. He was waiting at Phu Bai when I landed and taxied straight into the hangar. He had the crumpled section of skin cut off and wrote it up as a bird strike before the Old Man got there.

Ed Miler: At battalion headquarters Lieutenant Colonel Mullen told me that he was less than impressed by some of the Catkillers' habits, such as flying under bridges or lower than required by the mission. On my return to Phu Bai, I dutifully passed on those concerns to my intrepid young airmen. It wasn't two weeks later, on an unannounced visit to Dong Ha, when I came up behind a couple of pilots examining a Bird Dog and heard Capt. Roger Bounds say, "I sure hope that the Old Man doesn't find out about this." "Find out about what, Roger?" I asked. Bounds whipped around and turned as green as the leafy tree branches wrapped around the left landing gear.

Bill Hooper: Major Miler issued an ultimatum. Pilots were easy to replace, he pointed out, but Bird Dogs were long out of production and thus scarce. He knew that we were using the same low-level routes again and again. If the bad guys were around, he explained like a coach to a bunch of scratching and farting college football players, a Bird Dog flying low-level at eighty-five knots would not be a difficult target. He took the time to be explicitly clear. Henceforth, disciplinary action for any pilot caught low-leveling could well include a court-martial.

"Gentlemen, understand this. I'm giving each and every one of you a direct order to fly above minimums." He looked straight at me. "Captain Hooper, do you have any question about the intent of my orders?"

"Oh, no, sir. I'm quite clear on them. Thank you."

There were a few titters in the room. I slumped a little lower in my chair and wondered why I had been singled out. Okay, so maybe Wisby had gotten me on the rata-tat-tat stuff with the marine helicopters a few weeks before Miler took over, and okay, yeah, I'd been seen low-leveling back to Phu Bai a couple of times, but I wasn't the only one. Finch, with all his flying under bridges, was even worse at breaking the rules. It didn't seem quite fair.

For all the bluster and "it-doesn't-faze-me" façade we put up to hide it, facing multiple antiaircraft weapons on an almost daily basis took a psychological toll on all of us. Though we probably weren't aware of it, it was a poison that had to be drawn out. Heavy drinking in the club allowed us to forget and escape it for a few hours. Another antidote was low-level contour flying, the game being to see how close we could get to the ground and what grew out of it without hitting either. It demanded every bit of our flying skill, often frightening us so badly that the terror of those guns was momentarily neutralized. That it was against regulations added to its allure, of course, and checking our landing gear for incriminating leaves or grass prior to taxiing up to the revetment was a crucial part of our post-touchdown checklist.

Testing one's skills is an evolutionary process. Once we had the basics of low-level flying, there were additional games they could be applied to—such as sneaking up on the tower at Dong Ha. The rules were simple: how close could we get to the runway before the air traffic controller spotted us? Built on a low hill that gradually rose to about one hundred feet above the surrounding terrain, it was sliced along its flanks by some deep gullies. My favorite gully started just outside the runway's perimeter road and dropped away to meet the Dong Ha–Khe Sanh road at almost a right angle. It was wide enough and deep enough to hide us completely, and by getting right down on the gravel road, we were out of the tower's line of sight for the final two miles. Dedicated cheaters, we wouldn't make our call until we were already behind cover.

"Dong Ha Tower, this is Catkiller 1-2. Over."

"Roger, 1-2, this is Tower, go ahead."

"Uh, roger, Tower. What traffic do you have in the pattern? Over."

"Negative traffic reported at this time. Over."

"Roger, Tower, this Catkiller 1-2, advising an unobserved approach. Over."

"Roger, Catkiller 1-2, winds westerly at three to five knots, altimeter 2996, no reported traffic, call for final clearance on short final."

By now he would be trying to spot a Bird Dog diving for cover, but I'd already be less than ten feet above National Route 9 and about half a mile from the gully. Too low for a banking turn, I'd skid into the slot. The major concern now became the cables reaching down from three communications towers. Fortunately, they weren't built directly opposite each other, so we could slide from one side of the gully to the other and still stay out of sight. If I wasn't really on the ball in the last two hundred yards and had to climb a little to get over some wires, the tower would spot me and score a point. As the guys in the tower learned the game and what cheats we were, they'd watch this approach, which meant that as time went on, I just had to get lower and lower before popping into view.

Tying it down tight one day, I'd cleared the wires and had less than 150 yards to go when I called for clearance. When the tower acknowledged,

I immediately declared short final and looked up to see a green army truck roll into view, a bug-eyed driver staring down at me. The voice of the traffic controller came through my earphones.

"Catkiller 1-2, you're cleared for landing. Be advised the only reported traffic is a deuce-and-a-half crossing from your right to left, currently just above your flight path."

Hands moved at lightning speed on stick and throttle and I ballooned over him with inches to spare, laughing hysterically at coming so close to killing myself. . . .

Morning mission and debriefing report done, Anderson and I were relaxing in the Dong Ha line shack before heading back to Phu Bai. Normally we'd low-level back, but after Miler's last warning, discretion was in order. I knew Andy pretty well, and when I heard him sigh, I knew he was planning some mischief. He finished his Coke, paused expectantly, and issued a long, manly belch. He smiled with the satisfaction of a job well done.

I shook my head. "I thought you were supposed to be an officer and a gentleman."

"Look who's talking. You're the only pilot I know—and I use the term 'pilot' very loosely, you understand—who gases his observers. If the gooks ever got their hands on you they'd win the war." This was true. My farts were famous, guaranteed to clear a room in seconds. More than once I'd turned around in the Bird Dog to see my observer with his head out the window gasping for breath. I'd have cut one now just to watch everyone scatter, but I couldn't work it up on the spur of the moment. "Ready to head back, Fart Blossom?"

"Guess so." I stood. "Being the real pilot here, I'd better lead, unless you think you can find Highway 1 and know which way is south. Might be pretty tricky for you."

"What I think, Hooper, is that maybe we should have a little race. How does that grab you? If you think you can handle it, that is."

"Hey, what a great idea. Did you come up with that on your own? Yeah, that would be pretty exciting, all right. Balls to the wall and a blistering 100 knots."

Anderson stood and stretched, then shoved his hands into the pockets of his fatigue jacket. He shook his head sadly. "Hooper, you'll just never have the imagination that it takes to make a great pilot. I'm not talking about who gets there first. This is about who gets there *last*."

The next insult died on my tongue, and I looked at him in frank admiration. It was an inspired idea. Rather than sitting behind the controls and simply banging in full throttle, this would see who was better at controlling his airplane at its minimum air speed, a far more difficult task. I immediately accepted his challenge. Highway 1, which led directly to Phu Bai, would be our course. Our starting point would be Quang Tri, a few minutes south of Dong Ha, which would give us a distance of just over fifty miles. We had to maintain eight hundred feet and the course of the highway; S-turns were not allowed, and whoever was the first to cross the Perfume River, the southern boundary of Phu Bai, lost the race.

"Relax, Andy," I said as we walked toward the flight line. "You look a little nervous."

"The only thing I'm nervous about is being in the air the same time as you. The way you wander all over the sky is an insult to the profession. It worries me. So try to keep a straight course today, okay?"

"Hey. I'll be so far behind you, you won't have to worry about a thing. Just make sure there's a cold beer waiting for me when I land."

"Hooper, you're not only delusional, but for someone who got his wings out of a Cracker Jack box, you should show more respect for your betters."

"The only thing you're better at, Anderson, is talking about flying. But that's okay. Really. Another few years and I'm sure you'll get the hang of it. Some people just take a little longer than others. You probably lie awake at night, thinking, 'That Bill Hooper, I hope I'm as good as him some day.' Don't you? Admit it."

We reached my plane first and Anderson followed me around it as I did a quick preflight check. "Now, that's the propeller, Captain Hooper," he said with the cadence of a kindergarten teacher. He reached up and patted the leading edge of the airfoil. "And these things that stick out on each side? They're called wings. Maybe you've heard of those. All airplanes have at least two, and some old-timey ones actually have four. Isn't that funny? Oh, and back there is the tail. No, no, don't go touching anything unless a grown-up says it's okay."

Once the obligatory trading of insults had set the proper tone of the forthcoming contest, we took off and climbed to eight hundred feet. Taking up our positions either side of the highway, I glanced at my air speed indicator: seventy-five knots. To my left, Anderson's Bird Dog matched my speed exactly. I knew that he, like myself, was wracking his brain for a loophole in the rules that would allow some sort of cheating. But they were ironclad. As soon as we reached Quang Tri, the race was on. Throttles were chopped, flaps were dumped, and every window opened as our stall warning horns started blaring. A quick look at the air speed indicator showed a quivering forty-two knots. With sixty degrees of flaps and as high an angle of attack as I could manage and still maintain altitude, it couldn't have been very accurate but would make a good story in the club. We crossed the finish line in a dead heat, both accusing the other of every imagined impropriety under the sun. It had been fun, but nothing beat contour flying, and we returned to it at the first opportunity.

Chapter 15

Lean On Me

CHARLES FINCH: MOST OF US SWAPPED OBSERVERS a lot, but Hooper always flew with his assigned backseater. And he never returned from his three-hour missions on time. The rest of us extended our missions times, too, but Billy was always late. Bobby Goodspeed used to get so pissed off that he'd be pacing up and down hosing Hooper for not coming back on time. We'd tease him by saying that Hooper didn't like him and wanted to kill all the NVA before Goodspeed could get in the air. For a while Bobby could not find a gook and he blamed Hooper.

Bill Hooper: Since the bombing halt, we had been monitoring the buildup of a major NVA weapons cache in the DMZ. While the position was within range of our artillery, it had been left undisturbed: artillery was unlikely to destroy it, and the NVA would simply relocate the weapons stores following an attack. Once the rains stopped, however, the use of tactical air strikes would almost certainly guarantee destruction. But timing was crucial. The monsoon season had a reputation for ending abruptly. When it did, the NVA would quickly begin shifting the supplies to frontline units poised for the spring offensive.

It was 26 March 1969 when I returned from a mission into Laos and saw the weather was lifting. Working on my debriefing report, I kept glancing outside. I knew that the NVA were also keeping close tabs on the weather and were already making preparations to move the cache southward. By the middle of the afternoon, the conditions had improved dramatically, and the forecast was for a continuing clearing trend. The time had come. I would engage it the following day.

I walked over to DASC and laid out my plan, requesting three flights of air for the next afternoon and stipulating high-delivery bombs to keep the fighter-bombers above most of the anticipated ground fire. I next contacted the artillery commander whose battery I'd be using between flights. His 8-inch shells exploding above the site would create a slaughterhouse for any troops caught in the open. Everything was in place.

The next morning, I flew my early mission and, as usual, was late getting back. On final for Dong Ha, I saw another Bird Dog, prop turning, holding on the ramp. The pilot came on the radio to say he had my observer, Bill Norton, in his back seat and that I could take his observer for my next mission. I'd never flown without the one assigned to me and insisted he taxi back. After topping off the wing tanks, we climbed in and took off. I had no idea how fortunate I was that Bill was with me.

As soon as we were airborne I contacted DASC to confirm my request for three flights of air with high-delivery Delta-3s, the first fused with daisy cutters to detonate just above ground level, the following flights with point-detonation fuses. As I organized the air, Bill was on his FM radio behind me briefing the artillery. By the time DASC advised that the first flight would be on station in fifteen minutes, I had already picked out the target ahead and was descending. I passed over a freshly dug, donut-shaped AAA position just at the edge of a tree line and noted that it was empty. The target itself was situated on the side of a steep, east-west ridgeline, with at least a dozen bunkers dug into the north face. Making a low pass, I looked up and back to see roofed entrances large enough for a man to walk into. Spread over several acres, this was a major complex. I'd either taken them completely by surprise or they were playing possum; not a shot was fired at us.

Bill Norton was already talking with our artillery. We cleared the area, and within minutes the first round impacted north of the ridgeline. Bill made an adjustment, requested air bursts, and ordered, "Battery fire for effect." Five 8-inch shells shrieked out of the air to detonate a hundred feet over the target. We were orbiting to one side when the first air reported in.

"Catkiller 1-2, Catkiller 1-2, this is Barn Owl 449er. Over."

"Roger, Barn Owl 449er, this is Catkiller 1-2. Over."

"Roger, Catkiller, this is Barn Owl, flight of two Fox-4s with four Delta 9s and eighteen Delta-1-Alphas on board, and thirty minutes play time. Over."

"Barn Owl, say again your ordnance. Over." I wasn't sure I had heard him correctly.

He repeated and I shook my head—napalm and 250-pound snakes rather than the 1,000-pounders I wanted. Snakes were released low—around three hundred feet—but with no American troops in contact, there could be no justification for putting the Phantom pilots at greater risk than necessary. They were going to have to adjust their normal attack profiles.

"Barn Owl, be advised I requested high-delivery ordnance. I think the anticipated ground fire will be excessive for snake and nape, so let's make high-delivery approaches. The target is a large one, and we can't help but hit it. I want no shallow approaches. Repeat, no shallow approaches. Over."

I briefed him on the target, emphasizing that they should change heading between bomb runs to prevent the enemy from predicting their flight paths. Giving weight to my warning were the muzzle flashes from small arms as they made a pass over it. When they were ready, I lined up and fired a rocket into the southern edge of the target area. Barn Owl said he had the mark, and Dash 1 came in from the east. I was at about one thousand feet when his four Delta 9s passed my right wing by about four hundred meters, and hit just on the edge of the site. I adjusted for Dash 2, who came in from the west. His napes landed in the middle of the target. I had never seen napalm used as high-delivery ordnance and was impressed with the accuracy, but aside from a lot of satisfying flame and smoke, the bunkers were undisturbed.

By now the ground fire was building. So far it was pale-green tracers from AK-47s and light machine guns. I cautioned Barn Owl again about going in low. Dash 1 rogered, rolled in steep from the southwest, and released at about five thousand feet. Dash 2 came across the target from the west, dropped his snakes and continued east behind his leader. At this point the ground fire intensified, the muzzle flashes from dozens of small arms sparkling harmlessly in the wake of the two F-4s. Dong Ha DASC radioed that the second flight of air would be on station in less than twenty minutes.

Norton cranked up the artillery again. Because the bunkers were on the north slope, there was little chance of doing much damage, so he kept the air bursts coming to prevent the AAA sites from being set up and manned.

An air force Gunfighter flight reported inbound with gun pods and Mk 82 snakes on board. This combination of 20mm guns and high-drag 500-pounders meant that for the second time, I hadn't been given the ordnance I wanted. Then it dawned on me that these flights were probably being diverted from targets where the weather was still poor. We were committed now and I'd continue running everything they sent me.

"Roger, Gunfighter, recommend that you cross over the target at angels five. Be prepared for triple-A. We have received small-arms fire and observed a number of heavier gun sites that are not presently manned, but expect that they will be. We have covered the area with air bursts to suppress ground fire, but anticipate it will continue when we pull the artillery off. Over." I briefed them on the target and safest routes to approach and break off. The Ben Hai River was only about a mile away, and if they strayed too close to it, the 37mm and 57mm flak machines would be waiting for them. Norton shut down the artillery and I rolled in and punched off a rocket.

"Gunfighter, Gunfighter, do you have my mark? Over."

"Roger, Catkiller, I have your mark. Over."

I told him where there was a concentration of muzzle flashes and to choose his own heading. Three or four minutes had elapsed since the artillery had been pulled off the target, and there was a full welcoming committee of small-arms fire as he made a high strafing run, walking his rudder to hose down the area of heaviest ground fire with his 20mm gun.

"Dash 2, this is Catkiller. From Dash 1's gun hits, go west one hundred meters. You'll see a large stand of trees higher on the ridgeline. There is extensive ground fire coming from that location. Choose your heading." Dash 2 came in from the west, picked out the tree line, and swept through it with one long burst of 20mm. He released the trigger, lifted his nose slightly, and laid another burst that ended on the far side of the target, before pulling out at about eight hundred feet. Too damn low, but he had gotten through unscathed.

Although the attacks had cleared much of the tree cover, exposing more bunkers and undoubtedly inflicting numerous casualties, the bunkers themselves were still untouched. Concerned that the smoke over the target would hinder the Gunfighter's accuracy, I rolled in and fired my third rocket into the center of the complex. Staying above the range of small arms, Dash 1 released his entire load of 500-pounders. I watched them sail past my altitude, lost them against the green, and then saw a dozen bright flashes as they hit. Suddenly, there was a huge secondary explosion, followed almost immediately by another, both clearly audible through our helmets. Excellent. But there were still more bunkers that had not been hit.

"Dash 2, this is Catkiller, take it another hundred meters west with all your snakes."

Dash 2 delivered his ordnance precisely where I wanted it, and was rewarded with a massive detonation. Dash 1 announced they were Winchester, and the Gunfighters headed for Da Nang. Behind them, both impact areas were now the scenes of continuous secondary explosions as more bunkers began erupting. Flame and smoke shot into the sky. Tons of ammunition—bullets, mortar rounds, artillery shells, RPGs, mines, all painstakingly carried in over months, all destined to kill Americans—were going off in a chain reaction. This was the result I had hoped for.

Although we couldn't see them, survivors among the NVA logistics personnel and units assigned to guard the complex were undoubtedly running to escape the storm, and Bill Norton was determined to kill as many as possible. The next round of air bursts exploded over the target. Concentrating on the secondaries for the bomb damage assessment, I'd allowed us to get down to about four hundred feet above the ridge. I kicked right rudder to bring the aircraft around so he could make his artillery adjustments. Leveling the wings, I'd turned my head to verify that he had a clear view of the target when I heard a *pop*. Then it seemed like the right side of the airplane exploded.

Bill saw me spin almost 180 degrees in my seat, then turn back and slump against my harness. The airplane pitched forward into a dive, rolling slightly to the left. My first thought was that we'd been hit by a large-caliber antiaircraft shell. I knew we were going down, but I couldn't comprehend why I couldn't grab the stick right there in front me. I kept trying, but I just couldn't reach it. Then, in the negative G, I saw my right arm float up in front of me.

The Bird Dog has an auxiliary control stick stored next to the observer's seat. It fits so tightly into the socket on the coordinating bar between the front and back seats that it is usually a two-handed exercise to line it up and seat it. Sure that I was dead, Bill grabbed the stick. He had time for just one try before we hit the ground. With one deliberate move, Bill stabbed downward and planted the end of it in the socket between his feet. Still not understanding why I had no control of my arm, I grabbed my right wrist to pull the arm down just as Bill hauled back on the stick. When the nose came up, the arm fell like a dead weight into my lap. At that moment it crossed my mind that it had been severed.

I felt the airplane buffeting on the edge of a stall. In spite of my confusion, over nine hundred hours of concentrated combat time had made the Bird Dog almost a natural extension of my mind and body—in Doc Clement's words, I was wearing it—and I reacted instinctively by shoving the stick forward with my left hand. We were on the wrong side of the ridgeline, with ground fire still coming up, and I kicked left rudder to take us away from it.

Bill, who wasn't sure if I was alive or not, yanked the nose up again. It didn't take long for the airplane to start shuddering once more. I shoved the stick forward and then it became a tug of war between my left hand and both of his, and he was winning. Unable to hit the mike switch, I was screaming at him to release his stick when, through the fog of being injured, I saw that I still had a lot more throttle available. When I slammed it forward, Bill realized I was alive and gave me the controls. I clamped the stick between my knees, backed off on the throttle and trimmed the aircraft nose high so that we were climbing. As soon as we were clear of the target, I retrimmed the aircraft, turned southeast, and hit the button for the emergency frequency.

"Mayday, mayday, mayday. This is Catkiller 1-2 on guard. I'm hit, I'm hit. I say again: mayday, mayday, mayday. This is Catkiller 1-2 on guard. I'm hit. My position: zero-three-six-eight. Heading southeast, direct Dong Ha. I say again: I'm hit. My position is 0368. Request assistance. Over."

CHARLIE FINCH, SARGE MEANS, and Len Bumgardner had flown their missions that day and were on their way to Phu Bai.

Charles Finch: About five minutes south of Dong Ha I suddenly heard Bill on the radio, and from the tone of his voice I knew it was serious. Without a word on the radio, the three of us immediately reversed course and brought in full power. There was no point in all of us going up, so I told Sarge and Len to land at Dong Ha and then contacted the tower to get the crash crew, fire trucks, and ambulance ready.

Bill Hooper: Dazed, I began to examine my arm. It had turned blue-black, and the only sensation associated with it was the weight of it on my lap. I had little doubt that I'd lost it. Tracing upwards with my left hand, I found a piece of hot, jagged steel protruding from my right biceps. What would prove to be a piece of shrapnel four inches long and over an inch in diameter, it was from one of the last 8-inch air bursts. Blown into the air, it was falling back to earth when I flew into its path. The shrapnel had smashed through the windscreen to hit me point on, ripping through the muscle and splintering the humerus. (The doctors would later explain that what I had perceived as the side of the aircraft exploding was the shock wave going through my body when this pound of steel hit me.)

Dong Ha DASC advised they were launching two Huey slicks to intercept me in case I went down. I advised them that the aircraft was in good shape, that I'd lost my right arm, and should reach Dong Ha in less than twenty minutes. The next call was from Charlie Finch.

"Hoop, this is Charlie. Over."

"Uh, roger, Charlie, this is Catkiller 1-2. Go ahead."

"Okay, Bill, I'm coming up the West Trace. I think I should pick you up along there pretty easy."

My arm was aching badly, and I began having great difficulty concentrating. In spite of the wind blasting through the six-inch hole in the windscreen, there was an overwhelming desire to sleep. I was fighting to keep my eyes open. Only a small trickle of blood had collected on my rolled-up sleeve, so I knew I wasn't bleeding to death. Assuming that I was going into shock, I reached over my right shoulder with my left hand and unzipped the medical kit. Right after taking over as CO, Major Miler had ordered that amyl nitrate ampoules were included in the kit. We all thought it was a dumb idea. Not now. As soon as I broke one under my nose it jerked me awake, but it didn't last; within a minute or two, I was once more having real trouble staying awake.

Charles Finch: When Bill gave me his direction and altitude, the background noise of wind and engine made it sound like he had his head out the window. Sometimes he would key the mike and all I could hear was the noise of wind blast. I spotted his aircraft ahead, made a climbing left turn, and slid over the top to examine it. Looking down, I could not believe the size of the hole in the windscreen. I saw Bill sitting very rigidly, as though not to move his damaged arm. Norton was low in the back seat and leaning to the right to look forward. Norton came up on the frequency and said that he had the controls and was not injured. At one point I saw him lean forward and try to look over Hooper's shoulder to see the wound.

Bill Hooper: I broke another ampoule. Its effect had already dissipated when I heard a familiar voice in my earphones.

"Hey, Hoop, this is Charlie. I'm just off your right wing."

Struggling to stay awake, I turned my head. Another Bird Dog hung there, its wingtip a few meters from mine. Charlie's eyes were locked on me. "Hey, Charlie, uh, I'm having a real hard time staying awake. I . . . keep talking to me, Charlie, just keep talking to me."

"No sweat, Bill. How're you doing?"

"The ship is in good shape, but I've lost my right arm. I can't feel it. I feel absolutely nothing. Over."

"Stay with me, Hooper. We're not more than ten minutes out. Hang in there, we're getting close."

Charles Finch: Having two Bills was a little confusing, and when I asked Norton, "Are you OK, Bill?" Hooper thought I was talking to him and angrily repeated that he'd lost his arm. The strain in his voice had me concerned. I alternated staying on his wing, then pulling a little ahead and higher so he could see me without turning his head and I could look down into the cockpit. I kept talking, assuring him that he would be safely on the ground in minutes. Despite my assurances, I was worried about how he was going to flare on landing. I told Norton I would guide him in and tell him when to reduce power and flare. My biggest fear was a ground loop, and I explained to Norton that I wanted him to pull the stick full back after touchdown and keep it there even if the airplane started bouncing.

I told Dong Ha tower that there would be no go-around and not to let the crash crews get too close to the runway. Before the Hueys got to us, they heard my warning and flew ahead to land on the north side of the ramp.

Bill Hooper: Charlie and I talked back and forth, almost as though I was in a time warp. I wasn't aware of anything except his voice and his airplane. His constant and reassuring voice in my earphones was keeping me from sliding into unconsciousness, as though he were saying, "Lean on me, I'll take you home." Still talking, he pulled forward a little, and I flew formation on him.

Charles Finch: When I asked Norton if the rocket switches were closed, Hooper got pissed again and said the toggles were never opened today, which made no sense and convinced me he was going into shock. He was talking slower and slower, but I saw that he had a firm grip on the stick with his left hand. We were in sight of Dong Ha when the aircraft started to descend and climb more than before. They were both on the controls. When I told Hooper to just follow me to base leg, he managed to get right beside me, set up a nice glide angle and a slow turn to long final. With no wind, we were both too fast, and when he passed me, I told him to slow down. When more flaps came down and the aircraft did not balloon, I knew Hooper was flying. I told him he was doing great and I would be right beside him till touchdown.

Bill Hooper: Charlie told me that it was time to contact the tower and set up my approach. When I switched to the tower, the controller advised me that they were holding all other traffic and I was cleared to land. With Charlie still maintaining his position just off my wing, I turned east with him and set up a straight-in approach from almost three miles out. It was then I felt my thumb lying against the forefinger and the first twinges of real pain. The fog suddenly cleared and I snapped awake, my mind very clear and alert and focused on this one-handed landing. If there was any chance of saving the arm, I couldn't crash this airplane. It had to be the best landing of my life.

Charles Finch: Bill's last transmission was clear. I could see that he was focused and that there was nothing more I could say or do that would help.

Sarge Means: We'd gotten there well ahead of Bill, and when the siren in the tower went off, we knew that he was returning for a landing. We all went out to the runway in front of the Catkiller ramp to watch the excitement. The aircraft seemed to be doing fine until it got on short final. I could see that the flaps weren't down as much as they should be, and there were minor pitch excursions going on. He was having a difficult time.

Bill Hooper: I eased back the throttle, dropped some more flaps, and started a very slow rate of descent that I constantly adjusted with the throttle, concentrating on the touchdown point I was shooting for and wondering if I was going to get this airplane down safely. Whenever I needed to adjust the throttle, I had to hold the stick between my knees. Making this switch during the long approach to the runway was simple, but when I got to the touchdown point it would be necessary to cut power and keep pulling the nose up to bleed off the air speed. To do that using only my knees presented a bit of a problem.

Just before touchdown I pulled my heels back until only my toes were on the rudder pedals, held back pressure on the stick with my knees, and chopped the throttle. Just as I brought my hand to the stick and eased back on it, we made as perfect a three-point landing as I'd ever done in my life. Rolling down the runway, I looked up to see a Bird Dog go by. Charlie had followed me right to touchdown and had now throttled up and was passing over the tower and breaking left to come around for his own landing.

First Lieutenant Jim Lawrence, a marine fingerprint Bird Dog pilot from VMO-6, was there that hot and hazy day.

Jim Lawrence: I remember standing beside my O-1 at Dong Ha as my crew refueled and rearmed me. I looked around at the sound of crash trucks racing toward the runway and then saw two army O-1s on final from the west. It was obvious that one was chasing the other, which usually meant the lead bird had a problem. I watched as the lead Bird Dog touched down in a nice landing and rolled to a stop as the second Bird Dog went around.

Charles Finch: I sucked up half of my flaps and climbed straight up to watch Hooper roll out right down the centerline. I turned out left, and by the time I was on a quick base leg, I could see a lot of activity where Bill's aircraft had stopped on the runway. I landed short and turned into our ramp as one of our jeeps pulled toward me.

Sarge Means was the first to reach the Bird Dog.

Sarge Means: I opened the door and Bill was sitting there with a jagged piece of metal sticking out of his arm. He looked at me and said, "Sarge, now this is brutal."

Jim Lawrence: Fire trucks and medics soon surrounded the plane. They helped the pilot out and put him in the meat wagon, which sped toward a waiting Huey. The crew then pushed the plane off to the side to clear the runway, and I saddled up and went off to get shot at some more.

Charles Finch: When I got there, Bill was being loaded on the helicopter. He was very pale, in a lot of pain, and was talking to Sarge, who climbed onboard with him. I said something that was lost in the roar of the helicopter's engine and blades. Bill smiled, and I stepped back as the Huey lifted off for the hospital at Quang Tri.

Bill Hooper: Riding in that helicopter, I had an overwhelming sense of loss in knowing that my job as a Catkiller was over. I wasn't relieved to be alive or even considering the extent of my injury. Instead, I was filled with self-recrimination, anger, and bitterness. For the first time in my life I had been part of something very special, a group of men held together by great mutual respect, doing a job that saved American lives. And now in one unthinking moment I had let them down. It was a sense of loss I would feel for the rest of my life.

Charles Finch: I followed in my Bird Dog and got to Quang Tri in time to catch a glimpse of Bill being carried on the stretcher into the operating theater. As Hooper was being prepped for the first of what would be series of operations over the next eight months, I headed back to Phu Bai. I was numb all the way home. Not only had I lost a friend, but the Catkillers had lost a fierce warrior, a first-rate pilot with a real talent for running air and adjusting artillery. When I landed, everyone in maintenance was waiting to hear what had happened. With the loss of Harrison and Mac Byrd still fresh in everyone's mind, there was a great sense of relief that Bill was alive.

Bill Hooper: When I got to the emergency field hospital, I was lucky that they were having a slow day, which meant I got immediate attention. The impact of the shrapnel had temporarily stunned the nerves in my arm. As they recovered from the shock-wave trauma, the pain increased rapidly. Now it was severe. There were doctors and nurses all around, but they would not give me anything for it because I was going directly to surgery after X-rays. As they were rolling me this way and that way to take the X-rays, I remember hearing someone scream every few moments. I was thinking I was better off than some poor bastard there, until it registered that I was the one screaming. It wasn't long after that when they wheeled me into the operating room and pumped in the anesthetic. I had never felt such relief.

Charles Finch: We had a floorshow that night, and everyone who came in asked if there was any word from Quang Tri about Bill. Afterward, some of us ended up in the Super Hooch. It turned into kind of a hate session about the support we got and the taskers' poor understanding of our mission. While we were bitching and moaning, I remember Jim Hudson cataloguing Bill's personal effects for shipment to the States.

Although Bill was soon eleven thousand miles away in the orthopedic ward at the Fort Gordon hospital in Georgia, he remained a presence in the 220th. A blackboard in the club carried all the pilots' names and the number of days they had left in country. Bill's name must have gone down when the board was wet, because even after someone wiped it clean a ghostly Hooper remained, somehow embedded there. New guys would come in and ask why there were no days recorded next to the name, and we all wanted to be the one to tell the story of how Bill was hit and flew back.

My place at the poker table faced the board, and I was reminded of him every time I sat down. Hooper stories were in vogue, and we laughed about the things he did that drove us nuts. When I'd win a hand I'd stick my elbows out in that insect-like pose of his and just move my forearms to pick up the chips and stack them very slowly. People would laugh and say, "Hooper!" We missed him, but if Bill had come back and sat down with his messed-up arm, we'd have given him shit for dealing so slow.

Chapter 16

Busy Month of June

After the bombing halt, the NVA were not supposed to cross the DMZ into South Vietnam, but they did. The only way you could get air support was if you were receiving fire. So, if I saw enemy troops on the other side of the river, I'd tell my backseat to start firing his M16 out the window, and then I'd call DASC and tell them we were under fire and that I needed snake and nape. They would come back with, "Yes, we can hear it; we're scrambling some air for you."

–Doc Clement, Catkiller 18

CHARLES FINCH: IT WAS JUNE 2 1969. BEFORE taking off from Dong Ha, my backseater, marine Clyde Trathowen, said he wanted a photo of the big North Vietnamese flag that flew just the other side of Freedom Bridge. Almost every Catkiller had buzzed the flag at some time, so I said sure. We took off, and I started climbing to have a good look at the area before making a low pass for his camera.

We were around three thousand feet when I saw some NVA trucks about five miles north of the river. They were heading slowly in our direction down Highway 1, undoubtedly loaded with supplies to be used against American troops. It always infuriated me that all we could do was report our sightings. Since the November '68 bombing halt, the rules of engagement meant they were safe even in their side of the so-called Demilitarized Zone. Air was forbidden to cross the river, and no artillery would fire into North Vietnam unless the NVA fired on Americans first. There were times when we got around that by reporting we were receiving fire and calling in an artillery mission, but with these trucks a fair distance inside their haven, that wasn't going to work today.

But the longer I watched them, the juicier and more tempting they became. I finally decided I could get up there, make three quick passes with my rockets, and be back in about ten minutes, and nobody but the NVA would be any the wiser. Before the bombing halt, I'd destroyed a truck with a rocket, so I knew it could be done. When I told Clyde that I was going to engage them, he was not impressed. I turned south and started descending as though departing the area. When I got down to treetop level, I reversed course. We crossed the river into North Vietnam, still down on the deck and staying parallel with the highway.

A few minutes later they came into view. Back on the stick, and I started climbing, mentally computing where I wanted to roll in. At about eight hundred feet, I nosed over. Fixing on the windscreen of the lead truck, I armed both outboard tubes. The truck grew larger, and I could see the driver leaning forward to look up. Steaadyyy. Passing through five hundred feet, I squeezed the trigger, holding the dive for the split second it took the rockets to ignite and clear the tubes. In less time than it takes to describe, they hit. What happened next was not part of the plan.

A massive fireball blotted out everything in front of me. Then the shock wave slammed into us. The noise was deafening through the open windows, and we were in a dark cloud, the blast-furnace heat filling the cockpit. Blurred objects that might have been ammunition crates were flying past us. Bug-eyed, we came out the other side, and I was checking the controls to see if everything was still working and trying to get my heart back under control. Breaking right into a 180, I looked over to see that the first two trucks had been completely destroyed and that the third had slammed into the wreckage. Flames and thick black smoke were rising above them.

Worried that we might have serious damage to the aircraft, I put out a call. A Catkiller responded and asked for my position. When I told him to look north, he asked if I was "near that big, black cloud." As Clyde and I were trying to cook up a story, I looked out at my right wing and saw arming safety pins and fragments of plastic packaging, while the left wing had what looked like the tailfins from mortar shells embedded in it. I was in trouble. The other Catkiller flew alongside and reported that aside from things that were not U.S. Army issue stuck in my wings, the airplane looked okay.

Barely half an hour after taking off, we were back on the ground. I was met on the ramp by some very serious looking officers from the 108th and Dong Ha DASC. While they were grilling me, the crew chiefs started pulling fragments out of the bottom of the wings, puzzling over whether they were parts of mortars, grenades, RPGs, or artillery shells. One of the 108th guys asked me to take him back to the scene of the crime. We took off in another aircraft, and when it was clear that the column of smoke was well north of the Ben Hai, he said he had seen enough.

I spent that night at Dong Ha being asked by a lot of field-grade officers what I was trying to prove by violating agreements made between the North Vietnamese and U.S. governments at the Paris Peace Talks. Everyone in the chain of command right up to XXIV Corps was bouncing off the walls, and I was feeling distinctly uneasy about my future. I still don't know how I got out of that one, but when I got to the flight line the next morning, Mike LaFromboise said I was the talk of the marine observers. He wanted to go see the damage. I talked him out of it, and we spent the next two and half hours flying the safest mission we could. When we landed, my logbook entry took me over one thousand hours of combat missions in Vietnam.

On June 5 I took my first R&R since arriving the previous July and flew to Hawaii to meet my wife Nancy. I had postponed this for quite some time, as I was so wrapped up in the war. Nancy was not happy with the fact that I had just extended for another six months.

Ed Miler: Len Bumgardner's aircraft took a 12.7mm round through the belly of the bird that went through the upper leg and forearm of his backseater, marine Capt. Mike LaFromboise. There was nothing Bumgardner could do except put the ship on the ground as quickly as possible. Bum applied full throttle and kept it there for the thirty minutes or so it took to reach the field and land. It was not quick enough; LaFromboise bled to death in the back of the aircraft. Mike had only a few days left in country when he was killed.

"THINGS HAVE BEEN BAD TODAY," Jack Bentley wrote in his diary, "and the last few hours have built it up to a head. I've been so tired lately. Mike

LaFromboise was killed today in Len Bumgardner's back seat. They took a 12.7 in the bottom of the airplane. It came through Mike's right leg, and then blew his hand off several inches above the wrist. He bled to death before Bum could get to Quang Tri. Mike had nineteen days left. He was such a great guy and a damned good backseat. My first experience with troops in contact, I had Mike in my back seat. I can't believe the effect something like this leaves on me. It hurts at first, then heals over and becomes a permanent scar. I lean on Cathy at times like this and I know it's hard for her to understand without knowing what happened. It would be so very easy to forget everything and rely on booze. There's such a fine line dividing heroes and cowards. If I die, I'm dead; but I worry about my friends. I'm not trying to say I don't think about getting greased but it hurts more when a friend gets it."

Jack Bentley: After writing that, I spent hours with Bum trying to reassure him that it was not his fault and he had done all that one could. Sarge was Bum's main source of support, as they had been friends since flight school.

Their airplane became a problem. Mike's blood had drained into every nook and cranny in the tail section, and after a few days in the intense heat, the smell inside was overwhelming. Nobody would fly it. Sergeant Faustich or Al Lopez dismantled it and steam cleaned the interior of the tail section several times, but the odor remained. We finally got a disinfectant from the hospital and it became tolerable. Still, no one wanted to fly it.

I finally said, fuck it, the airplane was mine. We were prohibited from personalizing individual aircraft, but Al Lopez painted *Captain Jack* on the door and *Jack's Revenge* on the nose, and nobody said anything. As I recall, I flew all of my remaining missions in "0742." I always felt Mike was with me. I even got pissed when someone flew "my airplane" in my absence.

Charles Finch: I returned from Hawaii to learn that Mike LaFromboise had been killed the day before. His death hit me really hard, and the next day I flew eight hours, running air strikes and trying to kill every NVA I could find. When I landed that afternoon, Major Miler was there to meet me. He spent the night talking to an aviator just off R&R who probably should have been sent right back to Hawaii.

I had one mission scheduled the next day, but the ARVN were getting hit hard east of A-2, so I flew a second and killed a lot of NVA with Hellborne A-4s. When I landed at Phu Bai, the flight surgeon called me in for a talk. He knew that I had been flying the DMZ for over ten months, longer than anyone, and how much pride I took in that, but he'd also heard that I was flying unscheduled missions and taking unnecessary risks. He said I was probably suffering combat fatigue and that Major Miler wanted to take me off the DMZ.

I couldn't believe it. Flying the Z was my food, the air I breathed, everything to me. Finding the NVA, seeing their faces, and hearing the rounds snapping past as I went in for the mark, assembling the fast movers, seeing their approach and the bombs and napalm going in—how could anyone not want to do that for as long as he could? This was the ultimate in life for me. There was no one I knew who drank so deeply from this cycle of war and loved it as much as I did. I had only two more months to make it a full year with the 1st Platoon. Just give me those last two months, I asked. He finally promised to reconsider and told me to come back to see him on my birthday, just five days away.

Two days later I was covering an ARVN operation in the eastern part of the DMZ. Under attack by the NVA and completely disorganized, they went into a panic when I ran four air strikes and got twenty-one kills near their troops. Later that day, army and marine troops moved up to support them, and the action intensified the next day. The enemy hit an ARVN company defending the eastern flank, and then hit the main body with a coordinated rocket attack. Things were happening quickly and the enemy had the initiative.

Out of rockets and with a flight of marine Lovebugs on station, I came in low to mark the target with a smoke grenade. I felt the aircraft shudder as bullets went through the left wing and left elevator and dropped the grenade too soon. Dash 1 was already on final, and I had to wave him off, saying I needed to give him a better mark.

I was lining up when I got hit again, but I knew they could shoot at me all they wanted and not hurt me. I put the next smoke grenade on target, and Dash 1 laid his nape exactly where I wanted it. The Lovebugs had made about five passes when a Gunfighter flight checked in to say they wanted to join the fight. It was the first time I had ever used marine and air force in one traffic pattern, and it worked perfectly. This time it was the enemy who were in a shit sandwich, with no way to escape.

Keeping the F-4s spaced just far enough to avoid damage from the bombs dropped by the one in front, we mixed snake and nape with 20mm. They all took hits from ground fire, but we killed twenty-two of the enemy and stopped the rest. This was in the same area where Mike LaFromboise was killed, so I felt I had gotten a little revenge.*

Unable to stand the suspense of whether the flight surgeon was going to ground me or not, I dropped into his office a day early. He gave me a thorough physical, thought for a long while, and finally said to have a happy twenty-sixth birthday: he was going to recommend that I complete those last two months on the DMZ.

---

*Finch did not know that the marine and air force pilots and the U.S. ground commander had recommended him for the Distinguished Flying Cross until the paperwork and award caught up with him a year later at Fort Rucker.

Epilogue

220TH RECONNAISSANCE AIRPLANE COMPANY

Anderson, Quinton "Andy" (Catkiller 10/3): Following his tour with the Catkillers, Andy spent the last two years of his military obligation with the aviation section at Fort Bliss, Texas. He resigned his regular commission to pursue a civilian career, spending most of the next twenty-five years in the commercial real estate business where he used his "low and slow" flying skills doing land appraisals for the Nature Conservancy, Texas Parks and Wildlife, and U.S. Fish and Wildlife Service, much of them in the Big Bend area of West Texas. He quit flying in 1995, turning to the thrill of sport/touring on his BMW motorcycle, and changed careers by joining Merrill Lynch as a financial advisor. Today he manages the Merrill Lynch office in Lake Jackson, Texas, where he lives with his wife, Lee. They have four children and six grandchildren. "My association with the Catkillers was the most memorable year of my life," Andy wrote. "The bonds are stronger now than ever and if my country called, I would want to do the same thing with the same guys. Our reunion in October of '03 was a fantastic experience that I will never forget."

Bentley, Jack (Catkiller 17): Jack flew for the 220th from December 1968 to December 1969, logging well over one thousand hours with the 1st Platoon. Upon returning to the States, he married his fiancée Cathy, and they remain together to this day. After his departure from active duty in 1973, Jack completed his bachelor's degree in business administration at the University of Nebraska and then spent eighteen months flying a Cessna 421 for an oil and chemical company. The time away from his family made him pursue another career path as a salesman for a wholesale foods company. In 1978 he purchased a convenience store franchise, later built a car wash, and then co-founded an auto glass business. He is now retired and spends his days improving and developing the Myth Maker Ranch in northeastern Arizona, where he and Cathy reside with their five dogs, two cats, and two horses. They have four children and two grandchildren. Their firstborn son was named in honor of Mike LaFromboise and today serves on active duty as an army aviator. "In April of 1997 it was my honor to have Sarge Means attend my son's graduation from flight school at Fort Rucker, Alabama, and watch me pin on his wings. What a trip!"

Bruton, Bud (Catkiller 18): Leaving Vietnam with 850 hours of combat time, Bud joined the National Guard and flew helicopters until 1983, accumulating a total of 3,200 hours of both rotary and fixed-wing time. A 1966 graduate of Washington and Jefferson College, he has worked in the financial services industry since the 1970s, earning a position as a selected financial advisor with the Frank Russell Company. Maintaining his link to the company, Bud created Bruton Financial Advisors LLC in 2004, which, with its sister firm, Bruton Financial Partners, manage more than $240 million for high–net worth clients. He is a member and trustee at the Westminster Presbyterian Church in West Chester, Pennsylvania, and, along with Jacqueline, his wife of forty-two years, is an active choir member. Since 1990, he has done mission work in Puerto Rico for a Methodist Church camp destroyed by Hurricane Hugo, adding a medical and dental facility manned by volunteer doctors and dentists. Bud has also made five trips to Vietnam since the war. He and his son Ben helped to build a kindergarten in the A Shau Valley, which he had regularly flown over during his time with the Catkillers. His volunteer team was the first allowed to work in this remote area adjacent to the Laotian border. Bud serves on the board of the Veterans' Vietnam Restoration Project (VVRP), which each year sends veterans to assist those who have lost limbs to ordnance left over from the war. He and Jacqueline, a church deacon and hospice volunteer, live in East Brandywine, where he served for eight years as a township supervisor and chairman of the board for another five years. They are the proud parents of five sons and six wonderful grandchildren— as of this writing, two more are on the way.

Clement, Doc (Catkiller 18): After ten months as a Catkiller and two as a 219th RAC Headhunter in Pleiku, Doc extended another six months as a U-21 pilot in Nha Trang, transporting generals around Vietnam. He returned to Fort Rucker as a U-21 instructor and six years after joining the army, left to take a job as a corporate pilot for an Atlanta-based real estate company. But his taste for adventure remained unsatisfied, and he headed for Alaska as a bush pilot. "With my Cessna 185, I had a contract supplying mineral exploration camps. It was a demanding environment to fly in, and my Vietnam experience helped considerably. When winter set in, the camps closed and I'd head for Rio de Janeiro and party until it was time to go back to Alaska." Eight years later he took over as manager of the Killarney Fruit Company, flying regularly between its Florida and Georgia plantations, and then followed in his father's footsteps, joining Piedmont Airlines before it became US Airways. Doc retired in 2005, and he and his wife Brenda, an executive with Reynolds American, Inc., divide their time between their North Carolina home, a Miami beach-front condo, and the gaming tables in Las Vegas, the last an echo of those nights in the Catkiller Club.

Davis, Grayson (Catkiller 45/3): Returning to the United States at the end of his tour in 1969, Davis served out his last two years in uniform at Fort Hood, Texas, as the pilot for the commanding general of III Corps. He resigned his regular army commission in 1971 to attend law school and after graduating served as legislative assistant to a Texas state senator until 1977. He formed the law firm of Taylor & Davis, PC, to provide legal services in the energy sector, becoming a solo practitioner in 1988. Grayson is a member of the State Bar of Texas; Houston Bar Association; the Oil, Gas, and Mineral Law Sections of the State and Houston Bars; and has been board certified in oil, gas, and mineral law since 1994. He is also a member of the Development Council, Bush School of Government and Public Service, Texas A&M University, College Station, Texas. "To this day," he wrote, harking back to his days in Vietnam, "I still marvel at the bond that was formed so many years ago, and what an honor it was to have flown as a Catkiller."

Drechsel, Carl (Catkiller 30): His tour completed in 1970, Carl was assigned as instructor pilot and assistant operations officer at Primary Fixed Wing Training Center, Fort Stewart, Georgia. He left active duty in 1972; joined the U.S. Army Reserve, 75th Maneuver Area Command Flight Detachment, and flew U-8Ds as a senior army aviator; and retired as a colonel in 1994. He worked as quality assurance manager on several major projects for Saudi Aramco, Dhahran, Saudi Arabia, for seventeen years. Carl is now a consultant to Motiva Enterprises LLC, a joint venture between Shell and Saudi Aramco as quality manager on the $8 billion Mega Crude Expansion Project at Port Arthur Refinery in Texas, which will become the largest refinery in the United States. One of Carl's fondest recent memories is the 2006 Catkiller reunion in Houston, Texas, which he and his wife co-chaired. More than fifty Catkillers—enlisted, NCOs, officers, families, as well as past company and battalion commanders—were there to renew friendships and honor their missing and KIA Catkillers.

Finch, Charles (Catkiller 19): With a year flying the DMZ (longer than any other Catkiller), Charles extended for an additional six months to fly U-21s for the 62nd Aviation Company and then to Long Thanh with the Command Airplane Company. The death of his father, an army colonel who had participated in the D-Day landings in France, brought him home in February 1970. He served as a Bird Dog instructor at Fort Rucker until transitioning to helicopters in mid-1971. He was hired by Delta Airlines but remained in the army Reserves, logging thousands of hours in Hueys, OH-58s, and Blackhawks. His last assignment in the reserves was as 33rd Group commander at Fort Rucker, and he retired as a full colonel after twenty-eight years' service. A marathon runner with a long-term commitment to working with the disadvantaged, he was awarded the Olympic Medal of Honor in 1994 and ran with the Olympic torch two years later in Miami. By the time he retired from Delta in May 2003, he had been a lead check airman on McDonnell Douglas MD-88s and Boeing 757 and 767 aircraft and acknowledged as one of the company's top one hundred employees. He now concentrates on golf and maintaining a handicap of two. He and Nancy have been married since 1966 and their daughter Cathy, a pediatrician in Georgia, presented them with grandson Samuel in 2002. The Mercedes 280 SL he bought in 1970 with his Catkiller poker winnings is clocking up miles between the two households.

Hooper, Bill (Catkiller 12): With half his biceps destroyed, the radial nerve severed, and a section of the humerus virtually pulverized, Bill was flown from Quang Tri to Chu Lai to Japan, and then ten thousand miles across the Pacific and continental United States. Eight days after being hit, he was in the army hospital at Fort Gordon, Georgia. For the next eight months, he lived in a neck-to-waist Velpeau cast, undergoing five operations to reconstruct his arm, which included fixing a steel plate above and below the break and transferring a tendon from the inside of the wrist to the back of the hand so that he could open it. Eleven months after being wounded, Bill was discharged from the army and returned to the junior college he had left somewhat ignominiously in 1966. "Word got around that I'd been hurt pretty badly in Vietnam," he remembers. "A few weeks after starting school, a young couple with love beads and the obligatory peace emblems walked up. At first I didn't realize they were talking to me, until the boy said, 'You're nothing but a hired killer' whereupon his girlfriend spit on me. Very proud of themselves, they marched off, yelling more insults over their shoulders. I don't recall getting angry, but rather being utterly bewildered." Within six months he was a math tutor. He received a scholarship to Florida Atlantic University, where he completed his master's of science degree in ocean engineering in April 1976. After eighteen months as a research associate, he was hired by Brown and Root, Marine Division, Middle East, and headed to Abu Dhabi in the United Arab Emirates. He spent the next nine years in and around the Persian Gulf. He left the gulf in June of 1986 as Brown and Root's business development manager, Middle East, and turned his attention to the equipment side of the food-service industry. Today Bill is the owner of Food Equipment Sales and Marketing Agents, Inc., in Clearwater, Florida. When time allows, he and his wife Linda can be found scuba diving on their favorite spots in the Gulf of Mexico.

Hudson, Jim (Catkiller 12): On May 16, 1969, Jim was awarded the Distinguished Flying Cross for a July 1968 mission over North Vietnam. In 1970, Jim left the army and joined his father's foundry business in Huntsville, Alabama. Later that year he was diagnosed with rheumatoid arthritis, a disease that would eventually lead him to a career in biotechnology. After steady growth, Hudson Metals was sold in 1982 so that Jim's father could retire and Jim could go back to graduate school to study molecular biology. In 1987, he founded Research Genetics with the slogan, "Custom DNA, delivered in forty-eight hours." Starting with his son (born while Jim was a Catkiller) and later with his daughter and father, Research Genetics grew from two to over two hundred employees. The firm went on to develop tools for discovering the genetic causes of disease and played a significant role in the Human Genome Project. In 2000, Invitrogen (IVGN) acquired Research Genetics for $120 million. Today, Jim is the founding director of the Hudson-Alpha Institute for Biotechnology, a nonprofit research institute dedicated to using the knowledge gained from the Human Genome Project to find the causes and cures for disease. Jim and his second wife Susie have four children and five grandchildren and live in Jim's hometown of Huntsville, Alabama, where they have used part of their good fortune to help revitalize downtown. He still flies, but nowadays it's from the passenger seat of Susie's Citation VII. From the hours flying over the DMZ to the hours sitting around the poker table, Jim says he owes much of his success to the perspectives gained and the bonds he made as a Catkiller.

Means, Sarge (Catkiller 16): Sarge elected to stay in the army. After being passed over for major, he reverted to warrant officer and went on to become an instructor pilot in the UH-1 Huey, accumulating more than five thousand hours in type, and then working his way back into fixed wing. He flew Cessna Citations and Gulfstream IIIs for the U.S. Army Jet Detachment at Andrews Air Force Base and surpassed ten thousand hours of accident-free flight time in March 2004. "In June 1998 I was honored to have Charlie Finch promote me to CW5, but was finally booted out in 2005 for being too old—euphemistically called the Mandatory Retirement Date. It was probably time, although I wanted to put in one more year: serve forty and save someone a career! I feel extremely fortunate to have served, and traveled, all over the world. To this day I still tell people that my year in RVN was the happiest of my career. That shocks most of them, because it certainly is not a happy memory for many. But there is no doubt in my mind that it was the mission, the Bird Dog, and most of all the people: the male camaraderie, the bonding. It was present in Phu Bai, Republic of Vietnam, long before we had million-man marches and seminars and Promisekeepers. My life was forever touched by some wonderful guys, and this book has made it obvious that I wasn't alone."

Miler, Ed (Catkiller 6): His six months commanding the Catkillers ended in July 1969, and Ed returned to the States and the Command and General Staff College at Fort Leavenworth. After two years' graduate work at Tulane University in New Orleans, he served on the staff of the army's Ballistic Missile Defense Office. This led to an assignment as a battle staff officer with the National Emergency Airborne Command Post at Andrews Air Force Base. "I was the emergency actions officer, a JCS billet, and our job was to provide an airborne communications platform to all of the U.S. nuclear forces for the Joint Chiefs of Staff and the National Command Authority (the president). We trailed the president in our E-4B, a modified Boeing 747, whenever he left the country in Air Force One." Ed's last assignment was to the Army General Staff as a cost analyst in the office of the comptroller of the army. On retirement from active duty as a lieutenant colonel in 1980, he and his wife, Francine, went home to Summerville, South Carolina, where he is active in a family owned real estate business.

Norton, Bill: Despite a five-year, all-hands search through the Internet, no trace of Norton was found. Anecdotal evidence revealed he had gone to rotary-wing school after leaving Vietnam. Jack Bentley discovered on the Vietnam Helicopter Pilots' Association website that William W. Norton had died in 1994 of unspecified causes. Any information from readers will be appreciated.

Sharkey, Mike (Catkiller 46): Mike, an international aviation consultant, wrote to say, "I don't think of Nam that much, but when I do it usually is about the good times, the guys, and the funny things that happened. To me the missions were almost secondary. We were there to do a job and we did it to the best of our ability. But it was the comradeship that can only come from being in a place like Vietnam that got me through such troubling times and most certainly helped keep my sanity. John Kovach and I are very close these days and I try to see him whenever I'm in the States. His daughter was born while he was in Nam and his wife sent him a recording of her first cry. If I heard that recording once I heard it a thousand times. He used to walk through the mess hall while we were watching a movie playing that damn thing. Both our daughters live in Atlanta now and have become good friends. Life's cool sometimes, huh?"

Stewart, Rod (Catkiller 13): Rod was medevac'd three weeks after Operation Rich with crushed spinal disks. After recovery from surgery, he was medically grounded and assigned to the Infantry School at Fort Benning, where he later commanded a mechanized infantry company that included troops who had fought at Kinh Mon. He was granted a waiver to return to flight status and sent back to Vietnam to fly Bird Dogs with the 183rd RAC "Seashores" in II Corps. He was awarded the Soldier's Medal, two Distinguished Flying Crosses, a Bronze Star, a Purple Heart, and the Vietnamese Cross of Gallantry with Palm. His back injury then flared up and he was again medically grounded. He left the army and sailed a square-rigger around the world to "get my head screwed on straight." Returning to California, Rod became an air traffic controller, retiring from LAX control tower in 1983. He then operated his marine contracting company, invested, traveled extensively, and served with various civic and volunteer organizations. He has now retired for the third time and lives on an island in the San Francisco Bay area with his wife of twenty-eight years and their boats.

Strange, Glenn (Catkiller 2): Glenn's tour ended in April 1969, and he left active duty two years later. He joined Merrill Lynch and then spent four years in corporate finance, which was followed by four years in the Kentucky state government. A general malaise that began in Vietnam and grew steadily worse was diagnosed as multiple sclerosis in 1977. Its debilitating progression finally forced his resignation from the private sector, and he took the fallback position of a civil service employee. "After the MS diagnosis, wife #1 was so scared that she ended the marriage to save herself from being 'tied to a wheelchair,'" Glenn wrote. "Wife #2 found that as the MS worsened, she was also unwilling to deal with it; that marriage ended after six years. For all the grief and money those two marriages cost, it was well worth it to get to Vicky. She is the epitome of the perfect wife—best friend, lover, and soul mate. In addition to all that, through Vicky's family in Mexico I have found a clinic that produces an antigen that has *greatly* relieved the symptoms of the disease. People who knew me twenty years ago can't believe it when they see me now." Glenn worked as a budget analyst for the deputy chief of staff for resource management at Headquarters, U.S. Army Training and Doctrine Command at Fort Monroe, Virginia, retiring in early 2007.

Wisby, Jim (Catkiller 6): Returning to the States and attending the requisite courses at Fort Benning and Fort Leavenworth, Jim was assigned to the G-3 office at Fort Campbell, Kentucky, and tasked with bringing the 101st Airborne Division back from Vietnam. Judged to be lacking in patience, he was sent to Liberia in 1975 as advisor to the West African country's aviation commander and infantry commanding general. He flew the Liberian aircraft—Cessna 180s (both of them)—often landing in wing-wide jungle clearings. After twenty-seven months, he was reassigned to Fort Campbell's G-3 office and retired in 1980 as a lieutenant colonel. He spent six years as executive director of United Way, then turned to managing five sheltered workshops for the mentally challenged in the Pennyrile, Kentucky, area; he is in the Kiwanis Club and served as president and construction leader on the Habitat for Humanity board, helping to build more than a dozen homes. Now retired and an official Kentucky Colonel, he fishes, hunts, does odd jobs around the house, and helps his son Jeff in building furniture. His daughter Janet is first assistant on a heart team, while Jo, his wife of forty-two years, is the only woman in the area to bowl a three-hundred game. They have three grandsons.

USMC VMO-6 FINGERPRINT

Lawrence, James H.: Jim entered navy flight school as a Marine Aviation Cadet in 1965 and was still a teenager when he made his first carrier landing in a T2B Buckeye. Answering to the personal call sign "Nomad," he received his "Wings of Gold" as a twenty-one-year-old marine 2nd lieutenant, and flew F-8 Crusaders, A-4 Skyhawks, and O-1 Bird Dogs. He logged 432 combat missions over North and South Vietnam and Laos before transferring to the navy to fly A-7 Corsair IIs from the USS

Forrestal and USS *Eisenhower* and accumulating 103 carrier landings. Jim retired with the rank of commander to become an airline pilot, and joined the Air National Guard. He attended the USAF Fighter Weapons School, where he finished first in his class, and later flew forty-three combat missions over Bosnia and another twenty-eight combat missions in Iraq, all in the A-10 Warthog. He retired after thirty-eight years military service, with more than 2,000 hours in the Skyhawk and the Corsair II, and more than 1,600 hours in the Warthog. Of his 7,700-plus hours of military flying, more than 1,400 were in combat, for which he was awarded a DFC, two Single Mission Air Medals, thirty-five Air Medals, and sixteen other personal and unit decorations. After thirty-five years as an airline pilot, he retired in 2004 as a Boeing 777 captain. Jim is currently flight department manager and chief pilot for a major corporation in Atlanta, Georgia, flying a Falcon 20, a Falcon 10, and a King Air 200. With more than 34,300 hours total flight time to date, his recreation is flying a T-6 Texan and an RV-8 that he built himself—and he still answers to "Nomad."

1ST BATTALION, 61ST INFANTRY BRIGADE

Coopey, Tom: Nine months after Operation Rich, Tom received his discharge at Fort Lewis, Washington, and returned home to work as a telephone installer for New York Telephone Company. Tom attended the College of Staten Island at night for four years for an associate of applied science degree in business administration. He retired in 1998 due to disabilities and a retirement incentive from Bell Atlantic. He and Maureen Larsen were married in 1975 and have two grown children, Thomas G. and Mary Kathleen ("My red-headed challenge," Tom calls her), both of whom are soon to marry. Tom and Maureen live in Jackson, New Jersey, and are looking forward to the joys of being grandparents.

Krawcykowski, Joe: A shift commander for several years and the recipient of the New Jersey State Life-Saving Award in 1984, "Ski" retired as a captain from a busy city fire department after a twenty-six-year career. He held state licenses as fire inspector, official, and instructor; wrote for a number of trade journals; and still sits on a state fire committee. He has been married for thirty-two years, is the father of two sons, and is an avid outdoorsman, the latter prompting a "move to Montana to fish—soon!"

McKendree, Wayne: Drafted from a small Florida farming community in 1967, Wayne completed training as a reconnaissance scout, but a history of migraine headaches and surgery to remove a cyst on his spine left him with a medical profile that prohibited him from serving in combat. "I immediately went to my sergeant, tore up the paperwork in front of him, and volunteered for Vietnam, where I served until 1969." He moved to Atlanta after his discharge and became a salesman, then went into the construction business. He started his own commercial construction company that has been going for over twenty-five years. Married to a Georgia girl since 1974, they live in Kennesaw, Georgia, and have three sons and four grandchildren who are the pride of their lives. "I developed cancer in 2003," Wayne wrote, "but after surgery, radiation treatment, and chemotherapy, I am recovering. The doctor attributed the cancer to my exposure to Agent Orange in Nam, but if it came to defending my country, my family, and the American way of life, I would do it all again."

Ogawa, Alan: Until discovering the 5th Infantry Division website in 2004, Alan had had no contact with anyone from 1st Battalion, 61st Infantry since leaving Vietnam. "It was very emotional for me trying to remember things about Kinh Mon and many other battles that happened forty years ago," he wrote. "I was only eighteen years old then, but after seeing the good, the bad, and the ugliest sides of people and war, I came back an old man. I am now medically retired in Hilo, Hawaii, and went to my first DAV [Disabled American Veterans] meeting this year to become certified as a service officer. I thought I'd volunteer myself as an old veteran to help the new veterans returning from the war in Iraq. It was really lonely when we came back from Vietnam, and I surely don't want them to go through what we had to endure."

Roffers, Jim: In the years following his return from Vietnam, Jim's experience as a provider was primarily as an ASME welder, but in between layoffs and the pitfalls of factory work he served as a policeman, owned a small restaurant, had a gun shop, and contracted metalwork from his own premises. He is now "winding down," working as a welder for Country Flame Technologies in his hometown of Marshfield, Missouri, but says his real job is chasing after the grandkids. "Vietnam made me what I am. I try to be the best I can at whatever I'm doing and I treat everyone as if it will be the last time I'll ever see them. It's been a great life and I've enjoyed it immensely. I try to get out on the weekends with my kayak to enjoy the quiet and solitude. I still have the occasional adventure, though nothing like those I had when younger!"

1ST BATTALION, 77TH ARMOR BRIGADE

Van Haren, Peter: After returning to the "world" in July 1969, Peter spent the next year bumming around the beaches of Southern California before heading home to Arizona and attending law school. He started as a criminal trial lawyer and then as an attorney for several Arizona cities and towns, ending up in his current position as the city attorney of his hometown of Phoenix. He married late, but well, to his soul mate Jolinda, and they have three smart and beautiful daughters. He was recently appointed as chairman of the newly created City of Phoenix Veterans Commission and is thinking of retiring one of these days to devote more time to veterans' affairs and his many hobbies.

Appendix

I was called into the briefing, one cold and rainy day
Said they had a mission, they wanted no delay
I donned on all my armor, my rifle, pistol too
And headed for the briefing, to see what I had to do
The S-2 was awaiting, he said 'I'll tell you straight
Charlie's out in the A Shau, I hope we're not too late
The weather it should be OK, fixed wing is on the way
Let's go get old Charlie, before he gets away'

[The next lines are spoken.]
Hello Phu Bai tower, this is Catkiller 801
Sitting on the Bird Dog ramp, request to taxi one
Taxi to 27, that's the active for today
Hurry with your run-up, you're in a 130's way

I steered on to the active, I winged into the blue
Tower cleared me to change freqs, good day, good flight to you
I headed out to A Shau, the ceiling was too low
Told my marine observer, we'll try to make a go
When we arrived on station, just like the S-2 said
Charlie was in the valley, most were still in bed

[The next lines are spoken.]
Well hello Catkiller 801, this is Hellborne 852
Two A-4s on a 185, 30 miles from you

Lock on to channel 69, come out the 254
I'm an army O-1, skimming the valley floor

[The next lines are spoken.]
Tally Ho 801, now this is 852
I've got you at my three o'clock, now what are we gonna do

I'll run you on a 185, drop your Delta-nines
Then we'll use your pistols, I think that will work out fine

[The next lines are spoken.]
Number one on the base leg, now you're cleared in hot
From the target marking round, twenty meters one o'clock

Those A-4s were great that day
And they roared into the blue
Ran six flights on Charlie, Charlie only shot down two
We've given everyone the BDA, and now we're headed home
Jets, they've all left us, now we're out here all alone

[The next lines are spoken.]
Hello Phu Bai tower, this is Catkiller 801
Turning on the downwind, my prop is overrun
Engine's overheated, my chip detector's bright
So light up that old runway, cause I'm landing there tonight
Well hello Catkiller 801, now this is Phu Bai tower
I'd like to call the crash crew, but this is their coffee hour
Runway lights are broken, and the generator's down

[The last line is sung loudly.]
So Catkiller 801, you'll have to go around!

Glossary

1/5 (Mech): 1st Infantry Brigade, 5th Infantry Division (Mechanized).

1-61: 1st Battalion (Mechanized), 61st Infantry Regiment [of the 5th Infantry Division (Mechanized)].

1/77: 1st Battalion, 77th Armor Brigade.

12.7mm: Soviet-designed DShKM heavy machine gun of .51-caliber with a rate of fire of six hundred rounds per minute. Used by the NVA in both direct fire and antiaircraft roles. Often called a ".51-cal" or ".50" by some of the Catkillers.

37mm: Soviet-designed Type 55 antiaircraft weapon based the Swedish Bofors design of 1935. It has a sustained rate of fire of up to sixty rounds per minute.

57mm: Soviet-designed Type 59 antiaircraft weapon. Usually deployed in batteries of six and slaved to a radar control system.

108th FA: the 108th Field Artillery Group at Dong Ha supplied back-seat aerial observers for the Catkillers when their counterbattery missions took them to "Tally Ho"—North Vietnam.

212th CSAB: headquartered at Da Nang, the 212th Combat Support Aviation Battalion was the parent unit of the 220th RAC Catkillers and one of two CSABs under the 1st Aviation Brigade.

AA *or* **AAA:** antiaircraft artillery, often referred to as "triple-A," covered a range of North Vietnamese–manned weapons used against aerial targets.

A3: fire-support base at Gio Linh.

A4: fire-support base at Con Thien.

A-4: McDonnell-Douglas Skyhawk single-seat fighter-bomber used by marines and navy.

A-6: Grumman all-weather, two-seat fighter-bomber known for the heavy bomb loads it could carry and the accuracy of placing them on target. Used by marines and navy.

A-7: Chance-Vought Corsair II fighter-bomber flown by marines and air force.

ADF: automatic direction finder, which will give a bearing to a frequency broadcast by a nondirectional beacon. They were notoriously inaccurate, especially in mountainous terrain where signal reflection can cause fluctuations.

air: in the jargon, air support provided by marine, air force, or navy fighter-bombers.

Annamese Cordillera: a seven-hundred-mile-long mountain range lying parallel to the Vietnamese coast and rising steeply from the coastal plain to a height of eight thousand feet.

Arc Light: B-52 bombing mission. Because of their altitude, the heavy, eight-engined bombers could not be heard on the ground, and thus there was no warning before tons of bombs landed on unsuspecting NVA positions.

arty: artillery.

ARVN: Army of the Republic of Vietnam. Pronounced "Arvin," these were South Vietnamese troops allied with U.S. forces.

BDA: battle damage assessment.

Bde: brigade.

Bird Dog: Cessna high-wing, tandem-seat reconnaissance aircraft based on the Cessna 170. Its Continental O-470 flat six-piston engine of 213 horsepower gave it a top speed in level flight of 130 miles per hour (approx 114 knots). Adopted by the U.S. Army in 1950, the Bird Dog saw service during the Korean War as the L-19 (*L* for liaison). In 1962, it became the O-1 (*O* for observation) and was flown by the air force, army and marines, as well as the Vietnamese Air Force (VNAF). During the Vietnam War, 469 U.S.-flown O-1 Bird Dogs were lost to all causes.

Black Aces: 21st Reconnaissance Airplane Company, headquartered at Chu Lai.

Bn: battalion.

bogie: enemy aircraft.

CO: commanding officer.

Co: company.

Cobra: Huey helicopter gunship armed with rockets and miniguns.

comms: communications.

Dai Uy ("di wee"): Vietnamese for "captain."

DASC: Direct Air Support Control Center. Pronounced "dask" by the pilots, this was the Dong Ha–based tasking agency for air support in northern I Corps.

Delta-1: marine and navy designation for the 250-pound general-purpose bomb. The Delta-1-Alpha, commonly known as a "snake," was fitted with pop-out paddles (ballute) to slow the bomb after it was released. (The USAF designation for the D1-A was the Mk 81 Snake Eye.)

Delta 2: 500-pound bomb (USAF Mk 82).

Delta 3: 1,000-pound bomb (USAF Mk 83).

Delta 4: 2,000-pound bomb (USAF Mk 84).

Delta 9: napalm canister (USAF Mk 77).

DEROS: date of estimated return from overseas.

DFC: Distinguished Flying Cross.

DMZ: the Demilitarized Zone of one to two miles either side of the Ben Hai River, the border between South Vietnam and North Vietnam. Established by the Geneva Conference in 1956 after France withdrew and the country was divided. It became an area of regular battles between U.S. forces and the North Vietnamese Army.

dust off: Huey helicopters tasked with evacuating wounded troops.

East Trace: a half-mile defoliated strip that ran from Fire Support Base A4 (Con Thien) to FSB A3 (Gio Linh) to FSB A1 on the coast, part of the former "McNamara Line" designed to halt NVA advances into South Vietnam.

ETR: estimated time of return.

F-4: two-seat McDonnell-Douglas Phantom fighter-bomber used by navy, marines, and air force.

FAC: forward air controller. Though a U.S. Air Force acronym, it became a generic term for all O-1 Bird Dogs and O-2 Super Skymasters used for visual reconnaissance. Because of the high threat of ground fire in North Vietnam, the USAF flew two-seat F-100 Super Sabres known as "Fast-FACs" with the call sign "Misty."

feet wet: flying over water. If poor weather meant the possibility of hitting mountains when descending through cloud cover, aircraft would "go feet wet" and let down over the South China Sea before turning west.

FM (Fox Mike): frequency-modulated radio used for short-range communications. There were two FM radios in a Bird Dog—one for the pilot and one for the observer—that were used to communicate with ground units, including artillery batteries.

FNG: fucking new guy.

guard: a pre-set UHF radio frequency used for maydays and other emergency calls. The guard frequency was monitored by all aircraft and search and rescue. The survival radio carried by pilots in the event they went down also broadcast on guard.

HE: high explosive.

Highway 1: built by the French during colonial rule, this two-lane black-top road ran along the coastline of both South and North Vietnam.

Hillsboro: call sign for the C-130 that served as the tasking agency for U.S. aircraft operating over North Vietnam. When the Catkillers needed bombs dropped on a target in Tally Ho, they contacted Hillsboro, which scrambled or diverted marine, navy, or air force fighter-bombers.

hooch: generic term given to any semi-permanent structure used as a home or accommodation by Vietnamese peasants or U.S. forces.

Huey: turbine-powered Bell UH-1 helicopter that became one of the defining images of the Vietnam War.

I Corps: pronounced "Eye" Corps despite meaning *1*, this was the northernmost of four tactical combat zones in South Vietnam. All U.S. forces in I Corps were under the operational control of the 3rd Marine Division.

KIA: killed in action.

Kit Carson scout: former Viet Cong who was recruited to assist counterintelligence.

klick: kilometer.

LAW: light antitank weapon, a portable one-shot 66mm unguided rocket.

Leatherneck Square: an area with Dong Ha at the southeast corner, Fire Support Base A3 (Gio Linh) at the northeast corner, FSB A4 (Con Thien) at the northwest corner, and FSB C2 (Cam Lo) at the southwest corner.

Lima Charlie: loud and clear.

LRRP: long-range reconnaissance patrol.

LZ: landing zone.

MACV: Military Assistance Command, Vietnam.

nape: napalm.

NVA: North Vietnamese Army, more correctly known as the Peoples' Army of Vietnam (PAVN).

O-1: *see* Bird Dog.

O-2: fore-and-aft twin-engined Cessna Super Skymaster used by the U.S. Air Force.

OER: officer evaluation report.

PAVN: *see* NVA.

Phantom: *see* F-4.

push: pre-set frequency on the UHF radios. Pilots could switch frequencies by going to one of up to a dozen buttons that would connect them to Dong Ha DASC, various artillery batteries, or the guard (emergency) frequency.

R&R: rest and recuperation.

Skyhawk: *see* A-4.

SKS: Russian-designed semi-automatic carbine firing the same round as the AK-47.

smoke rocket: the 2.75-inch folding-fin aerial rocket. Most often used with a white phosphorus warhead, it was about four feet long and weighed 18.5 pounds. The white phosphorus warhead exploded on contact, generating a cloud of white smoke. Four fins flipped open on launch to spin-stabilize the rocket, but its accuracy was poor.

snake: high-drag 250-pound pound bomb with four paddle-like fins that extended at the rear after low-level release. These slowed it sufficiently to allow the delivering aircraft to escape before it hit and exploded. The nickname derived from the USAF designation of Snake Eye for the undulating, nose-up-nose-down flight caused by the drag of the fins.

SOI: signal operating instructions.

Spec 4: specialist 4th class; an E-4 specialist, similar to the rank of corporal.

TACA: tactical air coordinator (airborne).

tacair: tactical air support.

Tally Ho: code name for North Vietnam, though traditionally it is pilots' jargon for having something in sight.

TAOR: tactical area of responsibility. For the Catkillers, this included the DMZ and the southern fringes of North Vietnam; often shortened to "AO."

TDY: temporary duty.

TOC: tactical operations center.

UH-34: radial engine-powered Sikorsky medium helicopter used primarily by the marines in Vietnam. It was replaced by the Bell UH-1 Huey.

UHF: ultrahigh frequency. Bird Dog pilots had two UHF radios for communicating with Dong Ha DASC and other aircraft.

USO: United Service Organizations, which provides entertainment and recreation for U.S. forces around the world.

VC: Viet Cong. Often called Victor Charlie or just Charlie.

West Trace: a half-mile-wide defoliated strip running south from Fire Support Base A4 at Con Thien to FSB C2 at Cam Lo. Like the East Trace, this had been part of the McNamara Line designed to halt NVA advances into South Vietnam.

WIA: wounded in action.

Willie Peter: white phosphorus; also referred to in NATO phonetics as whiskey papa.

the Z: *see* DMZ.

Index

Places

Weapons, Planes, Ships, etc.

Other Terms